Public Policy Making in the Western Balkans

Margo Thomas • Vesna Bojicic-Dzelilovic
Editors

Public Policy Making in the Western Balkans

Case Studies of Selected Economic and Social Policy Reforms

Springer

Editors
Margo Thomas
International Finance Corporation
World Bank Group
Washington, DC, USA

Vesna Bojicic-Dzelilovic
Department of International Development
London School of Economics
and Political Science
London, UK

Disclaimer:
The findings, interpretations and conclusions expressed in this work are entirely those of the authors, and do not represent the views of The *World Bank*, its Board of Directors, or the governments they represent.
The World Bank does not guarantee the accuracy of the data included in this work. The boundaries, colors, denominations, and other information shown on any map in this work do not imply any judgement on the part of The World Bank concerning the legal status of any territory or the endorsement or acceptance of such boundaries.

ISBN 978-94-017-7946-3 ISBN 978-94-017-9346-9 (eBook)
DOI 10.1007/978-94-017-9346-9
Springer Dordrecht Heidelberg New York London

Printed on acid-free paper

Springer is part of Springer Science+Business Media (www.springer.com)

Foreword

This book is the final output of an ambitious programme of faculty development in the Western Balkans. Funded for the first 10 years by the Open Society Institute and led by Dr. Vesna Bojicic-Dzelilovic, the programme aimed to build the research and teaching capacities of junior and middle level faculty, to reconnect universities divided by war and partition, and to support critical and independent minded scholars. In the last years of the programme, the network of scholars who have participated in the programme formed themselves into a virtual think tank aimed at public policy research.

This book, undertaken in collaboration with Dr. Margo Thomas of the World Bank Group, represents the fruits of their endeavours. It enables the reader to assess policy-making in the Western Balkans, drawing on the insights of locally-based scholars who are able to analyse their situation from a wider global perspective. The book draws attention to contrast between the legalistic and excessively technical approach to policy-making undertaken by governments and their international backers and the context of policy-making characterised by weak governance, informality and all the multiple problems that arise from the double transition from totalitarianism and from war. Its strength lies in the fact that it is written by 'insiders' who are able to make use of their social science tools to enable them to stand back and analyse their countries from an 'outside perspective'.

London School of Economics and Political Science — Mary Kaldor
July 2014

Preface

This volume is a product of collaboration among a group of social scientists from the Western Balkans within the South East European Research Network (SEERN) which was convened under the auspices of the Faculty Development in South East Europe Programme at the London School of Economics and Political Science. The main objective of the Programme, supported by the Open Society Institute, was to support higher education institutions in the aftermath of the break-up of former Yugoslavia in rebuilding their teaching and research capacity, by modernising curricula and upgrading teaching and research skills.

Regional cooperation represented an important and strong aspect of the programme, with an ambition to pursue different types of activities where the partner institutions had common interest, enabling the best use of the available knowledge and expertise to address many common challenges facing this region. For most academics participating in the programme, the pressure and demand to generate policy-relevant knowledge spurred foremost by the international donors' involvement in the domestic governance was a novel professional experience, having come from a system where collaboration between academia and the policy making community was negligible.

Bridging that gap by strengthening the capacity to produce expert knowledge that can be used by policy makers, and strengthening the dialogue between the two communities, has been the main motive for partnering with the World Bank Group's International Finance Corporation Advisory Services initiative to set up the network of policy makers in South East Europe. In November 2010, the two networks met in Tirana to talk about the issues of competitiveness in the Western Balkans, and the kernels of most of the contributions to this volume were laid in the course of those conversations. All chapter authors are established experts in their respective area who were asked to shift their analytical gaze to the policy making process and elaborate on the theme of competitiveness, by looking at specific reform episodes and the role of policy makers and political factors that drive policy choices and policy implementation in their respective country setting. So, in an important way, the case studies collected in this volume are the product of a joint effort to strengthen the capacity of the academic community in the Western Balkans to produce policy-relevant knowledge and to engage in the policy making process. In terms of a broader contribution to the scholarship on policy making, these case studies provide a prism for examining the key elements of the policy making process in a region with a turbulent recent history of war and post-totalitarian transition, which has so far received scant attention in this area of social science. It is against this background that we hope this volume contributes to a modest body of empirical work on public policy making in the Western Balkans.

London, UK
Washington, DC, USA
2014

Vesna Bojicic-Dzelilovic
Margo Thomas

Contents

Contributors

Marija Babović Faculty of Philosophy, University of Belgrade, Belgrade, Serbia

Predrag Bjelić Faculty of Economics, University of Belgrade, Belgrade, Serbia

Vesna Bojicic-Dzelilovic Department of International Development, London School of Economics and Political Science, London, UK

Fikret Čaušević Department of Economics, University of Sarajevo, Sarajevo, Bosnia and Herzegovina

Dita Dobranja Good Governance and Economic Policy Program, Institute for Development Policy, Pristina, Kosovo

Saša Drezgić Faculty of Economics, University of Rijeka, Rijeka, Croatia

Danijela Jaćimović-Vojinović Faculty of Economics, University of Montenegro, Podgorica, Montenegro

Mimoza Manxhari Management Department, Faculty of Economics, University of Tirana, Tirana, Albania

Srdjan Marinković Faculty of Economics, University of Niš, Niš, Serbia

Andreja Marušić International Finance Corporation (Formerly with the Balkan Center for Regulatory Reform), Belgrade, Serbia

Silvana Mojsovska Institute of Economics, University St. Cyril and Methodius, Skopje, Republic of Macedonia

Slavica Penev Institute of Economic Sciences, Belgrade, Serbia

Margo Thomas International Finance Corporation, World Bank Group, Washington, DC, USA

Danilo Vuković Faculty of Law, University of Belgrade, Belgrade, Serbia

Abbreviations

AAK	Alliance for the Future of Kosovo
AAEN	Alternative Academic Education Network
ADA	Austrian Development Cooperation
ASBiH	Agency for Statistics of Bosnia and Herzegovina
ARZ	Agency for Work and Employment
ATM	Autonomous Trade Measures
BCPS	Bank Credit to Private Sector
BEONIA	Belgrade Overnight Index
BEU	Bureau of Education Services
BiH	Bosnia and Herzegovina
CAP	Common Agricultural Policy
CARITAS	Catholic Relief Agency
CBS	Croatian Bureau for Statistics
CSO	Civil Society Organisations
CEE	Central and Eastern Europe
CEFTA	Central European Free Trade Agreement
CEMI	Center for Monitoring
CNB	Croatian National Bank
CRR	Comprehensive Regulatory Reform
CSRD	Regional Development Cross-cutting Strategy
CSW	Centre for Social Work
DEP	Directorate for Economic Planning
DFID	Department for International Development
DP	Democratic Party
DPA	Dayton Peace Agreement
DPS	Democratic Party of Socialists
DSDC	Department for Strategies and Donor Coordination
EBRD	European Bank for Reconstruction and Development
EC	European Commission
ECB	European Central Bank

ECTS	European Credit Transfer System
EDF	Excessive Deficit Procedure
EHEA	European Higher Education Area
EONIA	European Overnight Index
EU	European Union
FBiH	Federation of Bosnia – Herzegovina
FDI	Foreign Direct Investment
FIAS	Foreign Investment Advisory Service
FIC	Foreign Investors Council
FMON	Federation Ministry of Education and Science
GCI	Global Competitiveness Index
GCR	Global Competitiveness Report
GIZ	German Development Agency
GMO	Genetically Modified Organisms
GoA	Government of Albania
GVA	Gross Value Added
HE	Higher Education
HERIC	Higher Education and Research for Innovation and Competitiveness
ICC	International Chamber of Commerce
ICJ	International Court of Justice
IDA	International Development Assistance
IMF	International Monetary Fund
ILO	International Labour Organisation
IPA	Instrument for Pre-accession Assistance
ISD	Integrated Support for Decentralisation
ISPP	Institute for Strategic Forecasting
ITA	Indirect Taxation Authority
LDK	Democratic League of Kosovo
LGU	Local Government Units
MCP	Ministry of Civil Affairs
METE	Ministry of Economy, Trade and Energy
MOES	Ministry of Education and Sport
MOI	Ministry of Interior
MONSTAT	Montenegro Statistics Office
MPS	Ministry of Education and Sports
NALED	National Alliance for Local Economic Development
NBS	National Bank of Serbia
NDI	National Strategy for Development and Integration
NGO	Non-governmental Organisations
NHI	Independent Croat Initiative
NSDI	National Development Strategy
NUTS	Nomenclature of Territorial Units for Statistics
OECD	Organisation for Cooperation and Development
OHR	Office of the High Representative
PDK	Democratic Party of Kosovo

PDP	Party of Democratic Progress
RIA	Regulatory Impact Assessment
RDP	Regional Development Program
RS	Republika Srpska, Bosnia – Herzegovina
R&D	Research and Development
RSD	Serbian Dinar
RSIS	Republic of Srpska Institute for Statistics
RZS	Serbian Institute of Statistics
SACII	Structural Adjustment Credit for Serbia
SBA	Stand-By Agreement
SBiH	Party for Bosnia – Herzegovina
SDA	Party of Democratic Action
SDC	Swiss Development Cooperation
SDP	Social Democratic Party
SEE	South East Europe
SFRY	Socialist Yugoslavia
SGP	Stability Growth Pact
SIDA	Swedish International Development Agency
SME	Small and Medium Size Enterprises
SMI	Socialist Movement for Integration
SNSD	Association of Independent Social Democrats
SORS	Statistics Office of the Republic of Serbia
TAS	Sarajevo Car Company
TEMPUS	European Training Foundation
TNC	Transnational Corporations
QA	Quality Assurance
Qark	Regional Council, Albania
UB	University of Belgrade
UIP	Uncovered Interest Parity
UM	University of Montenegro
UNDP	United Nations Development Program
UNICEF	United Nations Children's Fund
UNMIK	United Nations Mission in Kosovo
UNSCR	United Nations Security Council Resolution
USAID	United States Agency for International Development
USPRS	Trade Union of Serbian Education Workers
VAT	Value Added Tax
WEF	World Economic Forum
WTO	World Trade Organisation
WUS	World University Service
ZZ	Employment Agency

Chapter 1
Introduction

Vesna Bojicic-Dzelilovic and Margo Thomas

In broad terms over the past two decades or so, governments in the Western Balkans[1] have been transitioning from socialist regimes, centrally planned economies, and the legacy of armed conflicts. They have actively engaged in building new (and where appropriate transforming existing) economic, political, social and legal institutions to consolidate democratic and market-oriented regimes in the European Union neighbourhood. In this context, broad policy changes in the economic, social and governance spheres have been pursued, all aimed at stimulating competitiveness as a critical factor for generating sustained economic growth and development.

The first iteration of the global financial and economic crisis, starting in 2008 put the ongoing transition in the Western Balkans to the test. It is evident that the impact of the crisis has been much more severe in the Western Balkans than elsewhere in Europe (Bartlett and Uvalic 2013; Sanfey 2010; Myant and Drahkoupil 2012), and sustained economic recovery has been difficult to take root. The response of governments in the region has not been very effective in ameliorating the effects of the global economic and financial crisis in the economies saddled by various structural deficiencies (Bastian 2010; Dallago 2006), regardless of cross-country variation in the level of institutional development measured by a standard set of indicators compiled by international organizations such as the European Bank for Reconstruction and Development (EBRD) and the World Bank (Sanfey and Zeh 2013). This recent experience of responding to an externally triggered economic crisis is relevant in

[1] Western Balkans is comprised of the following group of countries: Albania, Bosnia-Herzegovina, Croatia, Kosovo, FYR Macedonia, Montenegro and Serbia.

V. Bojicic-Dzelilovic, Ph.D. (✉)
Department of International Development, London School of Economics
and Political Science, London, UK
e-mail: v.bojicic-dzelilovic@lse.ac.uk

M. Thomas, Ph.D.
International Finance Corporation, World Bank Group, Washington, DC, USA
e-mail: mthomas@ifc.org; thomaswgb@gmail.com

M. Thomas, V. Bojicic-Dzelilovic (eds.), *Public Policy Making in the Western Balkans*, DOI 10.1007/978-94-017-9346-9_1

that it has brought to light deep seated problems of general economic governance but also revealed a broad scope for further improvements across the policy areas affecting competitiveness in this set of countries.

Our review of the literature and active discussions with counterparts over the past few years, has led to the conclusion that there is a serious dearth of scholarship on public policy making in the Western Balkans. According to Petak (2006) this scholarship is necessary to provide for a better understanding of: (1) how the policy process is structured and managed; (2) how robust and credible policies are developed, adopted and implemented locally; and (3) the consequences for competitiveness and economic growth.

This book's ambition is to make a contribution to that body of literature by helping to build a foundation for examining economic and social policy making in the Western Balkans, and by supporting the work of the region's rising academics and policy makers. Therefore, the book examines the experience and outcomes of public policy reform in the economies of the Western Balkans by focusing on a selected number of policy issues in order to better understand the politics, process and dilemmas associated with policy making in a challenging post-socialist, post-conflict political and economic landscape.

Within this context, the contributors to this volume have looked at range of economic and social policy areas that have some relevance to national, sub-national, and regional competitiveness in the EU neighbourhood. These policy areas include: trade, fiscal and monetary regimes, foreign direct investment, human capital, as well as local and regional development. At the centre of this inquiry is the role of different policy actors in driving the policy agenda and the implementation of policy reforms, the bargaining process among these actors, their constituents, and special interests that collectively influence the scope, timing and the outcomes of policy reforms. Analytically, the onus is on understanding agency in the policy making process and the dynamics that drive economic and social reforms that are intended to contribute to improved competitiveness of the Western Balkan economies.

1 Policy Making: Theoretical Framework and Application

With the apparent institutional shift in the social sciences, it has become a commonplace to define international competitiveness by its institutional features. As a corollary, the idea that public policy plays a vital role in improving (competitive) advantages and removing disadvantages has gained in considerable traction (Pedersen 2010:631). This intellectual thread is of particular salience for the purpose of this study that aims to examine the policy making process in this particular group of countries. Over an extended period of time, these countries have been undergoing far reaching and sustained institutional change centred around a fundamental transformation of the role of the state in economic development – from a proprietor, producer, and allocator of economic assets – to a state that is market-oriented, concerned primarily with a regulation of economic exchange. With this changing role, the state is creating an institutional framework under which policy making process takes place and policy actors act (Bohle and Greskovitz 2012; Pedersen ibid). This implies a transformation in the relationship between the state and society that underpins and defines a new, emerging approach to fact-based, transparent policy making, while taking into account the political economy.

Public policy revolves around constant contracting, negotiations and re-contracting between the state and constituents (including the private sector and civil society) over the policies, actors and processes that contribute to improved competitiveness (Pedersen ibid). One approach to framing state-society relations is by way of policy networks as more institutionalized form of interaction and exchange (van Waarden 1992: 13). Policy network theories and analysis are rooted in the social networking concepts pioneered by social scientists in the traditions and disciplines of anthropology and sociology, such as Georg Simmel and Claude Levi-Strauss, who perceived social processes as the products or outcomes of "the purposeful interactions of individual actors" as opposed to an invisible hand that engineers social harmony (Kenis and Schneider 1991: 26). Building on this foundation of social actors and networks, the fundamental building block of policy networks is the policy actor and the relationships (including communities, coalitions, constituencies) that develop among actors-state and non- state- based on their beliefs, interests, and resources (Marsh and Rhodes 1992; Knoke 1998).

The term policy network refers to "a cluster of actors, each of which has an interest or 'stake' in a given ……. policy sector and the capacity to help determine policy success or failure" (Peterson and Bomberg 1999: 8). In a more comprehensive approach by Kenis and Schneider (1991: 41), "policy network is described by its actors, their linkages and its boundary. The linkages between the actors serve as channels for communication and for the exchange of information, expertise, trust and other policy resources. The boundary of a given policy network is not determined by formal institutions but by results from a process of mutual recognition dependent on functional relevance and structural embeddedness." Various definitions recognize that networks vary in formality, focus and the power controlled by respective actors but share common elements in terms of a common interest among the actors, incentives for affecting public policy, and a combined capability to affect policy outcomes. Policy network analysts "seek to explain the formation of state-interest organization networks, their persistence and change over time, and the consequences of network structures for public policy making outcomes" (Knoke 2007: 4). This analysis of the policy process makes a distinction between the policy domain and policy issue, the latter having an advantage of elucidating both group dynamics and the actors that influence relationships among policy actors (Kim and Roh 2008).

Each chapter in this volume interrogates a specific policy issue by asking the same set of core questions: What is the political, economic and social context and drivers of a reform? How was the policy designed/developed and implemented? Who were the stakeholders and policy actors involved in designing, implementing and evaluating the impact of the policy? What kinds of collaboration, collusion, or competition occurred? Was there an evidence of policy networks, and if so, who were the actors, leaders, their spheres of influence and special interests? How did the networks and coalitions influence the scope, timing and the pace of reforms?

2 Local Conditions for Policy Reforms in the Western Balkans: Context, Actors and Policies

Policy making takes place in a particular local political and social setting, and its forms are thus locally contingent (Bebbington and McCourt 2007; Malova and Haughton 2002). Therefore, before we outline a summary of individual chapters, and in order to situate analysis, it is worth reflecting on three key inter-related aspects of the local condition, which also allow to juxtapose, even in a somewhat general terms, the Western Balkans' experience of public policy reform to that of Central and East European countries. Given the paucity of research on the policy making process in the Western Balkans, we will draw on the findings from a more robust but still fairly nascent literature on public policy making in Central and Eastern Europe. At first sight the communist legacy may appear as the most obvious common ground, and the recent armed conflicts in the Western Balkans as a striking dissimilarity against which public policy making practices in those two country groupings have been shaped. There is in fact a more nuanced picture in terms of the context, actors and policies that ought to be considered to provide an intelligible account of the outcomes and the experience of public policy reforms in the Western Balkans.

The literature on transition in the Western Balkans is rich in analysis that usefully tries to decipher various aspects of internal and external context in explaining the different economic transition trajectories and outcomes. Acknowledging this important body of knowledge, we concentrate on a number of specific aspects pertinent to the analysis of the policy process along the lines of the policy network analysis outlined above. To begin with, the legacy of self-management in the successor states of former Yugoslavia and that of the 'hardest' form of totalitarianism in Albania (Dallago ibid) provide a distinct backdrop against which institutional change has been instigated by the public policy reforms explored in this book. Some of the key dimensions of the policy process such as mobilisation of interest based politics, participation of various policy actors, consultation process and coalition building manifest themselves differently against the self-management legacy[2] in ex-Yugoslav states and against the firmly hierarchical governance structures Albania inherited, despite an overall tendency to follow the West European institutional model (Malova and Haughton 2002).

The dissolution of the former Yugoslav Republic presented a unique challenge in so far as the successor countries have had to grapple with the consolidation of the

[2] Bohle and Greskovitz (2012) note that self-management legacy has been important in Slovenia developing a particular form of capitalism which they label 'embedded neoliberalism'; they furthermore argue that some features of 'embedded liberalism' can be also identified in Croatia.

state and market while undergoing political and economic reforms, with manifold implications for public policy making. Most critically, the instability and uncertainty within individual countries and the entire region, and its persistence long after the open violence ended, constituted a force and intensity that was not experienced by most Central and East European countries during their transition towards open market economies and pluralist democracies. Moreover, this has profoundly shaped the outlook of policy actors and the leaders of reform in the Western Balkans. The pending final political settlements which are necessary to complete the ongoing state-building projects in Bosnia-Herzegovina and Kosovo continue to cast a shadow over region's potential for steering governance in the direction that supports stable and sustained peace by promoting economic development and democratic political practice.

At the most basic level, the consolidation of national states and national markets out of what used to be a single polity and a single economic space meant that, alongside weak executive[3] leadership, limited availability of expert knowledge and capable public administration, these Balkan countries faced much more formidable constraints than the Eastern European transition frontrunners. As an example in the case of Serbia, the largest entity and seat of power in the former Yugoslavia, faced significant capacity challenges in implementing public administration reforms and even resorted to seconding expatriate staff to the key public offices, despite being the pole of attraction for the highly skilled public servants from across the former federation over several decades.

In the context of weak domestic institutions and limited capacity, the international community mobilized support and technical assistance in a form and of intensity unseen in other former socialist countries. This support was designed specially in response to the Western Balkans' complex, multiple transitions. In its extreme form, the role of international actors in conflict-affected Bosnia-Herzegovina and Kosovo was evident at all levels as international actors exercised executive authority and had the power to pass and even impose legislation in situations where there was a failure of the domestic governance and leadership.

A range of global, regional, bi-lateral and multilateral actors have mobilized to help steer democratic processes and economic development as a pillar of peacebuilding in the region. The European Union accession approach was adapted for the Balkans based on the approach used in Eastern Europe. The Stabilisation and Association Agreement (SAA) process and its ancillary structures, including the Stability Pact for South East Europe and European Partnership Agreements have been applied in parallel with other channels of support from bi-lateral organizations and international financial institutions. In similar fashion, membership in supranational governance entities such as the World Trade Organisation (WTO) and the Central European Free Trade Agreement (CEFTA) has been important.

[3]According to Malova and Haughton (2002: 104–107), the weakness of the executive branch of government was commonplace in early transition in the post-socialist world, partly because of the constitutional arrangements, and partly due to a sheer lack of expertise among the ministerial elites.

The particular context of the Western Balkans transition, i.e., conflation of the post-conflict, post-socialist transition and Europeanization through the adoption of the European Union type rules and regulations, has triggered a proliferation of policy mandates and actors. This in turn has shaped an exceptionally fluid environment for policy formulation, adoption and implementation, influenced the roles played by various policy actors and their interrelationships, and consequently the policy reform outcomes. This fundamental weakness of governance, institutions, and domestic state capacity[4] opened space for a much more interventionist roles on the part of international actors.[5]

On the one hand, the external actors have become pivotal drivers of the reform agenda, particularly the European Union (Sanfey and Zeh 2013: 19; Borzel 2013). On the other hand, fragmented policy making and blurred lines of responsibility have made informal actors, coalitions and political bargains not necessarily conducive to strengthening institutions play a more prominent role.

The problem of credible commitment,[6] coloured by those distinct traits of state *cum* civil society weakness in the post-conflict, post-socialist environment (Bojicic-Dzelilovic et al. 2013; Fink-Hafner 1998), has stymied the implementation of policy reforms and stumped the development of domestic economic governance mechanisms, albeit with some variations across the countries and policy areas. Some of the key preconditions for effective policy making, as a collective action involving a series of bargains (Bebbington and McCourt ibid; Malova and Haughton ibid; Hodgson 2006), including the independence of policy actors (particularly, the autonomy of the state *vis a vis* other interest groups), mutual trust, shared norms, and respect (Fenger and Klok 2001) have been deeply compromised in the Western Balkan countries, particularly those with an experience of armed conflict.[7] In sum, in a domestic set-up of weak state, weak civil society, and a pervasive international involvement, building complementarities among institutions and policy making structures to ensure policy coordination in support of economic growth, development, and competitiveness has been significantly impaired.

Some of the idiosyncrasies of public policy making in the Western Balkans can be attributed to the pace of economic reforms, compared to Central and Eastern Europe

---

[4] Using the example of environmental policy in Bosnia-Herzegovina, a country which has become something of a paradigm of weak state, Fagan shows how the state has been unable not only to implement and enforce the legislation but also to involve stakeholders in the policy making (Fagan 2013).

[5] The problem of 'stateness' has been identified as the key domestic condition which explains limited transformative role of the European Union in the Westen Balkans (Elbasani 2013; Bojicic-Dzelilovic et al. 2013).

[6] Problem of credible commitment to economic reforms is likely to arise due to complexity caused by the agency of multiple actors. It manifests itself in the time inconsistency of economic reforms which creates regime uncertainty, namely the instability of rules and institutions (Coyne and Pellillo 2011).

[7] There is large body of work in political science and conflict studies on the nature of the state and civil society in the Western Balkans which demonstrates that in this particular set of countries the notion of 'competitive arrangements' between the state and other policy actors that sustain public policy making process is quite problematic given the role of patronage network politics characteristic of those states which define the beliefs, interests and resources that various actors command.

in so far as the transition was pursued in a compressed time frame which restricted opportunities for learning and gradual adjustment (Gligorov 2007; Dallago ibid). From the perspective of policy analysis, the delay was largely due to weak or absent reform constituencies (Gligorov ibid). It was roughly around 2000, that the political climate changed towards more pluralist politics including the ascent of pro-reform oriented elites, and more concerted efforts to push through with the policy reforms particularly those promoted by the international actors began in earnest in some of the countries. One of the implications of the delayed transition and its 'condensed' character was the order in which the reforms have been sequenced. The transition experience of the Central and East European countries demonstrates that most governments focused initially on less costly 'first generation' reforms to consolidate market institutions (Szelenyi and Wilk 2010; Bohle and Greskovitz 2012) and subsequently to the more difficult and politically costly social and welfare issues. Although this pattern is not as clear in the ex-Yugoslav successor countries which could be related to the self-management legacy, it appears for example that social policy has received inadequate attention in the light of economic and social dislocation caused by the conflict in this region (European Stability Initiative 2003). Arguably this is a policy area where there was a strong need for substantive and effective reforms[8] that would balance growth enhancing policies and their redistributive effects.[9]

Another important factor influencing actual policy choice and the pace of policy reforms specific to the successor countries of former Yugoslavia, has been a national question in the context of politically and ideologically loaded state-building agenda. It was the political concerns surrounding the (nation) state building agenda that prevailed in shaping interests and policy priorities. This explains why for a very long time in most of former Yugoslavia successor states, there was little difference in terms of public policy agenda in the areas relevant to growth and competitiveness between the governing and opposition political parties. According to many scholars, this suggests that in fact, a lack of political will rather than a lack of reform capacity is a much more prominent factor that helps explain slow, conflictual, stop-and-go pattern of policy reforms with frequent instances of backsliding (Gligorov 2007; Elbasani 2013), that has ultimately delayed and deformed institutionalisation in the Western Balkans, including formalisation of policy networks and their stabilisation (Fink-Hafner 2007:8).

Yet another factor that has influenced the policy choice and the timing of policy reforms in the Western Balkans relates to a particular variation in the way the external actors have exercised their leverage over the local policy makers by applying a specific mix of political and economic conditions attached to financial aid. Often policy reforms were championed at the time and in a form not well-adjusted to local circumstances in term of local priorities, interests, local culture and administrative capacity, and, very importantly in view of recent history, regional political dynamic, which led to incomplete and/or distorted reforms, or normative compliance that ultimately failed to achieve intended policy outcomes (Borzel 2013).

[8] This applies to Albania as one of the poorest former socialist countries in Europe.

[9] For an argument for a different approach to social policy in the local condition shaped by the legacy of war, nation-state building and crisis management, see: Stubbs and Zrinscak 2009.

This selective and brief overview of some of the specific aspects of the context, actors and policies as a backdrop of public policy making in the Western Balkans discussed in the contributions to this volume highlights the utmost importance of the politics of the reform process in the post-conflict, post-socialist landscape in shaping the policy process itself and its outcomes. The conflation of war and post-socialist transition has engendered deep social transformation of the Western Balkans societies, which has reconfigured the relations between the state and society, and determined how policies, processes and the actors that participate therein (or not) are renegotiated.

3 Volume Overview and Main Conclusions

In looking at the formal policy making process in the Western Balkan countries as captured in the individual case studies in this volume, a picture emerges of a fundamentally legalistic approach that is rooted in the historical traditions of the Austro-Hungarian and the civil law system of the former Socialist Federal Republic of Yugoslavia (Thomas 2007). The constitution, normative legal acts and the rules of procedure of the government provide the foundation or the framework for policy and legislative processes as established under the former Yugoslavia with its particular tradition of economic and political self-management. The formal process for laws proposed by the government, as outlined by Penev and Marušić (2006) for Serbia, is fundamentally the same in the Western Balkans countries and the former Yugoslav Republics in particular. The formal process framed by the constitution and the rules of government procedure[10] establishes the main actors in the policy process as the government, members of parliament and parliamentary committees. These are the actors with the authority to propose policies that require legislative action for implementation.

The formal process does not reflect the conceptual development, design, articulation and political bargaining that is necessary even before the policy gets to the legislative stage. As Staronova (2002) argues, the actual policy conceptualization, formulation, and strategizing is not covered by the formal rules and procedures; instead, this part of the process varies depending on the politics, issues, government, and established norms. Those in turn are shaped by the indigenous context of local institutional arrangements, state-society relations and national culture, which in the Western Balkans bear the imprint of simultaneous, multiple transitions from communism, war and towards liberal market democracy anchored in the European Union membership. Consequently, each case study in this volume provides a contextualised account of a particular policy issue and traces the configuration of actors, interests and processes that define public policy choices and policy implementation.

In this context, the book is organised into three main sections (see Table 1.1 below): (1) A broad view of the economic and social policy reforms in the Western

[10] Legislative rules of the government, government procedure, and guidelines for law drafting.

Table 1.1 Overview

Chapter	Policy areas	Key issues
Introduction		
Part 1: the Western Balkans in the EU neighbourhood: economic and social policy reforms		
1. **Shaping social policies in the Western Balkans: legal and institutional changes in the context of globalisation and post-socialist transformation**	Social policy – higher education, employment and social protection	• Fundamental, paradigm shift in social policies of the Western Balkans with the transfer of responsibility for the provision of social security from the state to individuals, families and social groups
Marija Babović *Danilo Vuković*		• The cumulative impact of several waves of social disintegration motivated by: the disintegration or weakening of the state; conflicts between members of different ethnic and political groups; the collapse of socialist-era institutions compounded by the slow and inconsistent development of new institutions that are agents of social integration
		• Difficulty in realigning interests given the specific context of transition in the Western Balkans
2. **Fiscal policy and competitiveness in Croatia**	Economic and fiscal policy	• Political economy of economic and fiscal policy making in the context of EU harmonisation and accession
Saša Drezgić	Fiscal policy making in the context of EU harmonisation and accession rules and process	• Factors influencing policy direction, decisions, implementation and timing and their impact on economic performance and competitiveness
		• Conflict of interest among the key policy actors and constituents who influenced critical fiscal policy decisions,
3. **Building competitiveness and increasing trade potential in the Western Balkans: economic policy making in preparing for European integration**	*Trade policy*	• Trade policy reforms are required for the Western Balkan economies that are part of the EU Neighbourhood and signatories to the SAA agreement. These policies are influenced by three regional and global trade regimes: CEFTA 2006; the EU; and the WTO
Predrag Bjelić	Trade policy reforms, the Western Balkan economies	• There is a significant gap between policy reform and policy implementation. This gap is influenced by conflicts of interest among key actors and inconsistencies in the implementation of policies under different trade regimes. This gap adversely affects the competitiveness of the Western Balkan economies

(continued)

Table 1.1 (continued)

Chapter	Policy areas	Key issues
4. **The political economy of economic liberalization and competitiveness in Bosnia and Herzegovina**	Economic policy	• Complex political and economic segmentation at the national and sub-national levels in post-conflict BiH influences policy decisions, policy making and implementation in the areas of trade liberalization, financial liberalization and privatization
Fikret Čaušević	Trade liberalisation, financial liberalization and privatization	• The segmented political and economic structure of policy making is reflected in the lack of a coherent strategy for generating private investment and raises significant governance issues in policy implementation
Part II: policy making and governance – building markets and competitiveness in the Western Balkans		
5. **Strengthening regulatory governance – the case of Serbia**	Economic policy	• Regulatory governance has been one of the reform priorities, with strong involvement of international donors and the EU in establishing reform priorities, policy design and implementation
Andreja Marušić	Regulatory governance	• Mobilization of constituencies to support the reforms
Slavica Penev		• The critical importance of capacity building and resources for reform implementation
6. **Investment policy design, process and implementation in Kosovo**	Economic policy	Kosovo faces a range of challenges of creating a stable environment that is attractive for private investment
Dita Dobranja	Foreign investment	• Nascent institutions, weak governance and special interests undermine reform implementation and accountability
7. **Montenegro: enhancing competitiveness and accelerating European Union integration – the role of higher education**	Education policy	• The role of the international community, donors and the EU in shaping policy agendas
Danijela Jaćimović-Vojinović		• Limited capacity and resources for reform implementation
		• Strong opposition by vested interests among public higher education institutions

(continued)

Table 1.1 (continued)

Chapter	Policy areas	Key issues
8. **Managing the financial crisis: credit crunch and response in Serbia**	Financial policy	Serbia's policy response to the 2008 financial crisis
Srdjan Marinković		• Credit bubble, its development and credit crunch
		• Policy response by a tri-partite coalition between the National Bank, the IMF and foreign banks
		• Implementation challenges: winners and losers, limited capacity to conduct exchange rate policy in a small, open, transition economy
Part III: policy making and governance: national and sub-national policies		
9. **Strengthening competitiveness in the Republic of Macedonia: a regional development policy perspective**	Regional development policy	• Alignment of the policy with the EU regional development policies
Silvana Mojsovska		• Limited implementation capacity, absence of an established framework for implementation, inadequate expertise across key policy actors, limited resources
		• Importance of policy coordination in pulling resources and synchronizing different policies affecting competitiveness in a small country
10. **Local governance and regional development in Albania**	Local and regional development policy	• Weakness in the institutional framework for decentralisation
Mimosa Manxhari		• Limited implementation capacity, fragmented policy making, limited resources, weak reform constituency to implement regional development policy
		• Challenge of balancing local and regional level governance
Conclusion		

Balkan countries that constitute the EU neigbourhood, have signed the SAA reflecting the aspirations to EU accession, have embarked on the transition path with the goal of stimulating economic development and introducing market economies, and competing for private investment. This section is motivated by a regional perspective while highlighting the political, social and economic complexities inherent in many of the former-Yugoslav republics, with Bosnia-Herzegovina providing a particularly complex example; (2) Sect. 2 looks at policy making and governance in policy areas that include regulatory governance, financial policy, investment policy and trade liberalisation drawing on case studies of reform episodes from Kosovo, Montenegro and Serbia; (3) The third section focuses on local development and regional competitiveness drawing on case studies from Albania and the Republic of Macedonia.

The case studies demonstrate that despite Western Balkans complex local condition defined by prominent role of external actors in driving policy process, policy makers play an important role in building constituencies for reform, designing policies, and making policy choices in terms of policy scope, timing and sequencing. Across the Western Balkan countries, there is evidence of forms of collaboration on specific policy issues within government (i.e., inter-ministerial and/or inter-organizational) and between the executive and parliaments, although the extent of this collaboration is defined by government coalitions and often limited within party lines. In general, informal, unstructured and opportunistic policy coalitions exist. However, the nature of coalitions and collaboration between policy makers within government can be characterized as consistent with Granovetter's (1973, 1983) conceptualization of "weak ties" within a policy process that is dominated by small groups of policy elites, often powered by leaders in government and in some cases with the support of International Financial Institutions (IFI). Taken together, the observations provided in the case studies collected in this volume, and commentaries in the broader literature underscore the weak governance systems and the challenges faced by reform governments in modernizing the public sector and public policy making in the post-communist transition and developing economies of the Western Balkans.

References

Bartlett, W., & Uvalic, M. (Eds.). (2013). *The social consequences of the global economic crisis in South East Europe*. London: London School of Economics and Political Science.

Bastian, J. (2010). *External anchors to the rescue: Reaching out in a time of economic and financial sector crisis in South Eastern Europe* (Occasional Paper No. 10). Oxford: St Anthony's College.

Bebbington, A., & McCourt, W. (Eds.). (2007). *Development success: Statecraft in the south*. Basingstoke: Palgrave Macmillan.

Bohle, D., & Greskovitz, B. (2012). *Capitalist diversity on Europe's periphery*. Ithaca, NY: Cornell University Press.

Bojicic-Dzelilovic, V., Ker-Lindsay, J., & Kostovicova, D. (Eds.). (2013). *Civil society and transitions in the Western Balkans*. Basingstoke: Palgrave Macmillan.

Borzel, T. (2013). When Europeanization hits limited statehood: The Western Balkans as a test case for the transformative power of Europe. In A. Elbasani (Ed.), *European integration and transformation in the Western Balkans* (pp. 173–185). London: Routledge.

Coyne, C. J., & Pellillo, A. (2011). Economic reconstruction amidst conflict: Insights from Afghanistan and Iraq. *Defence and Peace Economics, 22*(6), 627–743.

Dallago, B. (2006). The local dimension of transformation: An introduction. In B. Dallago (Ed.), *Transformation and European integration: The local dimension* (pp. 1–20). Basingstoke: Palgrave Macmillan.

Elbasani, A. (Ed.). (2013). *European integration and transformation in the Western Balkans*. London: Routledge.

European Stability Initiative. (2003). *The road to Thessaloniki: Cohesion and the Western Balkans*. Brussels.

Fagan, A. (2013). Building environmental governance in potential candidate countries: Environmental impact assessment processes in Bosnia-Herzegovina. In A. Elbasani (Ed.), *European integration and transformation in the Western Balkans* (pp. 138–157). London: Routledge.

Fenger, M., & Klok, P.-J. (2001). Interdependency, beliefs and coalition behavior: A contribution to the advocacy coalition framework. *Policy Sciences, 34*, 157–170.

Fink-Hafner, D. (1998). Organized interests in the policy-making process in Slovenia. *Journal of European Public Policy, 5*(2), 285–302.

Fink-Hafner, D. (2007, 6–8 September). *Why Europeanization moves at different paces: The cases of Croatia, Serbia and Montenegro*. Paper presented at the 4th ECPR General Conference, Pisa.

Gligorov, V. (2007). Transition, integration and development in Southeast Europe. *Ekonomski Pregled, 58*(5–6), 259–304.

Granovetter, M. S. (1973). The strength of weak ties'. *American Journal of Sociology, 78*(6), 1360–1389.

Granovetter, M. S. (1983). The strength of weak ties – a network theory revisited. *Sociological Theory, 1*, 210–233.

Hodgson, G. M. (2006). Institutions, recession and recovery in the transitional economies. *Journal of Economic Issues, XL*(4), 875–894.

Kenis, P., Schneider, V., et al. (1991). Policy networks and policy analysis: Scrutinizing a new analytical toolbox. In B. Marin & R. Mayntz (Eds.), *Policy networks: Empirical evidence and theoretical considerations* (pp. 25–62). Boulder: Campus/Westview.

Kim, Y., & Roh, C. (2008). Beyond the advocacy coalition framework in policy process. *International Journal of Public Administration, 31*(6), 668–689.

Knoke, D. (1998). Who steals my purse steals trash: The structure of organizational influence. *Journal of Theoretical Politics, 10*, 507–530.

Knoke, D. (2007, January, 25–28). *Historical development of the national policy domain studies and comparing policy networks methods*. Conference presentation, COMPON Conference.

Malova, D., & Haughton, T. (2002). Making institutions in Central and Eastern Europe and the impact of Europe. *West European Politics, 25*(2), 101–120.

Marsh, D., & Rhodes, R. A. W. (Eds.). (1992). *Policy networks in British government*. Oxford: Clarendon.

Myant, M., & Drahkoupil, J. (2012). International integration, varieties of capitalism and resilience to crisis in transition economies. *Europe-Asia Studies, 64*(1), 1–33.

Pedersen, O. K. (2010). Institutional competitiveness: How nations came to compete. In G. Morgan, J. L. Campbell, C. Crouch, O. J. Pedersen, & R. Whitley (Eds.), *The Oxford handbook of comparative institutional analysis* (pp. 625–659). Oxford: Oxford University Press.

Penev, S., & Marušić, A. (2006). Enactment of new laws and revision of existing regulations. In S. Penev (Ed.), *How to improve legislative process in Serbia and Bosnia and Herzegovina*. Belgrade: Investment Compact for South East Europe and Economics Institute.

Petak, Z. (2006). Europeanization and policy making in the national context: The work of policy in Croatia. *Politicka Misao, XLIII*(5), 61–75.

Peterson, J., & Bomberg, E. (1999). *Decision-making in the European Union*. New York: St. Martin's Press.

Sanfey, P. (2010). *South-eastern Europe: Lessons from the global economic crisis* (Working Paper No. 113). London: EBRD.

Sanfey, P., & Zeh, S. (2013). Making sense of competitiveness indicators in South- Eastern Europe. In O. Anastasakis, P. Sanfey, & M. Watson (Eds.), *Defining a new reform agenda: Paths to sustainable convergence in South East Europe* (pp. 25–51). Oxford: St Anthony's College.

Staranova, K. (2002). Cultural change into professional policy making: The case of Slovakia. Centre for policy studies. http://www.policy.hu/staronova

Stubbs, P., & Zrinscak, S. (2009). Croatian social policy: The legacies of war, state-building and late Europeanization. *Social Policy and Administration, 43*(2), 121–135.

Szelenyi, I., & Wilk, K. (2010). Institutional transformation in European post-Communist regimes. In G. Morgan et al. (Eds.), *The Oxford handbook of comparative institutional analysis* (pp. 565–587). Oxford: Oxford University Press.

Thomas, M., et al. (2007). South East Europe: Opportunities and challenges for improving regulatory quality. In C. Kirkpatrick & D. Parker (Eds.), *Regulatory impact assessment*. Cheltenham: Edward Elgar.

van Waarden, F. (1992). Dimensions and types of policy networks. *European Journal of Political Research, 21*, 29–52.

Part I
Western Balkans in the EU Neighbourhood: Economic and Social Policy Reforms

Chapter 2
Shaping Social Policies in the Western Balkans: Legal and Institutional Changes in the Context of Globalisation and Post-socialist Transformation

Marija Babović and Danilo Vuković

1 Introduction

The scope of analysis in this chapter encompasses the reform processes in the field of social policy in the Western Balkans. Social policy is a public policy area, which defines and establishes the conditions under which individuals and groups gain access to different social subsystems and resources, and thus are protected from risks arising from the inability to access these. This means that social policy is actually a set of policies that define and shape the key conditions under which social integration is being achieved.[1]

Western Balkan countries have been exposed to more than two decades of change associated with the constitution of states, post-socialist transformation and globalisation. Their common socialist and state legacy was marked by a distinctive blending of economic and social policy. The absence of pluralism of economic and political power and the fact that the political nomenclature was the only active social subject (as other social groups were not able to form relatively stable class associations Lazić 2000, 27) have led to social policy that is based less on social rights and more on the care of a political state for its subjects (Petrović 2004, 67). The state had

[1] As Lewis noted, the term 'social policy' is sometimes used in the narrow sense to refer to a cluster of government policies designed to promote social objectives. This meaning is usually understood as policies intended to improve social well-being or the welfare of citizens and is often treated as equivalent to talking about 'welfare states'. On the other hand, more broadly, social policy is the interface between forms of integration and belonging and the administrative or organisational mechanisms devised for the delivery of welfare services and benefits (Lewis 2000, 4–5).

M. Babović (✉)
Faculty of Philosophy, University of Belgrade, Belgrade, Serbia
e-mail: bmarija63@gmail.com

D. Vuković
Faculty of Law, University of Belgrade, Belgrade, Serbia
e-mail: danilo.vukovic@ius.bg.rs

M. Thomas, V. Bojicic-Dzelilovic (eds.), *Public Policy Making in the Western Balkans*, DOI 10.1007/978-94-017-9346-9_2

the most important role in providing social security; many risks were socialised, while employment had a special role in the socialist social policy systems. The working place served a twofold function: as an economic unit, it had the function of employment and value production; but as a social protection unit, it had the function of (re) distribution of social resources. Disintegration of the single state, transformation from socialism to capitalism, as well as globalisation processes that have universally limited sovereign power of national governments to shape public policy are the context for social policy reform processes in the Western Balkans.

Precisely because of the importance of these policies in terms of social disintegration and transformation, it is important to examine under what conditions, by which actors, how and with what consequences these policies have been shaped. Certainly, this is not the first time that social policies in this part of Europe are being scrutinised, as evidenced by numerous studies (Deacon and Stubbs 2007; Stubbs 2009; Stambolieva and Dehnert 2011). Taking into account the findings of previous studies, the task of this paper is to specifically highlight social relations between stakeholders in shaping these policies, and to observe the extent to which these processes have incorporated or excluded certain social interest groups and how this is reflected in the key aspects of social policy.

Analysing social policies in the context of social transformation in the Western Balkans is too broad a subject for the scope of a single chapter, and this publication as a whole is strongly focused on economic policies. For these reasons, our analysis will be limited to the following: (1) the coverage of only a few key sectors or types of social policies, and (2) key indicators of their main features and types of changes.

In this paper, we will conceptualise social policy as previously done by Deacon and Stubbs 'as both real, having concrete impacts on the well-being of people, and epiphenomena with a logic derived from the interests of those engaged in the process' (2007, 2). However, our analysis will be limited to three areas of social policies—higher education,[2] employment and social protection policies. There are several reasons for this selection. In modern societies, economic participation is one of the central channels through which individuals integrate into society and achieve their socioeconomic status. Education and employment policies determine opportunities for economic participation of individuals and social groups, while social protection policies define requirements for protection against social risks, primarily those associated with the termination of or inability for economic participation.

The main objectives of the analysis are as follows: (a) to determine key content changes in the selected social policies in relation to the period of socialism, and to identify the trends of social changes based and reflected in such policy contents; (b) to identify key actors that shaped the given policies and, by defining their content, defined new terms of social inclusion and integration; (c) to describe the processes through which these policies are shaped, or rather to review the configurations of interests, their interrelationships and the actions of stakeholders, which led to the given outcomes in policy formulation. Such analysis will provide answers to certain

[2] Higher education policies have been selected because paradigmatic changes (privatisation, marketization, international integration, ideological justification of the education process) are the most visible in this area.

crucial questions: (1) Which social groups had access to the policy-defining processes, and (2) Which social groups have been ensured a better position in the social structure as a result of the new social policies. Therefore, analysis of the policy-shaping processes serves as a tool to understand important aspects of the deeper changes in the social structure.

The analysis is conducted on two levels. The first covers the Western Balkans with the exception of Albania (that is, Serbia, Croatia, Bosnia and Herzegovina, Montenegro and Macedonia). At this level, a comparative analysis on the 'sample' of social policies will inevitably be more general, with the aim to identify key directions for changes in policies and to pinpoint the most important stakeholders who have shaped these policies. The second level of analysis is a case study of Serbia in which, policy-making processes in higher education are analysed in more detail.[3]

The analyses carried out on two levels used different methodologies. At a comparative, regional level, the research was limited to secondary sources, which includes various studies, official documents and official statistics data. The analysis of social policies in Serbia also relies on an analysis of the content of key legislation and strategies to identify the content of policies. For the study of actors and processes, the analysis is based on the original research conducted by combining positional and reputational research methods to determine interrelations between actors and their relative influence on the policy outputs.[4]

The presentation will follow the same logic of the analytical framework: the first section will lay out a regional comparative analysis, whereas the second will focus more deeply on the processes of shaping select policies in Serbia.

2 Designing Social Policies in the Western Balkans

Within this section alone, it is not possible to point out a variety of complex and long-term structural and institutional legacies that marked the territory of the former Yugoslavia, and which still influence the configuration of social interests and the shaping of social policies. Several key determining factors, however, will be mentioned. It has already been pointed out in the introductory part that young states in this region have a common socialist legacy rooted in a distinctive merger of economic and social policies, a strong role of the state, an institutional basis of the social protection system, which is referred to as Bismarckian (Deacon et al. 2007; Vuković 2010) and distinctive forms of articulation of group interests through a system of self-government (with its own manifest and latent forms of alignment of interests and decision making) (Bolčić 2003). Nevertheless, that legacy does not stop at a common socialist past. The collapse of socialism and subsequent period of blocked and

[3] A wider and more detailed analysis of policy networks and social interests underlying changes in the employment, higher education and social protection analysis is the subject of a separate study (Vuković and Babović 2013), and we shall refer to these findings throughout this article.

[4] These methods will be further explained in another section.

delayed transformation in certain places[5] have been marked by conflicts in which state-building interests and the war were used as a cover for distribution of social wealth, and the construction of capitalism was pushed to the margins (Lazić 2011). Delayed transition to capitalism was obstructed by devastated institutions, destroyed or usurped economic wealth and permanent conflicts between political elites and social groups that have found themselves in positions of winners and losers of the transition (Bolčić 1997; Lazić 1995, 2000). Countries that started the transition to capitalism earlier and more mindfully have, after the initial economic downturn, also experienced a period of upswing. Unlike them, the countries of former Yugoslavia (except Slovenia) have failed to achieve long-term and stable economic development and to ensure that gains are allocated to many social groups, including those who are extremely marginalised (unskilled and factory workers, the elderly, people with disabilities, rural residents and others) (Lazić 2011; Milić 2002). The latest crisis of capitalism in the North-western hemisphere has also contributed to problems of transformation of these societies. Finally, inclusion into the global integration processes and EU accession rendered the fragile sovereignty of young countries even more so given the continuous conditioning of direction and character of changes imposed by international organisations and actors.[6]

Therefore, important determinants in the shaping and implementing of social policies in the countries of former Yugoslavia are as follows: (1) the above-mentioned institutional, Bismarckian legacy in which social rights are tightly linked to position in the sphere of labour; (2) weak state sovereignty, undermined from within by political and ethnic conflicts, and externally by international stakeholders who place conditions on financial assistance (such as the World Bank and IMF) or on joining the EU; (3) pressures of neoliberal interventions by international and some domestic actors; and (4) pressure by 'losers of transition'[7] to reverse the erosion of protection they once enjoyed. These countries have experienced multiple social disintegration: simultaneous disintegration of the state; conflicts between members of different ethnic and political groups; and collapse of socialist-era institutions followed by the delayed, slow and inconsistent development of new institutions that are agents of social integration. Under these conditions, shaping of social policy is extremely important for redefining of principles of social integration and transformation of social relations between groups and classes in the new societies of the Western Balkans.

Various insights into the changing social policies in the region (Deacon et al. 2007; Vuković 2010; Stambolieva and Dehnert 2011; Babović 2010) indicate that they assume a hybrid form whose modalities vary between a somewhat specific

---

[5] The notion 'blocked transformation' is used primarily to describe the situation in Serbian society during the 1990s when political elite sought to block change towards a market economy and political pluralism (Lazić 1995, 2000; Bolčić 1997).

[6] More on globalization aspects and trends in social policy and role of international actors in Deacon 2007.

[7] These are mainly classes of workers, primarily in the industrial sector but also in increasingly extensive service sector, as well as small farmers (Lazić and Cvejić 2004; Babović 2009).

constellation of interests and the above-mentioned determining factors. We will first focus on the characteristics of the reforms, or rather on the content of social policies in higher education, employment and social protection to identify the choices made in the shaping of these policies, as well as some of their most striking effects in social reality. We will then try to identify actors whose interests have had a decisive influence on shaping these policies and thus on the living conditions of different social groups. It is important to note that any attempt at systematic comparison in this region faces a serious problem of inconsistent data, which significantly limits the reach of such attempts.

3 Features of Social Policies Reform

A fundamental, paradigmatic shift in social policies of the Western Balkans can be observed in the transfer of responsibility for the provision of social security from the state to individuals, families and social groups. Therefore, the analysis of reforms in social policy raises questions about how and to what extent the state regulates the social security of citizens. Whether it does this indirectly through the creation of regulatory, economic and institutional conditions of protection, or directly through immediate provision of care in different spheres of social life, and the extent to which it does this. Or should we start at the other end and determine the extent to which responsibility for social security is transferred to an individual, who is expected to be extremely proactive and resourceful in key aspects of social participation, while the state acts as a background actor to define requirements, and intervenes only when individuals fail to 'take care of themselves on their own'. Within the same framework there is also the issue of social security costs—whether those costs are largely borne by the state or by an individual, and to what extent?

Starting from these basic issues, social policy reforms can be viewed through the following key dimensions: privatisation and marketization[8] in ensuring social inclusion and safety in different areas, individualisation of responsibility and activation of an individual in a given system of social inclusion and social protection. All these dimensions are associated with the general process of commodification that links social security of individuals and groups more tightly to the market. Our comparative analysis seeks to determine to what extent and in what forms these processes work in the Western Balkans, highlighting for similarities and differences. Attention will be paid first to higher education policies, then employment and finally, social protection policies.

[8] The two dimensions should be distinguished because while in the case of privatisation the private sector appears as a provider of services related to social inclusion and social protection, in the case of marketization, the state or the public sector can also occur as an actor offering the service under market conditions.

3.1 *Higher Education Policies*

Reforms in higher education are characterised by three key directions of change: *privatisation, marketization and Bolognisation*. The first is reflected in the fact that the offer of higher education is being privatised. In other words, in addition to state institutions of higher education, private ones also appear. These institutions offer programmes that are often better suited to market needs, in conditions when state universities are slow to adapt to the market system. At the same time, they represent an important area for economic positioning of the upper-middle class or, rather, those expert groups in the middle class who base their social status on academic careers.

Although the state still retains a dominant role in the field of higher education, there is a trend towards an increasing share among students in private higher education institutions everywhere. In most observed countries, the proportion of students at private faculties is about one-fifth, with Croatia varying considerably from this average, Serbia[9] digressing from it in recent years, while the two entities in Bosnia and Herzegovina manifest large differences. Namely, about 22 % of students[10] in the academic year 2009/2010 attended private faculties in Bosnia and Herzegovina, although the differences between entities are major—in the Republic of Srpska this share was 31 % and in the Federation of Bosnia and Herzegovina only 9 % (RSIS 2011; FMON 2010). In Croatia, private higher education institutions make up 24 % of all such institutions,[11] whilst only 6 % of students attend these institutions. As many as half of the faculties in Macedonia are private,[12] but still only a minority of students—21 %—attend these faculties. In Montenegro, the share of students attending private faculties is also around 20 %[13] (MPS 2011), while the share in Serbia amounted to 17.4 % in 2009/2010.

Another important reform direction is reflected in the broader process of marketization of higher education. Besides privatisation this also includes the trend towards commercial offers of services by public higher education institutions, which at the same time provide free or state-funded education services for some students. In some countries this marketization causes conflicts between users/clients or students on the one hand, and providers of services and their founders—the state—on the other.[14]

---

[9] All data on the number of students and higher education institutions were obtained by analysing websites of ministries of education, state institutes of statistics and related publications.

[10] In Bosnia and Herzegovina there are 22 universities with 147 faculties and 10 academies, to which 4 religious faculties should be added.

[11] Namely, Croatia has 10 universities, 7 of which are public and 3 private; 15 polytechnics, including 3 private ones and 27 colleges, of which 24 are private.

[12] According to the Ministry of Education and Science, Macedonia has 5 state and 9 private universities with a total of 134 faculties.

[13] In this country there is one state and two private universities, as well as seven independent private faculties (MPS 2011).

[14] In the last 3 years several student protests took place in Serbia and Croatia. Their main demands were for reduced tuition rates and changes in the rules of studying, which would be more in tune

The share of GDP spending on higher education in Croatia was 0.87 % in 2004, while 0.90 % of GDP has been allocated in Serbia and 1.10 % in Montenegro (Vukasović 2009). As we have seen, in recent years there has been an increasing share of students at private higher education institutions, and a significant number of self-financing students at state universities (57 % of all students in Serbia). Tuition fees for self-financing students at state universities in Belgrade range from EUR 560 to 2,500; this amount also includes costs of administrative fees and textbooks. At private faculties in Belgrade, 1 year of study costs between EUR 1,500 and 3,500. At the same time, the average take-home salary in Serbia is EUR 350. In these circumstances,[15] education becomes less accessible to the lower socio-economic classes and exacerbates inequality in education (Baucal and Pavlović Babić 2009; Farnell and Kovač 2010; Miličević and Danijela 2009).

The third key direction of reform of the higher education system is the alignment with the principles defined by the Bologna Declaration to enable increased efficiency,[16] harmonisation with European standards, better links with labour market needs, and stronger scientific and technological basis for broader development processes with the inclusion of students as partners in the educational process. These reform directions actually achieve two key effects: (1) the educational process and qualifications across Europe become more uniform and allow for quick conversion in conditions of increased mobility on the labour markets; and (2) knowledge and skills are shaped with a more direct connection to economic structures and development processes manifested through continuous changes to increasingly more volatile, unstable and flexible labour markets.

Bolognisation has taken a dual form. On the one hand, private higher education institutions have swiftly adapted to the new principle. They often provide an easy entry to the market, emphasising modern education profiles as well as those not requiring high investments in teaching facilities, research and development (hence, there is an underrepresentation of engineering, biotechnology and similar profiles at private higher education institutions). They have low requirements for students, and at the same time invest insufficiently in research and underperform in the various rankings when compared to public universities.[17] On the other hand, public higher education institutions have formally complied with the Bologna requirements, but a

with the needs of students. These protests were often contradictory, because on the one hand, they opposed the marketization of education, and on the other, public high schools were asked to accommodate the needs of clients and the needs of the market and to respond to the challenges and competition from private universities and colleges by introducing more exam terms and reducing necessary conditions for entry.

[15] It should be noted that we did not take into account the inadequate system of scholarships and student housing, which is not developing quickly enough to keep up with the growth and massification of university education and associated living expenses beyond tuition fees.

[16] In terms of faster passing through the system, higher percentage of successful completion of studies, and fewer dropouts.

[17] For example, at the Ranking Web of Universities, Belgrade University is ranked as 548th in the world, while the best ranking private university is Singidunum University with rank 5,371 (http://www.webometrics.info/en/Europe/Serbia). Similarly, Belgrade University is the only Serbian

large portion of curricula and teaching and examination practice has remained constant. Although the teaching staff is slowly changing, the system in general is still governed by senior academics whose professional socialisation took place during the socialist era. Finally, adjustment to market demands (for example, adjustments in curricula) is taking place with mixed results (cf. USPRS 2010; Branković and Šabić 2011; Popović and Đorić 2011; Uzelac 2009; World Bank 2008).

There is little research on the quality of higher educational programmes, and none that provides comparative insights. Rare studies indicate that, especially in the early years of privatisation of higher education before the system of accreditation was put in place, the quality of higher education was problematic. According to some analyses from 2001, three polytechnic schools in Croatia did not employ a single person. During this period, 91 lecturers (of whom only 25 had the rank of university teachers and were mainly outsourced from the universities) worked with almost 20,000 students. Due to low costs, high share of self-financing students and short courses, higher education has proved to be a very profitable business (Polšek 2004, 288–89).

Analyses show that the educational process is characterised by obsolete teaching methodologies and testing that assesses rote learning and factual recall. The quality of teaching is also affected by the fact that universities are decentralised, so it is difficult to establish multidisciplinary studies and governance structures that promote quality (World Bank 2008, 12). Concerns about the quality of teaching are related to both the public and private faculties. Western Balkan countries have introduced external systems of quality assurance and accreditation of institutions. However, transparency and accountability of this process is questionable because the system of control of public institutions is underdeveloped, and there is a considerable overlap between the university and the political elite.

3.2 Employment Policies

Employment policies cannot be effectively analysed in isolation from certain economic policies (such as policies relating to privatisation and taxation), or from labour policies. Since such comprehensive insights cannot be provided here, several key factors should be borne in mind when examining employment policies. Privatisation policies represent a broader set of policies, which encompass (1) regulations and requirements concerning the sale of state and former socially owned enterprises; and (2) shaping of conditions for private sector development (for example, through the establishment and development of small and medium enterprises and entrepreneurs). These policies create conditions under which resources required to initiate and carry out an economic activity (ownership of means of production) are distributed, define the responsibilities of owners of private enterprises, and

higher education institution ranked in the so-called Shanghai list (http://www.shanghairanking.com/ARWU2012.html).

foster or hinder development of the private business sector. The outcome of these policies partly affect the manner of restructuring of the labour market, and furthermore whether the public sector will retain a significant role in employment, and thus in the social integration of employees in this segment of the labour market. The policies also affect the conditions under which business is developed and jobs generated or labour supply created. Taxation policies define the layout of burden on the various economic actors and have a stimulating or inhibiting effect on the development and representation of different employment arrangements, especially the so-called flexible forms (part-time employment, freelance work, part-time engagement and 'job sharing'). It is important to keep labour policies in mind, because employment processes are affected by conditions related to workplace safety and sustainability, durability and quality of employment.

The effects of these policies, but also deeper and long-lasting economic and social processes in the Western Balkans have generated the following trends (with some differences and specifics): (1) privatisation was marked by misuse and often irresponsible transfer of public resources into private hands, with short-term profit interests and sometimes without any real and consistent intention to invest and regenerate, transform and develop privatised companies (Pavlović 2006; Vukovic 2005; Arandarenko 2010; Vuković 2011); (2) the state still remains an important employer, and employment in the public sector is significantly maintained[18]; and (3) whereas the government reduced the level of protection of workers,[19] particularly in the private sector, ineffective enforcement of laws and policies enabled informalization of the labour market and the existence of a large share of informal employment[20] and a grey economy. The system of taxes and contributions has often burdened the middle classes in particular (Arandarenko 2010), and has limited the development of flexible forms of employment.[21] In addition, labour markets in the region are highly segmented, whilst the position of employees in the public sector and white-collar occupations on average is significantly better than that of workers in the private sector (especially in SMEs) (Nestić and Rašić Bakarić 2010, 3).

In certain circumstances, employment policy should not be viewed as crucial in defining the odds of social groups' involvement in the labour market. It should be seen as a means that was, in the circumstances, doomed to have a very limited utility.

---

[18] Share of employment in the public sector is above the EU average, ranging up to 31 % in Serbia (in relation to all, including informal employment), 35 % in Croatia and 42 % in Montenegro (Monstat 2012; Bejaković et al. 2010).

[19] Measured by the OECD's index of EPL (employment protection legislation), countries in the region still have greater protection than the EU average (2.1 for EU-10 and 2.4 for EU-15), with maximum values in Macedonia (3. 2), Croatia (2.7), Bosnia and Herzegovina (2.6), and lowest in Montenegro (2.2), which until 2008 had the highest value according to this indicator of the protection of employees in the region (4.1) (ILO 2009a, 53–55).

[20] In 2011 this share amounted to 19 % in Serbia (RZS, ARS 2011), while it is estimated at 22.6 % in Montenegro (ISSP, ZZ 2007).

[21] Share of part-time employment is extremely low in the region and amounts to 4.6 % of total employment in Montenegro (Monstat 2012), 10.3 % in Bosnia and Herzegovina (ASBH 2011), 8.6 % in Serbia (SORS 2011), 9.9 % in Croatia (CBS 2010).

Table 2.1 Employment and unemployment rates for the population of working age (15–64) in 2011

	Employment rates (%)	Unemployment rates (%)
Bosnia and Herzegovina	38.7	28.0
Macedonia	43.5	31.9
Serbia	45.4	23.6
Montenegro	45.9	19.9
Croatia	51.5	14.3

Sources: Data from the Labour Force Surveys of the National Statistics Agencies

Shaping employment policies on the principles of activation, appropriate for modern employment policies in the EU and other developed countries, could not be effective, as serious problems occurred in the area of labour demand. The evidence of these problems can be found in extremely low employment rates and high unemployment rates in the region (Table 2.1).

According to available information, employment policies, which also include unemployment insurance, are poorly developed both in passive and active measures. Throughout the region there is relatively little unemployment benefit coverage for the unemployed, and the benefits that exist are low compared to average wages. In this aspect, however, significant differences are manifested; for example, the passive measures in Croatia cover 26.2 % of the unemployed (Bejaković 2011; Bejaković et al. 2010; World Bank 2010), while the coverage in Serbia is 11 % (World Bank 2006, 83), and 9 % in Montenegro (Krsmanović and Walewski 2006). The amount of compensation is defined at different levels. Hence in Montenegro, for example, it amounts to 40 % of the minimum wage defined by the general collective agreement (Ibid.), and in Bosnia and Herzegovina it is 40 % of the average wage (ARZ 2011, 35; DEP 2011, 26).

Increased importance is given to active labour market measures, but their coverage is still low. Thus, these measures include only 2.5 % of the unemployed in Croatia (Bejaković 2011; World Bank 2010). Funds allocated for active measures are relatively modest (0.07 % of GDP in Croatia, 0.11 % in Bosnia and Herzegovina,[22] 0.19 % in Macedonia,[23] and 0.10 % in Serbia[24]), which is lower than in some countries of Central and Eastern Europe (CEE) such as Czech Republic (0.31 % of GDP allocated for this purpose) and Slovenia (0.89 % of GDP) (World Bank 2010). Institutional capacities to implement these measures in individual countries are weak, and evaluation of their effects almost completely absent. Some authors observed that active measures often target more employable categories as in Bosnia with young people with higher qualifications (DEP 2011, 26) or some of the Serbian programmes (for example, First Chance, an active labour market programme)

[22] MCP (2010, 26).

[23] Uzunov (2011, 125).

[24] Arandarenko and Krstić (2008).

(Babović 2011). It is evident that the primary function of employment services is to register the unemployed and determine their rights to unemployment benefits and health insurance; however, provision of services such as vocational guidance, counselling, implementation of active measures is underdeveloped (MCP 2010, 26).

In most countries in the region, privatisation of employment mediation has not taken significant effect. Private employment agencies are registered, but rare estimates indicate that they do not play a large part in the recruitment process. However, it is assessed that the entry of private agents for employment mediation would contribute more to improvement of state institutions responsible for employment, as is the case in Croatia (Baturina et al. 2011, 21).

Formally, employment policies in the region were adapted to global trends in terms of increased emphasis on active labour market programmes and activation measures. In reality, these programmes have small budgets, are often inadequately targeted and have low impact (among other problems, due to low demand for labour). Unemployment benefits often do not represent an efficient mechanism for support because of the large share of long-term unemployment. Finally, there is a large share of grey economy and informal employment, which further decreases the impact of employment policies.

3.3 Social Protection Policies

Changes in the social protection policies will be registered here in the key aspects of the following three components: pension and disability insurance, social assistance to socially vulnerable groups and social welfare services.

In terms of pension policies, paradigmatic and parameter changes are taking place in the region. In the first group, two trends can be roughly identified: in Croatia, Macedonia and Montenegro, under the strong influence of the World Bank, three-tier pension systems have been introduced, which include compulsory pension insurance based on intergenerational solidarity (first pillar), mandatory pension insurance based on individual capitalised savings (second pillar), and voluntary insurance based on individual capitalised savings (third pillar). In Bosnia and Herzegovina and Serbia, these systems have not been introduced; thus the basic system is the successor of the former Yugoslav pay-as-you-go system based on the logic of intergenerational solidarity. Within the second category of changes, there is a noticeable increase in the retirement age and reduction of replacement rates, restructuring of funds and the like. Despite reforms, the pension funds still face an imbalance and deficit covered from the budget (ILO 2009b; Uzunov 2011; Guardiancich 2011; Matković 2009).

Some forms of social protection safety schemes have appeared everywhere, often with local variations in the amounts allocated and variable conditions of eligibility for assistance (Deacon et al. 2007). All systems of social protection are strongly influenced by the institutional framework of the former common state. In the social protection system (which includes material benefits and social services), the most important role is played by the centres for social work (CSW) as decentralized units of the ministry responsible for social affairs. CSWs administer social security benefits including social assistance and assistance for persons with disabilities, war veterans and the like. In all observed countries, social assistance is relatively low. In Croatia, for example, it is EUR 68 for the first adult (Bejaković 2011, 82); the conditions for receiving aid are strict (tests of behaviour and property); the targeting is good, but the coverage is low[25] as is total expenditure for social welfare.[26] These countries face problems such as limited coverage for vulnerable groups,[27] high-level expenditures for war veterans and other such politically motivated expenditures.

Social services are provided through a network of CSWs and accommodation facilities for users (residential institutions). Due to growing poverty and humanitarian problems caused by wars, ethnic conflicts and massive displacement of populations, centres for social work have prioritised the administration of financial support (also humanitarian aid in earlier periods). In such circumstances, insufficient resources could be devoted to counselling work and the development and implementation of social work services in the community. The main tendency in social services is a shift away from institutional care towards other forms of community support, including foster care and community-based welfare services. Another common feature of the whole region is the diversification of service providers and the introduction of private, non-profit sector, in particular. There are strong indications that the system still relies on the public sector (Papić et al. 2012), although many local and international actors have worked to develop alternative models for nearly two decades. One characteristic of social policies in the region is redefining social policy issues away from traditional sectoral policies and clear political choices within them towards policies that are more responsive to social problems of women, the elderly and young people (Deacon et al. 2007).

3.4 Social Policy in the Region: Common Trends

In all three areas of social policy, a relatively pronounced trend towards privatisation is observed. However, the state still remains the dominant service provider. In higher education, there are a growing number of private higher education schools, but only a minority of the student population attends them. Private agents appear on the labour market, but their role remains marginal. Social

[25] For example, only one-fifth of the poorest 15 % of Montenegro's population receives social assistance, which is still higher than in Serbia (7 %) and in Bosnia and Herzegovina (5 %) (Gotcheva and Strokova 2010).

[26] Allocations for social welfare range from 0.17 % of GDP in Serbia to, for example, 0.5 % of GDP in Montenegro, which is still less than 0.7 % in Slovenia (Gotcheva and Strokova 2010).

[27] For example, in Macedonia over 80 % of the unemployed are not covered by any social protection scheme (Uzunov 2011, 131).

protection services are offered by an increasing number of private for-profit or non-profit organisations, but social work centres and residential institutions in most countries are still the dominant network, and significant investments are being made to modernise and empower them.

Marketization is evident in higher education, where in addition to private universities, faculties and colleges, state universities are also providers of services at market prices. Marketization is also manifested through reforms of the pension systems in which a second and third pillar are introduced. However, marketization is reflected in the stronger binding of the results of these services to market needs—education is tailored more to the needs of the labour market; measures of employment and unemployment insurance are also designed to protect the unemployed as soon as possible and to equip them for successful re-employment. By the same logic, material social assistance is conditioned and restricted so individuals and families invest more effort to take care of their own viability in the market.

Although responsibility for social security is generally transferred to individuals, the state is not consistently in retreat, but remains sensitive to the influences and demands of specific social groups and coalitions. That last observation leads us to the next question: Who are the actors that have shaped the direction of changes in social policies?

4 Actors of Social Policies Reform

Identifying actors who have influenced the shaping of social policies in the described directions may not be detailed at this point because insights rely on available analysis and observations rather than on original research. Only in the latter part of this chapter will such analysis be conducted, and that only for a single country—Serbia. Therefore, here we will roughly assess the extent to which different actors played a role in shaping social policies.

The roles that states play as key actors and agents of reform differ throughout the region by type, capacity, nature and size of public administration. The role of states should be viewed in the context of political and social networks of key actors involved in social policy reform, who have been influential to a lesser or larger extent. We will briefly review the different roles of state and local actors in social policy reforms.

In Bosnia and Herzegovina, the state is weak at the central level; key social policy functions take place at lower levels of government. However, the state manifests itself in different ways at the two entity levels. In the Republic of Srpska, it is a centralised state within a state, ethnically homogeneous, with no major obstacles in the articulation and aggregation of interests, which significantly facilitates political decision making. In the Federation of Bosnia and Herzegovina, the situation is quite different because this entity is composed of ten cantons that are ethnically divided or mixed and have significant competences in shaping social policies. This leads to a diversity of social policies and even in social aspects of living between two neighbouring cantons. The Federation of Bosnia and Herzegovina has little means to influence these policies or to monitor their implementation (Maglajlić and Rašidagić 2011). Some authors suggest that one of the fundamental problems of social policy reform in Bosnia and Herzegovina is that the political scene, and even the state itself, is dominated by nationalist political parties that favour the interests of the ethnic group constituting their electorate in a way that ensures the survival of the elites in power. Due to this fragmentation, it is said that in Bosnia and Herzegovina there is not one, but rather 12 social policy systems (10 cantonal, 1 for the Republic of Srpska and 1 for the Brčko District), which makes the system significantly more expensive, reduces efficiency and leads to selective outcomes as the system offers better protection to groups that support the ruling political elites (Keil 2011).

In its state-building processes, Croatia, like Serbia, overthrew an authoritarian political regime and underwent democratisation processes. However, these political changes have not led to radical transformations in social policies but rather, implemented in a partial manner. Some authors suggest that the main reason for this is a political intention to retain the support of voters, which acts as a limiting factor for any future government. Thus far, every change in the shape or size of social protection has caused dissatisfaction among certain social groups. Political actors who were directly or indirectly involved in the processes of restructuring the social sector tended to have similar attitudes towards social security. In a way, the differences between political parties have disappeared in the field of social security. In addition, social policy reforms have been carried out primarily under pressure from the elites or under the influence of the World Bank and IMF, and later the EU (Vidović and Pauković 2011; Deacon and Stubbs 2007).

Macedonia has weak state institutions, a highly centralised government with poorly developed democratic principles, and a widespread system of patronage used for electoral purposes, including the distribution of key resources and positions to loyal actors. Additionally, underdeveloped civil society and a critical public have also shaped the conditions of social policy reform. Under conditions of widespread poverty and economic underdevelopment, but also due to interethnic tensions, social policy reform has been an extremely sensitive issue. In this context, international organisations have played a particularly strong role, which will be discussed later in more detail (Bornarova 2011).

Finally, the situation is only slightly different in Montenegro. Despite the severe conflicts that are sometimes referred to as bifurcation to show the duality of structure and policy in this country (undeveloped North versus developed South, orientation towards independence versus orientation towards liaisons with Serbia), political forces led by the Democratic Party of Socialists allowed for long-term continuity of government (Džankić 2011). The other actors were too weak to influence social policies reforms. These reforms were, as in other countries of the region, controversial, Thus social policies were not radically transformed as new forms of social integration were still fragile, and political conflicts threatened to escalate and jeopardise the continuity of government. Reforms have mainly occurred under external pressure, first through the World Bank, and then under the conditions of accession to the EU.

Therefore, it is clear that in all countries of the region an important role in social policy reforms has been played by the international community. However, its role should not be viewed in isolation from the characteristics and the role of the states themselves. The role of the international community was variable and depended on the strength of the state and civil society in the region. Namely, where the state was weaker and civil society more underdeveloped (as in Bosnia), international actors had a significantly greater impact (Deacon et al. 2007). Mapping the impact of various international actors in different areas of social policy, the authors observed that, generally speaking, the World Bank had the greatest influence everywhere, using loan conditionality or acting together with the IMF to push for changes in the desired direction. The International Labour Organization (ILO) had a weaker role, while other UN agencies—especially UNDP and UNICEF—have been important actors, often intersecting with bilateral donors (Ibid.). A great influence was exerted by bilateral organisations, primarily the British DFID, which often acted in partnership with the World Bank. Scandinavian organisations (especially from Sweden and Norway) also supported reform initiatives in social policy, as did the American USAID.

The European Union seems to have had a belated influence compared to other leading actors. Hence it is observed that the EU came into countries of the region with its demands, recommendations and funds, usually after the World Bank had already defined the agenda of social policy reforms. In addition, the manner in which the EU defines competences in the field of social policy—the absence of strong prescription—has made the impact of the EU weaker. The authors observed that the major impact of the EU is reflected in the transfer of discourse (if not immediately the practice as well) of social inclusion (Ibid.). However, the development of policies of social inclusion and social protection in the EU has progressed only after the Lisbon Strategy was passed in 2000; hence its more intensive transfer to the Western Balkans, which normally has a very slow accession to the EU (except Croatia), occurred only at the end of the previous decade.

The preceding discussion of actors and their roles in the social policy reforms in the region are just general observations. It is to be expected that in the context of different policies and different time periods various processes occurred, marked by a distinctive constellation of interests, liaising of or conflict between actors, and negotiations and use of decisive power. It is these processes as they occurred in Serbia that we will examine more closely.

5 Policy Actors and Policy Networks in Serbia: The Case of Higher Education

The analytical framework for case studies of actors and social policy reform processes in Serbia has been extended in several aspects: (1) (groups of) actors involved (directly or indirectly) in key reforms in higher education are identified in more detail; (2) types of connections formed in the given process are identified; (3) content of reform activities are more closely associated with interests of actors involved in the policy-making process; and (4) resistance and conflicts developed between various stakeholders are identified. Such an analysis should clearly identify the connection between broader societal interests and the process of shaping public policies and link social structure and the shaping of social institutions.

The focus of the analysis will be on a single policy area—higher education. A separate study is devoted to a more detailed analysis of three policy areas: higher education, employment and social protection (Vuković and Babović 2013). Here we will present a detailed analysis of higher education reforms while referring to the broader study when appropriate. The content and the process of reforms in these areas will be examined in terms of a key sector's law while the process of formulation of the public policy and articulation of social interests was studied using the network analysis approach (Babović 2005). The analysis was conducted using data obtained from research that combined two methods of data collection: (1) an analysis of the content of the law,[28] and (2) positional and reputational methods[29] of examining interrelations among actors and their impact in the given process. In the first phase of the study, all categories of actors involved in the adoption of key legislation were identified, and interviews were conducted with individuals representing the groups and institutions in the process (a total of 12 interviews, of which 4 were in the field of higher education). It is important to note that the interviews were conducted only with local stakeholders, and that the role of foreign actors was reconstructed based on the perceptions of respondents and the insight into other secondary sources (project documentation, related publications). In the following passages we will briefly outline the context in which policy changes have been designed, describe the content of the new policies and then inspect social interest and groups that participated in the process of policy formulation.

[28] In addition to the key law, the content of relevant strategies has also been analysed to gain broader insight into the content of changes.

[29] Positional methods are applied to network analysis in a situation where the set of actors in the network is known and when one needs to evaluate the shape and the strength of their relationship, and identify the centrality of the position of individual actors (Burt 1982). Reputational research methods are used to identify the relative influence and power of actors in a network, or in any process, based on a subjective assessment of participants in a given network/process on the relative power of other actors (Pfeffer and Salancik 1974). These methods have been applied with several limitations: (1) the analysis included key but not every actor involved in the process; (2) reputational methods are suitable for the highly politicised environment because the perception of different actors on the amount of power and influence of others is more unambiguous, since this power is more apparent, but these methods are more suitable for testing of current relationships and processes and do not provide detailed and accurate insights into the processes that occurred in the past.

5.1 Context of Policy Changes

When reform of higher education was prepared (2001–2004), key challenges were also identified: (1) to redefine and improve the institutional structure and management of universities; and (2) to provide a satisfactory quality of teaching. Universities were decentralised, and faculties had all the power to shape curricula and manage policies of employment and enrolment. This resulted in the multiplication of human and physical resources (teachers, administrative staff, libraries, laboratories) and hindered the establishment of multidisciplinary studies. Academic programmes and teaching methods were evaluated as obsolete and narrowly oriented, emphasising theoretical rather than practically applicable knowledge, with demanding studies that provided top-level students at the European average, but where intermediate-level students lagged behind the European average (Turajlić et al. 2004, 53–57). Two-thirds of the students were not completing studies in the pre-reform period. Those who managed to finish them, studied on average two times longer than the programme envisioned (Ibid., 51). Also, it was estimated that the educational system did not provide the knowledge required by the market.[30]

The Law on Higher Education (adopted in 2005) legalised the operation of existing private higher education institutions and liberalised higher education.[31] The overflow of resources from the public to the private sector has been regulated, if not stopped, with the system of accreditation in higher education. In school year 2011/2012, private universities or colleges in Serbia were attended by 17 % of all students. However, the marketization of higher education is not reflected solely through privatisation of the sector. At state faculties, there are two categories of students: those who study at public expense and those who finance their studies. Among the students of state faculties, 48 % belong to the latter category, while in the overall student population in Serbia, a total of 57% pay for their education.[32]

---

[30] The reform of higher education abandoned the idea of schools and universities as places where, in addition to preparation for work, socialisation of citizens in the spirit of democratic and civic values is being carried out (Jordan 2006, 113) or the idea of the university as a place where national identity was nurtured and developed (Turajlić et al. 2001, 7). The universities are expected to educate students for the market, to adapt to market needs and to include economics in their internal functioning, and even financing.

[31] At a time when the law was prepared (the period between 2003 and 2005), there were three private universities in Serbia and a number of private faculties and colleges that were not a part of a university. Nowadays, there are 7 state universities with 83 faculties and 10 private ones with 50 faculties (there are an additional 50 state colleges and 22 private colleges that do not operate within a university).

[32] Other elements of higher education also show the increasing burden of education on families and individuals: (1) scholarships and loans from the national level are used by 13 % of students at state universities, and (2) the network of dormitories is insufficient and unevenly developed. In Belgrade, there is one place in dormitories for every seven students at state universities (no new dormitory has been built since 1978), in Novi Sad, one for every 13 and in Niš, one for every 20 students.

As for the goals of legal and institutional reforms, a major point of conflict was changing the management system of universities—that is, the issue of integration of universities. This reform goal has not been achieved to this day. Faculties have maintained the status of legal entities and are self-managing the process of teaching (including quality control), enrolment and employment. Among national authorities responsible for management of the entire system of higher education, they have a majority of votes.[33]

5.2 *Actors, Networks and Outcomes*

If we disregard the fact that the concept of higher education reform was essentially predefined by the Bologna process, and that in this sense the most important actor was the international community—that is, the EU, which Serbia hopes to access—two key interest 'camps' can be identified in the reform of higher education. The first is the Ministry of Education of Serbia—more specifically, a group of experts gathered within and around this ministry; and the other is the universities. In addition to these two key actors, the process also involved students as well as international development partners. Let us briefly look at the positions of these groups and their interests in terms of reforms.

The Government of the Republic of Serbia was entirely for change. The official policy in Serbia at the time was for reform and Europeanization, and adopting the Bologna reform of higher education—a clear pan-European process—was to be expected. However, the government had already confronted several painful political 'fronts': it had to cooperate with the International Crime Tribunal for the former Yugoslavia, was under pressure due to difficult economic and social situations, and had dealt with large security issues (which in 2003 culminated in the assassination of the prime minister). In such circumstances, there were certain limits to the government's willingness to exert greater reform pressure in this area. This is also evidenced by the assessment of a respondent included in the process of drafting a new law on behalf of the Ministry of Education. According to this respondent, in conditions of low social support, the government did not want to face a politically influential university public as its opponent.

The main promoter of reforms was the Ministry of Education (MoE). However, the very composition of the ministry was peculiar. Immediately after the political regime changed in 2000, new management arose from the ranks of the Alternative Academic Education Network (AAEN) and from the circles of

[33] The National Council for Higher Education is responsible for development and improvement of higher education. Most of the members are representatives of higher education institutions, although the ministry's intention was for this body to be constituted so that universities are no longer managed by universities themselves (Branković 2010, 62).

university professors[34]; even the minister was a university professor.[35] The new leadership of the ministry took time to become acquainted with the work because they had no experience in public administration. Furthermore, the administrative officers of the ministry were unfamiliar with the reform of the European higher education system, and great efforts were invested to improve human resources. Serbian public administration was at that time (as well as now) characterised by a very hierarchical structure (Ben-Gera 2009; Grupa autora 2002), and all major decisions relevant for work of a ministry were made by a few figures. This is why the Ministry of Education was faced with a paradoxical situation: Decision making was at the top, the top was not familiar with all aspects of the work of ministries and sectors and relied in its decisions on the lower professional and administrative structures. The lower structures, however, were sceptical about changes, but powerless to take initiative except to passively or actively sabotage and slow down the changes.

The eight universities (five public and three private) operating at the time resisted change. The views of representatives of private and state universities converged on one point: university representatives felt that reforms threatened the interests of all university stakeholders: in the new system, professors would have to work more, external sources of income would be threatened, and the position of faculties (especially the economically powerful ones) would be compromised because decisions would be made at the university level. Opponents of change thought that the reforms paid little attention to traditional values and concepts of education. Bologna reforms were associated with the new type of mass higher education that would significantly change the previous, well-entrenched and prestigious Humboldt-type of university 'for the elite' (Popović and Đorić 2011). They also undermined the governance structures at universities—where real opportunities lay to adapt to changes and so on.

Students who participated through representatives of their organisations in the working group to draft the law were the most opposed to change. According to the interpretation of one respondent (a representative of the ministry), the students were already primarily interested in reforms that would principally facilitate studies, even if solutions were not in accordance with the principles of the Bologna Declaration.[36]

[34] AAEN is a nongovernmental organisation (NGO) established in 1998 by a group of professors who were expelled from the University of Belgrade (after the adoption of the restrictive Law on University in 1998) or who were looking for ways to restore or maintain the academic freedom and offer new courses and new models of work to students. AAEN had great international support and participated as an observer in all major international initiatives. Within the organisation itself, human capacities necessary for the reform of higher education have been developed. When government changed, experts associated with AAEN had international contacts and knowledge necessary for the higher education reform.

[35] Member of the Civic Alliance of Serbia, a small party close to the Democratic Party of then prime minister Zoran Djindjic.

[36] Later legislative amendments in 2008 and 2010 were largely a response to the demands of students to facilitate studying.

The influence of student organisations and student representatives in working groups that prepared the law was, in the opinion of the respondents, insignificant.

The influence of international actors is the result of internationalisation of sector policies and social policy in general (Stubbs 2003; Deacon and Stubbs 2007). Council of Europe, WUS Austria, the World Bank, the Fund for an Open Society and others were active in the higher education sector in Serbia. Some financed reforms through loans (World Bank), and some through grants (WUS, Fund for an Open Society). According to the respondent from the ministry, at the beginning of the process ideas about higher education reform were supported only by these international actors. Moreover, it was the international partners who, after a change of government, pressured the next ministry to continue reforms (Branković 2010). However, the main dynamics of the reform process were carried out through negotiations between two key interest groups, or rather, institutions—the ministry and universities.

Insight into the characteristics and dynamics of the process indicates that it was not straightforward, that it was conducted in conditions of a very complex conflict of interests, and that in parallel with the confrontation over reforms—which the university community resisted—attention had to be paid to preserving the autonomy of institutions of higher education which had been compromised in the past decade. The reform was designed by a circle of experts associated with the then MoE. During the preparation of legislation (2003–2004), there were as many as four working groups for drafting the Law on Higher Education, and there were different conceptions of reforms and legislative changes (Branković 2010). At no time was there a consensus on the content of changes; the greatest differences were between the concept advocated by ministry representatives and the prevailing mood at the university. According to respondents involved in the process for the government, the ministry had to be cautious in negotiations with university representatives because the university was just emerging from a period of repression and lack of autonomy; hence the interest of the reform-oriented government was to further strengthen this autonomy.[37]

From the very beginning, the structure of university management—that is, the issue of university integration—caused the greatest conflict of interest. All faculties were uniformly resistant, although the academic community in Serbia widely believed that the biggest opponents of change were the large and powerful faculties. However, the assessments of respondents show the University of Belgrade (UB) had the greatest impact, as illustrated by the observation of one respondent from university circles, '… if UB does not want something, others will grumble, but will not complain publicly'. UB's political influence was measured by, among other things, the fact that many

[37] That is exactly why one of the first steps after the change of the Milosevic regime in 2000 was the abolishment of repressive legislation of 1998 and return to the force of law on universities from 1992. This solution was not considered optimal, but it was deemed necessary to make positive changes in higher education in a short time span.

professors also had political careers.[38] However, even UB comprised, at that time, a set of faculties as independent units. Thus, the analysis of university interests really meant analysing the interests of individual faculties.

After the elections in 2003, the minister of education was chosen from the ranks of the Democratic Party of Serbia, former prime minister Vojislav Koštunica's party. During this period there was a change and a mutual convergence of attitudes of MoE and the university public. The researchers recorded more positive attitudes among the most influential representatives of academia towards the new minister and his associates (Branković 2010, 56 ff.). It is obvious that in the new circumstances, the university interests were better represented, and the new law was drafted and passed in the parliament soon after. It is interesting that today, 8 years after its adoption, all players in the process have an equally negative attitude about both the law itself and its implementation. Representatives of the former ministry feel the law did not transform the higher education system sufficiently and did not dissipate the old power relations and governance structures. On the other hand, representatives of the university public say that the implementation of the Bologna reforms was full of compromises (for example, with students on the conditions of studying) and that it devalued the teaching process, reduced the quality of teaching and its outcomes, and over-commercialised knowledge.

The limited reform reach of existing laws is explained by some respondents as arising from an unfavourable social context: 'You cannot make the most modern European system of education and not change anything else. In a country where everything is falling apart, one cannot tighten anything'. Many participants in these processes now point out that one of the reasons for failure of the concept of deeper changes in higher education lies exactly in what its opponents were saying 10 years ago: the country was not ready. In the words of a respondent from the ministry:

> The prime minister was not popular […]. He had a respectable government and hoped to create something in four years that will give him another four years, only to be able to make something serious then. To do this, he had to avoid antagonising people. He was prepared for a higher risk with primary and secondary education. There were people who were ready for reforms […]. He was definitely not ready to confront the people in higher education that were loud, public figures, had access to the media […]. Political support is misleading […] We had full political support until we would pull a move that would stir up the academic public, but not from that point on.

We, on the other hand, conclude from the analysis that the Law on Higher Education was a result of specific social interests articulated and resolved in a particular institutional environment. The resistance from the universities was largely due to the fact that the new system would transform them into institutions more appropriate for a market society, and force teachers in terms of selection and promotion, into a market position, demanding a more proactive stance and competitiveness. At the same time, the law introduces the mechanisms of monitoring and quality checks, which again in market conditions, threatens the protected university

[38] The entire modern history of Serbia is characterised by engagement of the intellectual, particularly university elite, in politics (cf. Čalić 2004; Prpa 2003).

community. Universities and faculties organised in a short-term policy network managed to adapt the initial reform concepts to their interests and to preserve what, in the public, is perceived as the most important interest (autonomy of the faculty). MoE was faced with deeply entrenched interests and perceptions. It failed to create a policy network of representatives of interested institutions and remained isolated in an attempt to change higher education in Serbia.

6 Conclusions

Overview of key aspects of reforms in three areas of social policy (higher education, employment and social security—in the narrow sense), and the analyses of roles of different actors in their making, aimed to show how the conditions of social integration are being redefined in certain areas of societies of Western Balkan countries. Namely, the task was to examine the content of the reforms in the chosen subsystems and to recognise how these changes redefine the terms of access for different social groups. Furthermore, the task was to identify groups with access to the policy-making process whose interests affected the actual form of selected social policies.

The first part of the analysis was conducted more as a review of key policy directions with mapping of roles of key stakeholders in this process, especially international institutions and organisations as well as local, state and political elites. This comparative regional analysis has shown that essential directions of change are basically the same in the observed societies of the Western Balkans and that differences are demonstrated in the range, level and proportion of established changes, or certain specific features in detailed operationalization of individual components. Processes of privatisation of services have been identified everywhere (private high schools, employment agencies, various providers of social protection services, private pension funds), as have marketization of services where the public sector also acts as a bidder in the competition with the private sector (especially in higher education and community social services), with small state funding for certain programmes of social inclusion and social protection (for example, in active employment). In general, the described changes indicate a specific shift in key social integration mechanisms: responsibility to engage in production and other social processes and to ensure adequate living conditions lies primarily with the individual. The state converted its role of direct integrator to one of defining the conditions and was seen in a more competitive context as a service provider.

Pressures or influences from the international community primarily support these directions of changes. On the other hand, the structural legacy of the socialist era and the burdened transition of Western Balkans societies, marked by severe political instability and rising inequalities between the 'winners' and 'losers' of transition, act in the opposite direction. They put pressure on the state or rather the political elite to preserve elements of social policies in which the vested interests of certain social groups are particularly strong.

The deeper analysis in this paper was conducted for higher education reforms in Serbia. The analysis revealed that unlike reforms in employment and social protection (Vuković and Babović 2013), which were marked by developed networks (as in social protection) or lack of entrenched interests and corresponding networks (as in employment policy), higher education reform was characterised by confrontation between two competitive networks. The process of policy changes itself took place mostly under the influence of external factors as it was necessary to align the system with the Bologna model. Internal stakeholders were strongly divided between the supporters and opponents of reform, while the enactment of the law was marked by numerous conflicts. Interim policy networks have been formed on the side of the university community. The Ministry of Education, as a proponent of reform, did not manage to similarly develop networks of political support, thus limiting the reach of higher education reform. The reform model was imported from the EU, but its national operationalization was strongly influenced by the conflict between pro-Bologna and status-quo groups. Pro-Bologna players gathered around the ministry and the government, while the other group came from the university and claimed that elements of the reform—if not the entire reform—were at odds with the university's position. The ministry's expert team also originated from the university, but failed to provide the same level of organisation and support as the stakeholders from the university. Therefore, we can observe that this process was in large part shaped by the internal conflicts within the university community, with the authentic pro-Bologna option remaining a minority position. The outcome of this process has been that reforms were carried out according to the Bologna model, but with frequent changes within the basic framework (through various legal acts) and with outcomes that, in the end, satisfy no one.

The outcome of the struggle for higher education reforms was determined essentially by structural factors. The pro-Bologna network was in the minority and relied on the university and political elite. It was opposed by a broader and more heterogeneous network that united around basic common interests. These interests included the protection of certain privileged and unchallenged positions that could have been endangered under open market conditions, as well as the privilege to trade off positional capital in the public sector for higher remunerations in the private higher education sector. Public discussion also encompassed the deterioration of knowledge, loss of social influence and prestige of the university as well as other more general issues.

References

Agencija za rad i zapošljavanje (ARZ). (2011). *Bilten br.6*. Sarajevo: Agencija za rad i zapošljavanje Bosne i Hercegovine.

Agency for Statistics of Bosnia and Herzegovina (ASBH) (2011). Labour force survey 2011, final results. Sarajevo: ASBH.

Arandarenko, M. (2010). Politicka ekonomija nezaposlenosti. In M. Arandarenko, A. Prascevic, & S. Cvejic (Eds.), *Ekonomsko-socijalna struktura Srbije* (pp. 71–86). Beograd: Naucno drustvo ekonomista i Ekonomski fakultet u Beogradu.

Arandarenko, M., & Krstić, G. (2008). *Impact analysis of employment policy and active labour market programmes in the Republic of Serbia, 2003–2007*. Belgrade: Government of Republic of Serbia.

Babović, M. (2005). Socijalne mreže—povezivanje društvenih aktera u sferi ekonomskih aktivnosti. *Sociologija, 47*(4), 351–370.

Babović, M. (2009). *Post-socijalistička transformacija i socio-ekonomske strategije domaćinstava i pojedinaca u Srbiji* (Post-socialist transformation and socio-economic strategies of households and individuals in Serbia). Belgrade: Institut za sociološka istraživanja Filozofskog fakulteta.

Babović, M. (Ed.). (2010). *Izazovi nove socijalne politike: socijalna uključenost u EU i Srbiji* (Challenges of new social policy: Social inclusion in EU and Serbia). Belgrade: SeConS—Grupa za razvojnu inicijativu.

Babović, M. (Ed.). (2011). *Socijalno uključivanje: koncepti, stanje, politike* (Social inclusion: Concept and policies). Belgrade: SeConS i Institut za sociološka istraživanja Filozofskog fakulteta Univerziteta u Beogradu.

Baturina, D., Bežovan, G., Matančević, J. (2011). Local welfare systems as part of the Croatian welfare state: Housing, employment and child care. WILCO Publication no. 05, Zagreb, www.wilcoproject.eu

Baucal, A., & Pavlović Babić, D. (2009). *Kvalitet i pravednost obrazovanja u Srbiji: obrazovne šanse siromašnih: analiza podataka PISA 2003 i 2006*. Belgrade: Ministarstvo prosvete Republike Srbije, Institut za psihologiju Filozofskog fakulteta.

Bejaković, P. (2011). The national model of the welfare state tradition and changes: 1991–2010. The case of the Republic of Croatia. In M. Stambolieva & S. Dehnert (Eds.), *Welfare states in transition: 20 years after the Yugoslav welfare model*. Sofia: Friedrich Ebert Stiftung.

Bejaković, P., Bratić, V., & Vukšić, G. (2010). Komparativna analiza zaposlenosti i naknada za zaposlene u javnom sektoru u Hrvatskoj i u Europskoj uniji'. *Društvena istraživanja, 21*(1), 101–111.

Ben-Gera, M. (2009). *Horizontal policy coordination*. Belgrade: Ministry of Public Administration and Local Self-Government.

Bolčić, S. (1997). *Ownership transformation and the problems of redistribution of the social power in the post-socialist societies*. Balkan forum 2.

Bolčić, S. (2003). *Svet rada u transformaciji* (The world of work in the transformation). Belgrade: Plato.

Bornarova, S. (2011). Development of the social protection system in post-communist Macedonia: Social policy making and political processes. In M. Stambolieva & S. Dehnert (Eds.), *Welfare states in transition: 20 years after the Yugoslav welfare model* (pp. 135–165). Sofia: Friedrich Ebert Foundation.

Branković, J. (2010). *Decision making on decision making: Deciding governance in higher education in Serbia 2002–2005*, MA thesis, Faculty of Education, University of Oslo.

Branković, J., & Šabić, N. (Eds.). (2011). *Research policy, financing and performance: Croatia, Serbia and Slovenia in comparative perspective*. Belgrade: Centre for Education Policy.

Burt, R. (1982). *Toward a structural theory of action: Network models of social structure, perception, and action*. New York: Academic.

Čalić, Ž. M. (2004). *Socijalna istorija Srbije 1815–1941*. Belgrade: Clio.

Croatian Bureau of Statistics (CBS). (2010). *Labour force survey*. Zagreb: CBS.

De la Porte, C., & Deacon, B. (2002). *Contracting companies and consultants; the EU and social policy of accession countries* (Globalism and Social Policy Programme (GASPP) Occasional Paper 9). Helsinki: STAKES.

Deacon, B. (2007). *Global social policy and governance*. London: Sage.

Deacon, B., & Stubbs, P. (Eds.). (2007). *Social policy and international interventions in South East Europe*. Cheltenham: Edward Elgar.

Deacon, B., Lendvai, N., & Stubbs, P. (2007). Conclusions. In B. Deacon & P. Stubbs (Eds.), *Social policy and international interventions in South East Europe*. Cheltenham: Edward Elgar.

Direkcija za ekonomsko planiranje (DEP). (2011). *Bosna i Hercegovina—Ekonomski trendovi 2010. godina* [Bosnia and Herzegovina: Economic trends 2010]. Sarajevo: Savjet ministara BiH—Direkcija za ekonomsko planiranje.

Džankić, J. (2011). Political transformations: Welfare states in transition Montenegro: A long drive down a tough road. In M. Stambolieva & S. Dehnert (Eds.), *Welfare states in transition: 20 years after the Yugoslav welfare model (202–28)*. Sofia: Friedrich Ebert Foundation.

Farnell, T., & Kovač, V. (2010). Uklanjanje nepravednosti u visokom obrazovanju: prema politici »proširivanja sudjelovanja u« Hrvatskoj. *Revija za socijalnu politiku, 17*(2), 257–275.

Federalno ministarstvo obrazovanja i nauke (FMON). (2010). *Informacija o upisnoj politici na visokoškolskim ustanovama u Federaciji Bosne i Hercegovine i uskladjivanje sa potrebama tržišta rada*. Mostar: Federalno ministarstvo obrazovanja i nauke.

Gotcheva, B., & Strokova, V. (2010). *Social safety nets in the Western Balkans: Design, implementation and performance*. In Presentation at the Policy Round-table. Podgorica, March 2011.

Grupa autora. (2002). *Izazovi reforme—dijagnostička studija organa državne uprave Republike Srbije* [Challenges of the reforms – Diagnostic study of the public administration in the Republic of Serbia]. Belgrade: Vlada Republike Srbije.

Guardiancich, I. (2011). Penzije i socijalna uključenost u tri zemlje bivše Jugoslavije: Sloveniji, Hrvatskoj i Srbiji' [Pensions and social inclusion in three countries of former Yugoslavia: Slovenia, Croatia and Serbia]. In D. Vuković & M. Arandarenko (Eds.), *Socijalne reforme: sadržaji i rezultati* [Social reforms: Content and results]. Belgrade: Fakultet političkih nauka.

Institut za strateške studije i projekcije i Zavod za zapošljavanje (ISSP, ZZ). (2007). *Radna snaga i zaposlenost u Crnoj Gori* (Labour force and employment in Montenegro). Podgorica: Institut za strateške studije i projekcije i Zavod za zapošljavanje.

International Labour Organization (ILO) (2009a). *Delivering decent work in Europe and Central Asia* (Vol. I, part 2). Report of the Director-General. Geneva: ILO.

International Labour Organization (ILO) (2009b). *Report on the pension reform in Bosnia and Herzegovina: First assessment.* Budapest: ILO.

Jordan, B. (2006). *Social policy for the twenty-first century*. Cambridge: Polity Press.

Keil, S. (2011). Social policy in Bosnia and Herzegovina between state-building, democratization and Europeanization. In M. Stambolieva & S. Dehnert (Eds.), *Welfare states in transition: 20 years after the Yugoslav welfare model* (pp. 41–58). Sofia: Friedrich Ebert Foundation.

Krsmanović, A., & Walewski, M. (2006). *Labor market institutions in Montenegro—a barrier to employment?* (Working Paper). Podgorica: Institute for Strategic Studies and Prognoses.

Lazić, M. (1995). The features of global social transformation of Serbia. In S. Bolcic (Ed.), *Social changes and everyday life: Serbia at the beginning of nineties*. Belgrade: Institut za sociološka istraživanja Filozofskog fakulteta u Beogradu.

Lazić, M. (Ed.). (2000). *Račji hod. Srbija u transformacijskim procesima* (Crab's walk. Serbia in the transformational processes). Belgrade: Filip Višnjić.

Lazić, M. (2011). *Čekajući kapitalizam. Nastanak novih klasnih odnosa u Srbiji* (Waiting for capitalism. The creation of new class relations in Serbia). Belgrade: Službeni glasnik.

Lazić, M., & Cvejić, S. (2004). Promene društvene strukture u Srbiji: Slučaj blokirane post-socijalističke transformacije (Changes of social structure in Serbia: The case of blocked post-socialist transformation). In A. Milić (Ed.), *Društvena transformacija i strategije društvenih grupa: svakodnevica Srbije na početku trećeg milenijuma* (Social transformation and strategies of Social Groups: Everyday life in Serbia at the beginning of third millennium) (pp. 39–70). Belgrade: Institut za sociološka istraživanja Filozofskog fakulteta u Beogradu.

Lewis, G. (2000). Introduction: Expanding the social policy imaginary. In G. Lewis, S. Gewirtz, & J. Clarke (Eds.), *Rethinking social policy*. London: Sage.

Maglajlić, R. A., & Rašidagić, E. K. (2011). Socio-economic transformation in Bosnia and Herzegovina. In M. Stambolieva & S. Dehnert (Eds.), *Welfare states in transition: 20 years after the Yugoslav welfare model* (pp. 16–41). Sofia: Friedrich Ebert Foundation.

Matković, T. (2009). Pregled statističkih pokazatelja participacije, prolaznosti i režima plaćanja studija u Republici Hrvatskoj 1991–2007 [An overview of the tertiary education participation, completion and tuition fee indicators in the Republic of Croatia 1991–2007]. *Revija za socijalnu politiku, 16*(2), 239–250.

Milić, A. (2002). Dobitnici i gubitnici u procesu tranzicije iz ugla porodične svakodnevice (1991–2001) (Winners and losers in the transition process from the perspective of everyday family life). In S. Bolčić & A. Milić (Eds.), *Srbija krajem milenijuma: razaranje društva, promene i svakodnevni život* (Serbia at the end of millennium: Destruction of the society, changes and everyday) (pp. 251–281). Belgrade: Institut za sociološka istraživanja Filozofskog fakulteta u Beogradu.

Miličević, F., & Danijela, D. (2009). *Razvoj socijalne dimenzije u obrazovanju: izvještaj za Hrvatsku* [Development of social dimension in education: Report for Croatia]. Zagreb: FES i Institut za društvena istraživanja.

Ministarstvo civilnih poslova Bosne i Hercegovine (MCP). (2010). *Strategija zapošljavanja u Bosni i Hercegovini 2010–2014* [Employment strategy for Bosnia and Herzegovina 2010–2014]. Sarajevo: Ministarstvo civilnih poslova Bosne i Hercegovine.

Ministarstvo prosvete i sporta (MPS). (2011). *Strategija razvoja i finansiranja visokog obrazovanja u Crnoj gori 2011–2010* (Strategy of development and financing higher education in Montenegro 2010–2011). Podgorica: Ministry of Education and Sport.

Montenegro Statistical Office (Monstat) (2012). *Labour force survey 2011—release*. Podgorica: Statistical Office.

Nestić, D., & Rašić Bakarić, I. (2010). *Minimum wage systems and changing industrial relations in Europe*. National Report Croatia. Zagreb: Ekonomski institut.

Papić, Ž., Dmitrović, T., Vuković, D., Delova-Miladinova, P., & Ninković-Papić, R. (2012). *Who, how, why? Regional cooperation of NGOs in reducing social exclusion and poverty*. Sarajevo: Inicijativa za bolju i humaniju inkluziju and Fondacija za socijalno uključivanje.

Pavlović, D. (2006). Zarobljena država [Captured state]. In S. Mihailovic (Ed.), *Pet godina tranzicije* [Five years of transition]. Belgrade: Friedrich Ebert Foundation.

Petrović, M. (2004). *Sociologija stanovanja. Stambena politika: Izazovi i mogućnosti* (Sociology of housing. Housing policy: Challenges and opportunities). Belgrade: Institut za sociološka istraživanja Filozofskog fakulteta u Beogradu.

Pfeffer, J., & Salancik, G. R. (1974). Organizational decision making as a political process: The case of a University budget. *Administrative Science Quarterly, 19*, 135–151.

Polšek, D. (2004). Higher education in Croatia and requirements of the European Union. In K. Ott (Ed.), *Croatian accession to the European Union: Institutional challenges, vol. 2*. Zagreb: Institute of Public Finance.

Popović, N., & Đorić, G. (2011). Od uzgajališta za elitu do masovne proizvodnje visoko obrazovanih stručnjaka' [From a nursery-base for the elite to a mass production of highly educated experts]. *Nacionalni interes, 7*(3), 301–325.

Prpa, B. (2003). Neuspešni reformisti: Srpski intelektualci u Kraljevini Srba, Hrvata i Slovenaca (1918–1929) [Failed reformers: Serbian intellectuals in the Kingdom of Serbs, Croats and Slovens]. In L. Petrovic (Ed.), *Srbija u modernizacijskim procesima 19. i 20. veka: 3. Uloga elita* [Serbia in modernization processes 19th and 20th century: The role of elites]. Belgrade: Izdanje autora.

Republic of Srpska Institute for Statistics (RSIS) (2011). *Higher education: Statistical bulletin* no. 8, Banjaluka: RSIS. Available at http://www.rzs.rs.ba/PublikObrazCIR.htm

Republicki zavod za statistiku. (2011). *Anketa o radnoj snazi. Izvestaj za 2011*. Beograd: godinu.

Stambolieva, M., & Dehnert, S. (Eds.). (2011). *Welfare states in transition: 20 years after the Yugoslav welfare model*. Sofia: Friedrich Ebert Stiftung.

Statistical Office of the Republic of Serbia (SORS). (2011). *Labour force survey 2011*. Belgrade: SORS.

Stubbs, P. (2003). International non-state actors and social development policy. *Global Social Policy, 3*(3), 319–348.

Stubbs, P. (2009). A missed opportunity? Social and labour market policies in the Western Balkans. In M. Weichert et al., (Eds.). *Dialogues: Ownership for regional cooperation in the Western Balkan countries*. Sofia: Friedrich Ebert Stiftung.

Turajlić, S., Babić, S., & Milutinović, Z. (Eds.). (2001). *Evropski univerzitet 2010?* [European university 2010?]. Belgrade: Alternativna akademska obrazovna mreža.

Turajlić, S., Andrejić, M., Rudić, L., & Todorović, L. (2004). *Visoko obrazovanje u Srbiji* [Higher education in Serbia]. Belgrade: Alternativna akademska obrazovna mreža.

Unija Sindikata Prosvetnih Radnika Srbije (USPRS). (2010). *Obrazovanje u Srbiji danas* [Education in contemporary Serbia]. Belgrade: USPRS.

Uzelac, M. (2009). *Priče iz Bolonjske šume* [Stories from Bologna forest]. Vršac: Visoka škola strukovnih studija za obrazovanje vaspitača.

Uzunov, V. (2011). Socio-economic transformation and the welfare system of the Republic of Macedonia in the period of transition. In M. Stambolieva & S. Dehnert (Eds.), *Welfare states in transition: 20 years after the Yugoslav welfare model* (pp. 115–135). Sofia: Friedrich Ebert Foundation.

Vidović, D., & Pauković, D. (2011). Welfare state in transition: Political transformations. The case of Croatia. In M. Stambolieva & S. Dehnert (Eds.), *Welfare states in transition: 20 years after the Yugoslav welfare model* (pp. 92–115). Sofia: Friedrich Ebert Foundation.

Vukasović, M. (Ed.). (2009). *Finansiranje visokog obrazovanja u Jugoistočnoj Evropi: Albanija, Crna Gora, Hrvatska, Slovenija, Srbija* [Financing higher education in South-East Europe: Albania, Montenegro, Croatia, Slovenia, Serbia]. Belgrade: Centar za obrazovne politike i Državni univerzitet u Novom Pazaru.

Vukovic, S. (2005). *Pravo, moral i korupcija* [Law, morality and corruption]. Belgrade: Filip Višnjić.

Vuković, D. (2010). Izazovi oblikovanja socijalnog režima u Srbiji' [Challanges in creating Serbian welfare regime]. In *Izazovi nove socijalne politike: socijalna uključenost u EU i Srbiji* [Challenges of new social policy: Social inclusion in EU and Serbia]. Belgrade: SeConS—Grupa za razvojnu inicijativu.

Vuković, D. (2011). Društvene osnove pravne države: slučaj Srbije' [Societal foundations of the rule of law]. *Sociološki pregled, 45*(3), 421–451.

Vuković, D., & Babović, M. (2013). Social interests, policy networks, and legislative outcomes: The role of policy networks in shaping welfare and employment policies in Serbia. *East European Politics and Societies*. doi:10.1177/0888325413495088. published online.

World Bank. (2006). *Serbia: Labor market assessment*. Washington, DC: World Bank.

World Bank. (2008). *From fragmentation to cooperation: Tertiary education, research and development in South East Europe*. Washington, DC: World Bank.

World Bank (2010). *Social impact of the crisis and building resilience*. World Bank report no. 55111-HR. Zagreb: World Bank and UNDP Croatia.

Chapter 3
Fiscal Policy and Competitiveness in Croatia

Saša Drezgić

1 Introduction

The debate on fiscal policy and competitiveness[1] has been recently revived in the light of the global financial crisis triggered by the U.S.A. sub-prime mortgage crisis in 2008. The effect of the global economic downturn was the strongest in the European Union due to the specific concerns that fiscal tensions in the monetary union could jeopardise stability of the whole community. Since the monetary policy of the EU is run by the European Central Bank (ECB) and fiscal policies are the prerogative of national decision makers, pressure was placed on the member states to introduce a number of corrective measures with an emphasis on the use of fiscal policy instruments to strengthen economic competitiveness[2] in dealing with the impact of the global financial crisis (Gros and Alcidi 2010). This regional policy has determined the national policies of both EU members as well as EU- dependent countries in so far as the less competitive countries have had to engage in fiscal consolidation processes in the circumstances of unfavourable monetary conditions (high interest rates) while more competitive countries have enjoyed low interest rates and have increased space for fiscal manoeuvres.

[1] Fiscal policy can be defined as a set of government activities that uses taxation and spending to achieve goals of high and stable rates of economic growth, low unemployment and stable and low inflation rates (and a number of other goals depending on the priorities of a particular society). Competitiveness is a set of institutions, policies and factors that determine the level of productivity of a country (WEF 2013). Fiscal policy, affects every pillar of competitiveness, and directly and indirectly determines the level of productivity.

[2] This refers to the efforts towards decreasing the labour costs by wage reductions. In public sector directly, and by reducing taxes in private sector.

S. Drezgić (✉)
Faculty of Economics, University of Rijeka, Rijeka, Croatia
e-mail: sdrezgic@efri.hr

M. Thomas, V. Bojicic-Dzelilovic (eds.), *Public Policy Making in the Western Balkans*, DOI 10.1007/978-94-017-9346-9_3

In Croatia as one of the more recent entrants to the European Union (EU), since October 2001 when the Stabilisation and Association Agreement (SAA) with the European Union was signed, macroeconomic and fiscal policies have not produced sustainable and high rates of economic growth. Croatia's GDP growth per capita in 2000–2011 averaged 2.5 %, below most middle-income countries and Croatia's emerging Europe peers. Croatia's underperformance is particularly notable since 2009 (IMF 2012). According to the World Economic Forum (WEF) competitiveness ranking, Croatia has been classified among less competitive countries in the area of South-east Europe (WEF 2013). Croatia's macroeconomic performance since 2001 has been characterised by a low average rate of economic growth and unstable growth rates dynamics, high levels of long term unemployment, rising income inequality, a drop in the volume of private investment and in the rates of return, rising costs of capital, inefficient government spending and increased tax burden. The key favourable macroeconomic indicators have been low and stable inflation rates, coupled with stable exchange rates.

The scope of this chapter is to analyse the reform of the fiscal system in Croatia from the perspective of its impact on country's overall competitiveness. The period of analysis is set by the ratification of SAA document which set boundaries of possible fiscal reforms under the fiscal and harmonisation rules of the EU. Several factors are the key when it comes to outcomes of economic and fiscal policy in regards to competitiveness of Croatian economy:

1. Historical and political background of the country which created unfavourable initial conditions in terms of reaching the goals of high level of competitiveness;
2. Crucial impact of international community, institutions and organisations in shaping the boundaries of economic policy in Croatia (small open economy under strong influence of EU economic policy – preparing for accession and becoming an EU member);
3. Specific structural problems and issues which define national economic landscape that affects overall competitiveness level of the country;
4. Interplay and clashes of different policy actors that affected the pace and content of fiscal reforms in the period since 2001.

Due to the complexity generated by the interconnected nature of the above four sets of factors, in this chapter, the relation of fiscal policy and competitiveness is limited only to a narrow aspect of macroeconomic stability. The main focus is therefore on the overall effects of government spending, tax level and structure effects and specific effects pertaining to the interaction of monetary and fiscal policy.

The main argument of the paper is that the fiscal policy in Croatia was not able to deliver higher level of competitiveness due to generalised lack of quality of economic and fiscal policy. This lack of quality predominantly comes from inability of main political forces to devise a consistent, sustainable and feasible long-term plan of economic development. This is the reason why features of fiscal policy in Croatia were shaped by both external and internal factors which are both exogenous. This exogeneity refers to the fact that fiscal policy was not active in a sense that it changes economic system in favourable direction, but instead, adapts on an "ad hoc" basis to the economic conditions. In fact, such exogenous nature of fiscal policy determinants in Croatia worked to create a preference among policy makers for a 'status quo' type of economic and fiscal policy. There is clear evidence that Croatian fiscal policy is procyclical which is common for countries with weak institutional system. Arguably, there is a sort of voracity effect[3] (Lane and Tornell 1999) ongoing in Croatia due to the presence of strong interest groups that prevent formulation and execution of rational economic and fiscal policy.

In order to achieve goals of high and stable economic growth, economic and fiscal policy decision makers have to provide clear, strategic direction of economic and fiscal goals and measures, adapted to specific features of national economic structure and social preferences. Even prior to 2001, it can be argued that EU membership was the most important goals of every successive Croatian government. From that perspective, the task of the fiscal policy was to comply with the EU fiscal rules set by the Maastricht criteria and the Stability and Growth Pact (SGP). Croatia in the final line succeeds in accomplishing these goals and joined the EU with fiscal positions which were EU- compliant in the fiscal rules provisions. However, such unidirectional fiscal policy is not sustainable; worsening macroeconomic imbalances for the first time led to breaching the limits of fiscal rules in 2012 and, most certainly, activation of EU excessive deficit procedure (EDP). Therefore, continuation of present inertial policy with narrowly set goals is not sustainable and is damaging to the prospect of improving competitiveness in Croatia.

In developing the argument, this chapter has several key objectives: (a) to provide insights into main components of fiscal policy that affect the level of a country's competitiveness; (b) to discuss dynamics of fiscal reforms in Croatia since 2001 which reveals tendencies and dominant factors which shape fiscal policy features and outcomes; (c) to present dominant policy actors and networks with specific interests which affect fiscal policy reforms; (d) to analyse interactions of actors and processes which form specific regime of fiscal (and monetary) policy in Croatia.

The research methodology in this chapter relies on application of contemporary theory of fiscal policy onto the regulative framework of EU and Croatia. Such theoretical background is supported by the empirical data from various sources (Eurostat, WEF, IMF, and Croatian Ministry of Finance). The interviews with selected economic experts serve as a benchmark for defining the attitudes and the role of key actors of fiscal policy reforms. In order to demonstrate the mechanisms of voracity effect and procyclical fiscal policy, the examples of interactions of different interest groups will be discussed.

[3] The " voracity effect" is defined as a more-than-proportional increase in discretionary redistribution in response to an increase in the raw rate of return in the efficient sector (Lane and Tornell 1999, p. 34). This effect increases with the strength of the leading interest groups in particular society which exploit their position to increase transfers from the government and appropriate higher share of government redistribution. This has a negative effect on lower rate of economic growth.

The second section of the paper, after the introduction, describes specific context of fiscal policy in Croatia. Section 3 presents an overview of the dynamics of fiscal policy reforms in Croatia and is followed by a section analysing specific positions of key actors that shape fiscal policy outcomes. Section 5 elaborates interactions of actors and networks and processes that come from such interplay; the final part of the paper concludes by offering a set of policy recommendations.

2 Fiscal Policy in Croatia: Theoretical Considerations

Economic (and fiscal) policy in Croatia has its roots in the stabilisation program which set off in 1994. The main goal of this program was to stop galloping inflation which was considered the number one threat to macroeconomic stability of the country (see Družić 2012). Coupled with such an economic policy platform, there was a scenario of fast pace liberalisation and transition which eventually led a path to a number of both market and government failures. Principal responsibility for those failures belongs to fiscal authorities. Their root cause is the decisions making process driven by low level quality of fiscal institutions and public sector, which resulted in the formation of tax and spending budget structure with low multiplication effects. More broadly, inappropriate policy decisions led to exertion of market failures through the processes of privatisation which either eliminated existing companies or created market monopolies and oligopolies (banks, telecommunications, energy sector and other). Regulatory provisions under the fiscal authorities disabled the scope for monetary policy action by banning borrowing to the government and by setting the price stability as the main goal by the Croatian national bank. The result of such policy was non-competitive exchange rate set by passive monetary regime (fixed to EURO) and passive fiscal policy supported by increasing revenues from privatisation and rising capital inflows. The path towards EU accession officially set in 2001 created favourable circumstances to change the existing model of economic policy, but this opportunity was never used.

Even before signing the SAA, Croatian fiscal authorities were keen to follow EU fiscal rules even though, other than the political goals, there was no reason to pursue such policy. Institutional framework for Europe's monetary union is provided by the Maastricht Treaty. Provisions set up by the Maastricht Treaty define a framework for inflation, exchange rate, interest rate and fiscal consolidations targets within the EU. The set requirements limit the public debt and the budget deficit as a share of GDP to 60 % and 3 %, respectively. The most important reason or justification for introducing the convergence criteria is the goal of preserving the stability of the common EU market. Having no constraints on the EU members fiscal policy could lead to excessive public debt, rising interest rates and undermine the stability of EU monetary system. Therefore, some of the member countries could expect bail-out procedure by the European Central Bank in response to the recent economic crisis. The Pact for Stability and Growth (SGP), which was finalized at the June 1997 meeting of the European Council in Amsterdam, was set up in order to prevent inflationary debt bailouts, neutralize inflationary pressure more generally, offset political bias towards excessive deficits, internalize international interest rate spill-overs, and to encourage policy co-ordination. SGP consisted of more restrictive set of provisions than those laid down by the Maastricht Treaty, which only stipulates that the general government deficit may not exceed its reference value (3 % of GDP) unless the deficit has declined significantly and continuously to where it is close to that reference value, or the excess of the reference value is only exceptional and temporary and the deficit remains close to the reference value. The SGP says nothing about the size of the output decline producing that exceptional and temporary excess deficit, or the period over which it must occur. In this sense the SGP implied less flexibility than the Maastricht Treaty. One of the heaviest criticisms of such fiscal rules was directed towards their impact on growth. The empirical evidence of the possibility that a declining share of public investment in GDP could have adverse consequences for economic growth over the long term is inconclusive. There are a number of reasons why the many studies on this topic do not yield clear-cut conclusions. First, it is difficult to control for all the factors, in addition to public investment, that affect growth over the longer term. Second, a sizable portion of public investment is directed to supporting broad functions of government, including redistribution and provision of social services, maintaining law and order, and administration, which do not directly boost productive potential. And third, the lumpy nature of much infrastructure investment implies that the full impact of investment on roads, telecommunications, and other infrastructure on growth can only be realized with considerable lags, once effective infrastructure networks have been established (see Eichegreen and Wyplosz 1998).

There is, however, evidence that public investment has fallen because of fiscal adjustment, and on this account, there are reasons to be concerned particularly if the cuts in public investment are not reversed, and thus fiscal adjustment contributes to declining public investment ratios, or if cuts are reversed and there is substantial volatility in public investment instead (which can reduce the efficiency of both public and private investment). For OECD countries, Roubini and Sachs (1989) observe that public investment is often quickly and drastically cut during periods of restrictive fiscal policy. More specifically for the euro area, it has been claimed that the SGP deficit limits have contributed to the recent decline in public investment. It has to be noted that even a fraction of a percentage point of the growth rate can become important when allowed to accumulate over time; some simulations suggest that, after accumulation over the last two decades, the levels of real output would have ended 5 % lower in France and the U.K., and 9 % lower in Italy (Eichegreen and Wyplosz 1998). There is no proof yet that any of the EU economies in the course of the consolidation process succeeded in increasing the rate of growth and volume of the fixed capital. Research on OECD economies has showed that decrease of gross GDP by 1 % automatically leads to an increase in deficit of 0,6 % (see, Levit and Lord 2000). The danger is that the SGP could divert effort from fundamental reforms needed for accelerating the pace of economic growth. Fiscal rules linked to the provisions of the SGP are by no means capable of providing a radical swerve in European economic growth. In such circumstances the SGP could become even more binding, and have additional negative impact by increasing the volatility of output, and hence depressing growth further. This could trigger a mechanism generating a sort of a vicious circle and keep the EU member states trapped at the low-level economic equilibrium.

Government spending and taxation are important categories that determine dynamics of economic growth of every country. Of course, in the short term, increase in government spending raises economic growth by a "multiplier effect" and taxation changes patterns of personal and investment spending. Therefore, it is very likely that fiscal consolidation will cause negative effects on growth regardless of the fact whether it is conducted by the contraction in government spending or by increasing taxes. However, some of the recent research shows potentially positive effects of fiscal consolidation. Such effects are explained by the fact that a decrease in the tax burden as a consequence of a reduction in government spending increases available income of private sector, which can then be directed towards investment. This is accompanied by positive expectations of smaller tax burden in future (Giavazzi and Pagano 1990, 1996; Alesina and Perotti 1997; Alesina and Ardagna 1998; Perotti 1999; Gupta et al. 2003; Ardagna 2004). However, more recent research refutes the expansionary contraction thesis and focuses on determining specific factors that lead to positive effects of fiscal discipline in short and long term (Favero and Giavazzi 2007; Guaijardo et al. 2011).

Based on the evidence (Spillimbergo et al. 2008) all things being equal, fiscal consolidation is an effective tool for reducing bloated governments across the EU and for gaining competitiveness by the reduction in the tax burden in future. However, the problem is in timing. Fiscal consolidation has to be conducted during the expansionary phase of the business cycle. The notion that fiscal consolidation is necessary in the time of crisis means that fiscal policy is unable to boost economic growth. Therefore, positive effects of fiscal multipliers are considered to be smaller than the negative effects from government borrowing which results in increased interest rates. Such a thesis lies at the heart of neoliberal theory and is confirmed by the empirical results mentioned earlier. Potential problem with this line of thinking is in the activity of the private sector in time of uncertainty and crisis. If there is no an increase in the private sector activity, a recessionary spiral sets in with classical traits of a "paradox of thrift". Empirically speaking, these avenues of business cycle are poorly researched. Theoretical analysis draws conclusion that the effects of fiscal activity are country specific, depending on specific structural (endogenous) and external (exogenous) factors. For example, we can assume that a reduction in interest rates (at least in the short time) will have significantly larger effects on export-oriented economy. However, the problem is that within the European economic space there is a pressure to endorse a platform of uniform fiscal policy (although nominally divergent) by following a one-fit-for-all recipe regardless of the country specific economic parameters. While such policy suits some of the countries, it is dangerous for the others, such as Greece, Spain, Croatia, to name but a few.

Even though, prior to accession, it was not obligatory for Croatia to follow EU fiscal rules set up by Maastricht Treaty and the Stability and Growth Pact, Croatian economic and fiscal policy tried to fit into that framework. The acceptance of these criteria was one of the most important external factors that defined outcomes of fiscal policy in Croatia. A second one was rapid liberalisation of the economy which aggravated the prospects for survival of traditional industries unable to adapt quickly to the global competitiveness level. Such shock therapy, which marked the transition processes in the broader set of countries in South East Europe (SEE) through privatization and liberalization, has created systems conducive to market failure. Many manufacturing companies have been shut-down because they could not cope with competitive pressures of the world market, in the context where the state provided no support. At the same time a number of private monopolies were created, especially during the period of privatization of large systems – telecommunications, financial system, the oil industry, etc. The result of such privatization was not an increase in competitiveness and the welfare of society. Throughout transition period in Croatia and, similarly, in the SEE countries, an ad hoc economic policy was pursued. On the one hand, this had negative effects on the efficiency of the public sector, and on the other, it contributed to market failure as state failed to intervene in functional spheres. Therefore, the resulting gap in terms of competitiveness compared to other countries that have conducted a functional economic policy is not surprising.

Croatia does not rank particularly well in terms of competitiveness (Fig. 3.1). As argued in the preceding discussion, this is partly to do with the institutional framework which was not conducive to improvement in the level of competitiveness. In Croatia, as in the rest of SEE, there has been a prolong tendency of growing foreign trade balance deficit which testifies to this lack of competitiveness. Furthermore, the structure of exports is unfavourable in that it is primarily oriented to products and

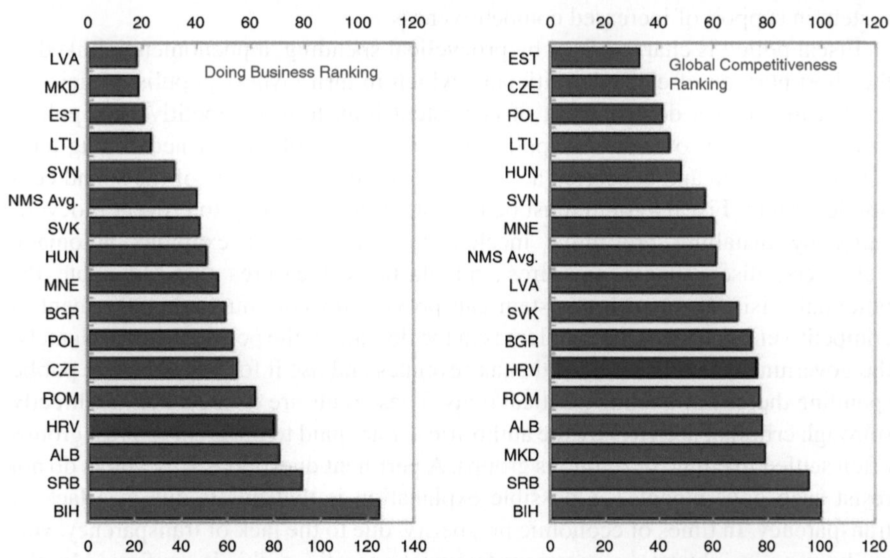

Fig. 3.1 Croatian competitiveness, 2011–2012 (Source: IMF (2012), based on World Bank (2012) and World Economic Forum (2012))

services with low value added, and with low technology content. Therefore, the emerging attitude among the policymakers that efforts are needed to move away from the concept of market fundamentalism toward more active role of the state in the framework of industrial policy should come as no surprise. Government measures are intended to overcome constraints related to a lack of finance, infrastructure, innovation capacity and human capital in order to boost competitiveness.

The problem is that the present model of development pursued by Croatia and other SEE countries was concerned primarily with the reduction of the tax burden – especially tax exemptions on corporate income tax and taxes on capital. However, rough and non-selective measures allowed development of financial markets and in some countries tax structure perfectly aligned with the interests of the import lobby. In this model, there were no adequate incentives to technological upgrading and the growth of productive capacity. On the other hand, in terms of expenditure, the state sector has remained too large, and presents too high a burden on taxpayers and the private sector. Government incentives have been channelled to inefficient enterprises in which different lobbies and political elite have been installed, so that the overall effect in terms of improved competitiveness and strong economic performance has been disappointing.

The economic crisis which began to be felt in SEE countries during 2008, presented an opportunity for a radical reorientation of economic, and especially of fiscal policy. Sudden stop in capital inflows led to a drop in economic growth rates through the reduction of aggregate demand, particularly due to the fall in personal consumption. As a consequence, imports fell much faster than exports. This turn out required functional and selective government intervention in order to overcome the consequences of the crisis and, more importantly, to restructure the entire economic system in support of increased competitiveness.

Fiscal policy is characterised by procyclical spending, a phenomenon linked to the short horizon of elected politicians, which in turn favours populist policies at the detriment of a development of consistent long term competitiveness policy. Procyclical effects of economic policy are an indicator of the absence of long-term planning horizon and concerted action to create the fundaments of the sound economic system. Fiscal system must be formatted in such a way to prevent procyclicality by installing preventive mechanisms such as for example, automatic stabilizers, discretionary measures and elasticity measures that anticipate the potential crisis. Only such a system can provide for continuous improvement in competitiveness. Part of the problem is in the domain of the political arena. Namely, the governments claim a part of the tax revenues and use it for unproductive public spending thereby collecting political rents. These rents are collected either directly (through criminal activity) by the authorities or are paid to different interest groups often settled in ethnic or religious groups. A pertinent question is why voters do not resist such governments? A possible explanation is that this is due to a lack of transparency. In times of economic prosperity, due to the lack of transparency, voters have no insight into government financial operations; this is confirmed by the fact that more corrupt countries exhibit stronger features of procyclical government policy.

3 Dynamics of Fiscal Policy Reforms

3.1 Tax Policy

In addition to inappropriate volume and structure of government spending, Croatian tax system was also deficient in economic and social sense. Stabilization of public finance (budget) and more appropriate distribution of income are only possible by changes in tax structure. Croatian Constitution defines the Republic of Croatia as a social society. Does Croatian society come close to such a goal?[4] Sever et al. (2009) argue that the distribution of income in the Croatian economic system is suitable to typical liberal social models and not to the models (left) of social societies in Europe. The relations between capital and labour share of national income have not changed since the transition from the socialist economic model in Croatia. On the contrary, the focus has been on the expansion and strengthening of capital-relations at the expense of labour costs cuts. It follows, therefore, that for the redistribution of income towards stimulating economic recovery and stabilization, changes of the tax system and taxation policies are necessary. This can be achieved by the combination of property taxes, income from capital and extra profits. Dividends, shares in profits, interest from capital and other stock speculation, speculation in real estate, property taxes, etc. in general, are non-taxable within the Croatian tax system. In this respect, it is clear that fiscal burden does not fall on businesses and primarily pressures general population. At the same time, however, fiscal relaxation of labour factor is necessary in order to protect savings and ensure economic growth. Compensation for reduced revenues is provided by taxation of capital incomes (which are not taxable at the moment). New research has in fact proved that there is no need to fear taxation of capital income from the standpoint of endangering savings and economic growth (Uhlig and Janagawa 1996).

Table 3.1 presents a comparison of average labour costs in OECD, the EU and Croatia in 2008. In recent period labour costs are the most highlighted factor that

Table 3.1 Comparison of labour costs for OECD, EU and Croatia (2008)

Association/country	Personal income tax as % of gross wages	Contributions of employees as % of gross wages	Personal income tax and contributions of employees as % of gross wages	Personal income tax and contributions of employees and employers as % of labour force costs
¢OECD	15.9	10.7	26.6	37.7
¢EU-15	20.0	11.4	29.5	39.3
¢EU-19	16.8	12.5	29.3	42.6
Croatia	10.0	20.0	30.0	40.3

Source: Sever et al. (2009), OECD: taxing wages 2008, Paris, 2009

[4] If 800–900,000 members of the society have the opportunity to claim only 9–10 % of the total (gross) income, it is a society that is away from such social goals.

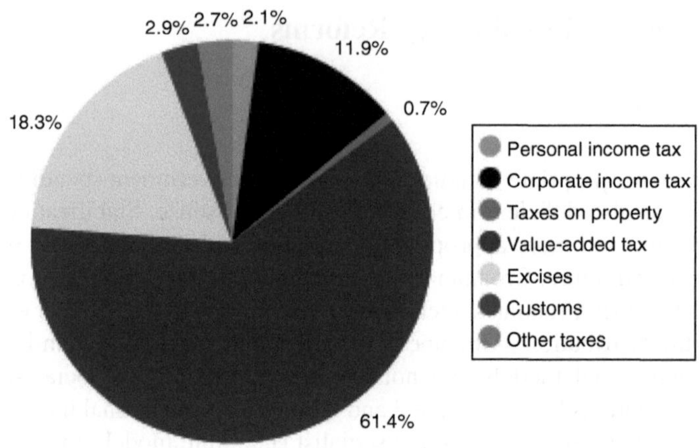

Fig. 3.2 Tax revenue structure in 2011 (Source: Ministry of Finance: Annual Report for 2011)

affects competitiveness which is particularly valid for countries under common monetary regime. As the data in the table show, Croatian tax system exerts the highest burden on labour costs among selected groups of countries. Since consumption tax in Croatia is also one of the highest in EU, in order to improve competitiveness, the tax system will have to shift towards taxation of capital and property.

Figure 3.2 presents a tax revenue structure in year 2011. It can be observed that indirect taxes – value added tax and excises take almost 80 % of the tax revenues, which indicates strong repressiveness of the tax system in Croatia. Even though the tax burden on personal income tax and corporate income tax is low, the labour costs for companies are heavily burdened by social security contributions that match the volume of revenues of value added tax.

These unfavourable effects of Croatian tax system are not caused only by the tax system itself. The problem is that long term rate of growth is not sufficient to provide relaxation of the tax rates. In addition, Croatian economy is characterised by long term unemployment and one of the lowest rates of employment in the EU (57 % of the active population). This creates imbalance and need for high level of taxation in order to preserve living standards of a large stratum of social welfare dependent population.

3.2 Expenditure Policy

As it was elaborated in the previous section, the main goal of the Croatian government spending policy was to control social tensions by providing generous social safety net. Of course, that was possible by reducing the level of public investments. Sever et al. (2011) have looked into the dynamics and the relationship of budget spending and economic growth in Croatia in the past two decades and Sever et al. (2009)

provide more extensive approach with overall analysis of economic policy and role of fiscal policy as one of its components. The main propositions of this study were based on short-term and long-term measures. Short-term, it was proposed to urgently suspend investment in new infrastructure projects in the foreseeable future, correct income taxation, change social security system, introduce taxation of extra-profits, reallocate budgetary expenditures, reprogram debt and; to start preparations for a thorough reform of the tax system. Long-term, the study proposed to pursue additional investments in education, increase the role of property taxation in the tax system, tax income from capital, and pursue a comprehensive reform of the public sector alongside territorial reform as a prerequisite for the successful decentralization.

As it was previously mentioned, throughout the period covered by this research fiscal policy was skewed towards current spending. Since the opening of international financial markets to Croatia in 1997, Croatian economy experienced high level of foreign capital inflow which originated mostly from portfolio investments (privatisation of state monopolies), foreign direct investments and increased borrowing. The strong inflows enabled a rise in living standards and favourable conditions for increased government revenues. In turn, rising government revenue led to the proliferation of unproductive and inefficient government spending and also hidden corruption (hidden by a voracity effect[5]).

Such spending dynamics was unsustainable and already in 2005, the outflow exceeded the inflow of foreign capital. The "scissors" were closing on the two sides: on the one side, the debt repayments had been reaching the GDP growth rate. On the other, repayments had surpassed the growth rate of the capital inflow (Sever et al. 2011). The economic and financial outflows were among the initial causes of the latest crisis of the Croatian economy followed by the outflow of capital. Further aggravating factor was the effect of unproductive spending of borrowed capital, which overall intensified the poor state of Croatian economy and public finances.

The dynamics of public expenditures is presented in Fig. 3.3. Due to the changes of budgetary methodology or adjustment to the new budget classification, it is possible to analyse expenditures by quarters from the second half of 2004. The data refer to the consolidated central government although for the purposes of our analysis it would be preferable to use consolidated general government data.

It can be observed that the bulk of budgetary spending is related to the compensation of employees and social benefits. Since the onset of the economic crisis in 2008, the structure of expenditures shifted in an unfavourable direction in that in relative terms, the ratio of expenditures in GDP increased. In particular, the expenditures for the compensation of employees and social benefits increased. In addition, capital expenditures contracted both in relative as well as in absolute terms, a confirmation of a pro-cyclical nature of the government budget. Government spending has been consistently financed by borrowing. However, in recessionary

[5] A phenomenon where government resources are misused by interest groups in times of economic prosperity and high level of government revenues. Due to the fact that all interest groups gain share of government revenues, there are no incentives to reveal corruption.

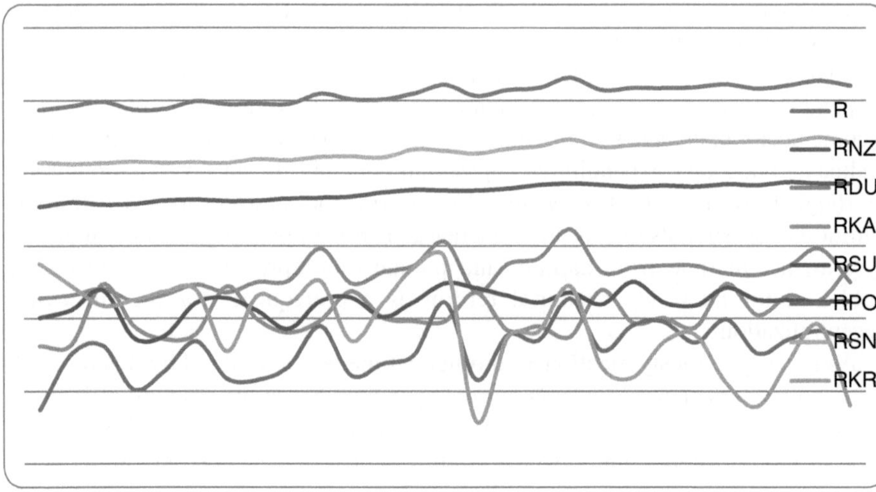

Fig. 3.3 Government spending (Q2 2004–Q1 2011) – natural logs, constant prices based on previous year (Source: Sever et al. 2011, Online databases of the Ministry of Finance (www.mfin.hr, *R* total expenditures, *RNZ* compensation of employees, *RDU* expenditures for goods and services, *RKA* interest, *RSU* subsidies, *RPC* grants, *RSN* expenditure on social benefits, *RKR* Capital expenditures)

conditions the relative increase of expenditures is caused by reduction of GDP and does not represent devised "ex-ante" operation of the government, but "ex-post" reflection of negative economic dynamics. Hence, government borrowing is not anti-recessionary because it lacks the multiplier effects due to its orientation towards filling the fiscal gap (Sever et al. 2011).

3.3 *Fiscal-Monetary Coordination*

A further element in assessing the effects of fiscal policy on competitiveness is the relation between the fiscal and monetary policy regime. As it has been already mentioned, the analysis of fiscal-monetary system is specific for every economy given that the effects of such interaction depend on specific structure of the economy and specific features of fiscal and monetary policy. Thus, besides the macroeconomic perspective, it is very important to clarify specific features of institutional system that can lead to certain problems in regards to macroeconomic stability.

Alongside fiscal policy, monetary policy carries important share of responsibility for macroeconomic condition of Croatian economy. A debate on the validity of Croatian monetary regime starts from the stabilisation program in 1994 which was successful in curbing galloping inflation rates and ensured the price stability of economy until present. In the conditions of rapid liberalisation and capital inflows underdeveloped domestic economy was not able to compete with foreign companies.

Gradual increase in demand for foreign products had an appreciation effect on the domestic currency. From that point there was no significant changes of fiscal and monetary regime and the economic structure took the form of "import based structure" which was also suitable for boosting budget revenues (there was a parallel growth of balance of payment deficit and budget revenues due to increased value-added tax revenues from imports). Therefore, in the long run the effects of fixed exchange-regime determined by the monetary policy focus on stability were unfavourable for economic growth; economic growth was based on capital inflows and after the crisis, when capital flows reversed even in gross terms, economic growth stalled.

Against such economic, fiscal and monetary trends in Croatia, a question about sustainability of the fiscal system is an important one. The sustainability of fiscal system is dependent on the endogenous factors related to fiscal system such as the level and structure of government spending and taxation, but also on the interaction with the monetary policy. As it mentioned earlier, economic growth in Croatia was largely determined by government consumption, i.e. expansionary fiscal policy. Private sector has been exposed to conditions of double pressure both by fiscal and monetary policy. Tax system which burdens the economy near the top of the Laffer curve and financial system which extracts value added from the private sector (due to over excessive costs of borrowing) make production activities very difficult. In such circumstances only industries enjoying monopolistic and oligopolistic position can prevail. The policy choice of maintaining fixed exchange rate meant that monetary policy gave up the sovereignty in order to keep price stability through the appreciated exchange rate. Coupled with the difficulties to control monetary in the context of majority foreign owned, privatised banking sector, the possibilities of the monetary system to promote economic growth in the country have been severely limited. Thus, the monetary system in Croatia does not fulfil its basic role but the banks are, instead able to accrue profits without a pressure to improve efficiency and creativity. The spread between passive and active interest rates coupled with explosive growth of indebtedness has enabled high profits (only deteriorated by nonperforming loans which increased by worsening economic conditions). The negative effects were reinforced by the failure of fiscal policy to tax incomes from capital savings which ultimately stimulates reallocation of investments from real economy to financial system.

This monopolistic position of the banking sector in Croatia has interesting repercussions on the ability of monetary authority to conduct monetary policy. Even if the central bank relaxes the monetary policy, why would banks decrease their active interest rates? In such a scenario, only bank profits would increase. Since Croatian market is over-indebted (citizens, companies and government), it is unlikely that the banks will have incentives towards reducing the interest rates burden and provide additional financing (and thus increase the balance sheet risks). Such specific position of the banking system creates new phenomena in financial field which can be named *crowding out of private sector investments by financial institutions* whereby high rates of return on deposits in the conditions of high fiscal and monetary burden reallocate funds from real investments towards financial ones.

Problem of Croatian monetary system, by its nature, is similar to many other countries. Monetary system regulation focuses on the protection of financial system and does not account for the systemic risk which derives from interaction of financial system with real economy. Private banks maximise profits without need to consider societal goals of welfare maximisation. This is primarily the responsibility of monetary and fiscal goals.

The unfavourable effects the interactions of fiscal and monetary regime has on competitiveness via high costs of government spending which raise tax burden and cost of capital for the private sector, have another dimension which concerns income inequality. The regressive nature of the tax system which exerts relatively higher burden for populations with lower income levels, coupled with a lack of capital income taxation creates tendencies towards rising inequalities. Monetary system creates additional asymmetry through high passive and active interest rates; additional monetary burden is put on heavily indebted lower income groups against high rates of return from savings of higher level income groups.

The outcome has been a worsening of overall competitiveness in Croatia in the course of the recent crisis triggered by the global economic downturn. Negative rates of economic growth lead to fiscal contraction and widening budget imbalances and additional fiscal contraction in the context of restrictive monetary policy added to the economy's recessionary cycle. Rukelj (2010) in his empirical paper confirms that monetary and fiscal policy in Croatia act as substitutes with negative effect on economic growth. In a period of restrictive fiscal policy and expansionary monetary policy, there was an explosion of borrowing, particularly in the private sector. In another regime of interaction, when the fiscal policy was expansionary and monetary policy restrictive, the costs of borrowing were high and hence crowding out of private investments and stagnation of economy.

Therefore, despite a high level of dependency of both fiscal and monetary policy on external factors and domestic economic structure, it is possible to create expansionary growth conditions. However, both fiscal and monetary authorities have to coordinate their activities under the framework of same goals. Next section takes a closer look at policy making process and its actors.

4 Key Actors of Fiscal Policy

It is interesting to observe that political economy issues in Croatia are heavily under-researched even though this kind of research provides most relevant answers for the reasons of the Croatian sluggish economic growth and the lack of improvement in competitiveness in recent decade. Besides Radosevic (2012) which directly covers political limitations in resolving the economic crisis, most of the research is directed to more narrow fields such as issues of political corruption (Ravlić 2007, 2010; Bađun 2011).

In Croatia, following actors play the key role in the area of fiscal policy:

- The government, and the Ministry of finance as the key institution;
- The Croatian National Bank (CNB) which partly affects the costs of government borrowing and, thus, creates manoeuvre space for fiscal policy;
- Supranational institutions, the EU (the European Commission) and the IMF which directly or indirectly pressure fiscal authorities to comply with regulations of guidelines;
- Large companies (foreign and domestic);
- Unions and nongovernment organisations (NGOs).

Regarding the government role, there are two main determinants that shape fiscal policy. First, the fact that Croatian governments since 2001 have been formed by the coalitions of political parties and thus, have been weak governments. Basically, two main parties – the Social Democratic Party (SDP) and Croatian Democratic Union (HDZ) have been the core of all coalition governments since 2001. Thus, all governments have run similar economic policies based on ad hoc decision making process driven mostly by major interest groups. Both parties could be defined as right wing parties in economic sense – that is to say pursuing economic programs that promote neoliberal economic agenda. However until recently, both parties have refrained from dealing with a reform of the extensive social security system which heavily and unsustainably burdens the government budget[6]. Second determinant which defines fiscal policy outcomes is related to a problem of negative selection in a sense of predominant influence of politics when appointing the leaders of key government institutions and companies. This kind of governance mechanism undermines the quality of institutions, not least by intensified rent-seeking activities which provided a wider basis for political corruption in Croatia. Compounding the problem of human capacity across government institutions is a problem of relatively low wages which has been conducive to the "brain drain" from government institutions. Consequently, the government has lacked the expertise and technical capability to formulate economic programmes and a set of policies in regards to managing public goods and services.

From the beginning of the stabilisation programme in 1994, the Croatian National Bank pursued the policy of fixed exchange rate to EURO with the primary goal of stable inflation rate which alongside liberalisation of capital flows led to quick Euroisation and loss of monetary sovereignty. This kind of policy effectively followed a kind of dogmatic position of contemporary economic theory and practice until the global financial crisis in 2008 that national banks have to be independent from the fiscal authorities. However, this concept was quickly rejected at the very beginning of the crisis and worldwide, monetary authorities heavily supported government fiscal measures. Nevertheless, Croatian National Bank has never changed this monetary regime. The positive result of such regime notwithstanding- stability of the financial system because fixed exchange rate policy protected banks from market risk and enabled creation of foreign reserves – such monetary system increased transaction costs for economy via higher interest rates and exchange rate

[6] The main reason has been political sensitivity of the required reforms.

burden, and increased systemic risk in a longer term. A lack of the Bank's proactive engagement can be further illustrated by its regulatory role in so far as it failed to create a financial system that provides capital to economic subjects with low transaction costs and protects citizens from financial risks related to credit expansion underway since 2001. The CNB was very careful in terms of regulation of mostly foreign banks and restrained from any regulations that might affect allocation of funding which was based on market decisions. This is why banks mostly supported less risky financing of real estate purchase and refrained from financing companies in the times of crisis. In addition, due to currency clause credit contracts, banks were protected from volatility of exchange rate and all the risks were transferred to citizens, companies and governments.[7]

Supranational institutions, both the EC and the IMF paid a considerable attention to the fiscal position of the country. During the whole period since 2001, there was a pressure to further liberalise the economy, particularly by privatizing the remaining portfolio of government owned companies. Both institutions supported fiscal consolidation efforts in order to comply with deficit and debt limits of EU. It is interesting to note that the IMF's policy which previously supported monetary-fiscal setup in Croatia, from 2011 has suggested potential changes in regards to exchange rate policy – in direction of devaluation of currency which would enable quick restoration of competitiveness for the export sector. However, such suggestion was rejected by the CNB arguing that the export base is too small to have substantial output effects and the financial risks are too high (IMF 2012).

Position of large companies in Croatia is specific due to the origin of their formation. There are two types of large companies in Croatia. One portion is still owned by the government (such as Hrvatska elektroprivreda d.d., Croatia osiguranje d.d. etc.), and one portion is privatized during the 1990s–the beginning of the 2000s (telecommunications, financial sector). Government companies are plagued by corruption and lack of efficiency. The crucial reason for such a state is in weak institutional powers of the government where mostly political criteria dominate in terms of managing these large systems. This provides ground for political corruption and rent-seeking. According to Rajković (2011), the extent of direct and indirect financial damage during the administration headed by Prime Minister Sanader[8] (government lead by the HDZ from 2003 to 2011), was at the level of more than 80 % of government annual budget.

Overall, the outcomes of the privatisation process in Croatia can be evaluated as extremely harmful for the country's growth prospects. The key government monopolies were privatized through unfavourable contracts and by undervalued price, which created private monopolies and oligopolies. Those in turn affected economic system through high prices and low quality of services. The problem of 'domestic' corruption is directly linked to 'imported' corruption mainly channelled through the large multinational companies operating in Croatia (Transparency International 2012).

---

[7] However, in the long run systemic (credit) risk that stem from unsustainable burden of financial costs for declining economy presents a major threat for banks.

[8] Sanader resigned from position of Prime minister and all functions in HDZ on July 1st 2009.

A number of cases illustrate this deleterious symbiosis of domestic and imported corruption: Enron-HEP, Bechtel-HC, Barr-Pliva, BLB – Riječka banka, BLB – Hypo banka Hrvatska, Daimler – TLM, MOL – Ina (Radosevic 2012). According to Radošević (2012), there are powerful business lobbies that act both on the side of Government and the CNB. These interest groups push towards a policy of stronger fiscal discipline by cutting wages and pensions in order to raise competitiveness by internal devaluation. However, due to the fact that Croatian governments run populist policies with large share of budget directed to social security spending, there were no significant cuts before the latest economic crisis. Such institutional and political circumstances led to preservation of so called "status quo economic policy". However, economic crisis characterised by long-term recession and growing fiscal imbalances does not allow the continuation of such policies. The mainstream consensus of most of the Croatian parties is that the fiscal policy should be based only on fiscal devaluation (reducing costs of labour) and on structural reforms (more flexible labour market).

The unions and nongovernmental organisations (NGO) from the beginning of 2000 have increased their relevance in the face of weakening government credibility. This particularly refers to the fact that the government did not take considerable efforts in protecting the workers and citizens in the redistribution of value added between owners of the capital and the workers. According to Grdešić (2006), the interplay of government and unions in Croatia is based on constant conflict and a lack of consensus. This has its origin in the political interventions and attitudes of political elites at the beginning of transition process in Croatia. The gains of privatisation processes were accrued to the elites that were connected with political parties and they resulted in mass unemployment and sharp reduction in wages. This created a basis for a continuous clash between union representatives and political elites that almost never involved consultations and joint platforms. This clash was intensified since the financial crisis in 2008 in particular. The inability of governments to sufficiently protect citizens has spurred the emergence of NGOs that try to protect citizens from the private sector (for example, 'Udruga Franak' that lobbies for the reduction of credit burden of the citizens who took out loans with foreign currency close offered by the local commercial banks) or from the government (for example, 'Udruga Zviždač' that tries to protect individuals by revealing the cases of government corruption).

5 Interaction and Relationships of Key Networks in the Light of Fiscal Reforms

When analysing interaction and relationship between key actors that have direct and indirect effect on fiscal policy, the evidence demonstrates their persistent conflict. Throughout the period covered by this study, there were episodes of a conflict of interest with some other interest group. Decision making on fiscal policy was increasingly becoming dependent on political pressure and the direction and strength of that pressure was mainly formed by media coverage. This part of the paper presents some examples of the struggles between different networks which led to preserving the status quo and holding back on the reforms. In terms of providing the evidence of voracity effect, the times of crisis from 2009 much more clearly present how interest groups lead to socially irrational decisions.

Since 2001, when increased capital flows from privatisation processes, alongside borrowing and foreign direct investments raised the economic growth rate and government revenues, there was far less attention on the government fiscal decision making. The effects of inefficient government spending in this period were hidden by abundant tax revenues and fiscal illusion created by inflow of foreign capital. Perfect platform for redistribution of government transfers between the interests groups was provided by large scale public investments, mainly in highway infrastructure. However, when by 2009 the effects of the crisis hit through a decline in living standards and tax receipts, the struggle between interest groups led to revelation of systemic corruption in Croatia.

From the beginning of the crisis, the government was reluctant to pursue any significant countercyclical measures. One of the first attempts to act against the crisis was to introduce "crisis tax" in August of 2009. The introduction of this tax shows the potential of government for coping with the crisis. The tax was successful in collecting revenues but it was based on ad hoc political decision, without prior analysis and it was full of erroneous stipulations and based on theoretically unacceptable tax policy method. Parallel to the introduction of this tax was a dramatic decrease in public investments from the beginning of 2008 (see Fig. 3.1). All these decisions were based on fiscal goals without any broader consideration of overall effects of fiscal policy on economic system; such fiscal policy goals remain predominant up to present time.

It is very useful to depict a clash of interest groups which prevent reforms in the system. The most recent example is an attempt to introduce a property tax. As it was presented in the section 3 of this paper, the Croatian tax system is based on VAT receipts and taxes on labour. At the end of 2012, the new coalition government presented plans for new property tax scheduled for April 2013. However, from the very presentation of the tax proposal, there was a fierce battle through media even between the coalition parties. The HDZ as a coalition partner from the beginning strongly rejected this tax. This party has a more liberal approach to economic system than the leading Social Democratic Party and this creates struggles particularly in the field of fiscal policy. These different programs of the coalition partners provide strong incentive for the status quo policy. In addition, both parties are supported by somewhat different voting groups. The HDZ is supported by business sector and the SDP by the section of voters demanding more redistribution. In addition, property tax was very much unpopular by both of these groups. Businesses demand lowering of taxes in general. Property tax would damage banks financial sheets in particular due to the large accumulation of property based on mortgages on loans. This tax would put pressure for sale of these properties which would lead to bank loses. Therefore, there were strong incentives to prevent introduction of this tax. On the other hand, political opposition was struggling to prove that this tax will put additional burden on overtaxed Croatian taxpayer. The outcome of this contest is that it is highly unlikely the tax will be introduced although it was recommended by the IMF), and that other tax reforms would follow soon.

In discussing the issues of fiscal and monetary coordination, besides the official policy of the CNB's independence and its chosen monetary policy regime which does not allow for extensive monetary intervention, it is worth taking a note of numerous accusations of the close relations of monetary authorities and government with large private companies and foreign banks which generate political corruption at this level as well (Radosevic 2012, p. 37). For example, former Governor of the CNB was accused of the conflict of interest due to a lack of transparency in providing information about relation of his family company with the large import company (which favours the current monetary regime). Nevertheless, without further analysis of potential rent-seeking incentives that come from the CNB, it can be concluded that the monetary policy regime suited the large foreign banks and import based companies. The financial burden and the risks were transferred to the export based companies and citizens. It is interesting to note the position of the NGO Udruga Franak, founded to champion the interests of the citizens who took loans pegged to the Swiss Franc and who endured significant rise in their repayment annuities. In an open letter to the CNB, the Ministry of finance, and the Croatian Union of Banks[9], they express a hope that the Ministry of finance will continue to eliminate illegal practices in the financial system. They argue that the CNB should join the Ministry in these efforts because so far, the CNB was not supportive, but, on the contrary, was an obstacle to such a process. "Open support of the CNB to the arguments of the Croatian Union of Banks is out of the domain of preserving financial stability and enters the sphere of supporting the extra profits of banks. By this manner we appeal for cooperation due to the fact that country which financial stability is protected by the CNB consists of citizens and not from few business subjects".

Supranational institutions, the EU and the IMF, provide a form of political pressure which directs general regime of both fiscal and monetary policy. Their propositions were more uniform when it comes to fiscal policy. In regards to monetary policy, particularly the IMF was occasionally prone to suggest more flexible exchange rate regime, and thus, flexible and active monetary policy. Both the European Commission (EC) (2013) and the IMF (2012) have similar evaluation and measures proposed for running economic and fiscal policy. The efforts towards fiscal consolidation and structural reforms are welcome and both argue for further efforts to reduce high budget deficit and to resolve the liabilities carried by state-owned enterprises while safeguarding investment and other growth-enhancing expenditure. There are also suggestions to increase the efficiency of taxation, deal with labour market rigidities and an unfavourable business environment. In the past, the ruling political parties very often used recommendation of these institutions to

[9] http://www.udrugafranak.hr/index.php/stavovi-udruge/item/602-otvoreno-pismo-ministarstvu-financija-hub-u-i-hnb-u

justify some politically unpopular measure. Due to the fact that Croatia in 2014 enters the excessive deficit procedure[10] this will provide additional support for continuation of consolidation reforms.

As it was already stated, the business class in Croatia was mainly created on the basis of privatisation processes where the criteria for selecting the members of business elite were political and not the professional one. These business elite entrenched both in domestic and foreign companies developed strong ties with political parties. In this way the privatisation process actually served to redistribute national wealth and strengthen business elites in the long run. Foreign companies that participated in the privatisation processes recognized the possibilities to exploit such systemic corruption and used local elites to take over most profitable government companies that had monopolistic features. This kind of approach created adverse effect for the economic development of the country because the key industries were not interested in the development of these companies, but were focused on profit-maximising policies in order to transfer capital to the foreign owners. Compounded by the tax system that does not prevent such negative dynamics, such capital outflows heavily damage economic potential of the country. According to Radosevic (2012), Croatian transition oligarchy does not have entrepreneurial orientation, lacks capacity for modern management and innovations and tries to transfer financial burden to the wider population. This can be most clearly observed through the tax system dominated by indirect taxes, a lack of certain types of taxes which exist in developed economies and conducive to legal outflow of capital.

Finally, the unions and pressure groups under the large NGO umbrella, will most likely increase their importance despite the fact that conflict between them and the government is becoming sharper with extended recession. The present setup of fiscal policy which is directed to the policy of fiscal consolidation and internal devaluation (shift in tax structure towards additional decrease in direct taxes and decrease of wages) necessarily creates high resistance due to declining living standards and increase of unemployment. Lack of social dialogue aggravates social tensions and reduces chances for overall support of rational government policies. The latest open letter[11] to the Prime Minister by the President of the Great Council of Independent Union of Science and Higher Education supports this thesis.

Based on previously described relations of key networks in Croatian society it can be concluded that Croatia has a long-term crisis of social relations between different social groups where relations are not based on joint interest but each actor tries to gain maximum redistribution gains for itself. This leads to overall inefficiency of the system and worst case scenario outcomes for all of the interest groups. In a way, short term benefits for each network will be lost by the realisation of long-term systemic risk which will lead to loses for all actors.

---

[10] http://ec.europa.eu/economy_finance/economic_governance/sgp/pdf/30_edps/126-06_commission/2013-12-10_hr_126-6_commission_en.pdf

[11] http://www.nsz.hr/vijesti/umjesto-kukurijekanja-postenije-bi-bilo-ispricati-se-svima

6 Conclusions

Fiscal policy is a powerful instrument within economic policy that can affect competitiveness through many channels. Even in the case when the manoeuvre space is severely limited, as in EU countries whose fiscal policy is bonded by fiscal rules, there are still many alternatives. The paper presented an elaboration of key factors of fiscal policy in a critical perspective. A clear policy recommendation comes from the main argument of the paper. Even though Croatia became a member of EU, nothing changes in regards to achievement of vital macroeconomic and societal goals. However, these goals will not be achieved if there is no systematic approach of running an economic and fiscal policy that respects specific national needs and preferences. The competitiveness of the national economy will not be improved by continuation of present inertial (status quo) fiscal policy.

One of the directions of fiscal policy has to be towards short-term measures for the stabilization of the economy. It is necessary to identify opportunities for implementation of expansionary fiscal policy, primarily in the direction of government spending and infrastructure investment with high multiplicative effects. Problems with public debt present a barrier to such policy and, therefore, there is a need for rescheduling the public debt. Significant savings are possible within the structure of the budget. In addition, changes in the tax structure that would lead to higher taxation of capital savings and property could provide relaxation of labour tax burden and, thus, raise competitiveness of the labour market. The other direction focuses on radical structural reform and rationalisation of the public sector. Such an approach requires a longer time period and it has to be carefully conducted due to potentially unfavourable effects of economic crisis. Among other measures it is necessary to radically revise the organization of the state apparatus, implement rationalization of territorial organization, and of functionality of operations of the state institutions as well.

In general, a significantly different fiscal policy has to be applied. A target-oriented policy which directs public resources to promote growth of new activities, easing credit constraints, infrastructure and human capital has to be promoted. Public sector should be reduced both in terms of government spending and government employment. It is possible to achieve higher level of productivity by informatisation of the state apparatus and the installation of decision-making mechanism for consistent and planned directing of economic flows. The benefits of these measures would spillover directly through the unloading of the tax pressure and indirectly by more effective action in terms of creating a quality business environment. The whole functioning of the public sector should be focused on increasing the technological forces in society that within the existing production factors raise the production function of the society. This concept replaces the previous unsuccessful one which was based on cost competitiveness. Raising the level of fiscal transparency and public financial management is the prerequisite for the success of such reform.

Finally, it has to be noted that, under extreme scenario, fiscal policy can affect competitiveness in two ways. One is proposed by the current mainstream model based on internal devaluation which aims at reducing wages and reducing public goods and services, and thus, tax burden. This path inevitably leads to clashes of social groups and social tensions. The second one is to run flexible and adaptable economic-fiscal policy that requires fine tuning of economic structure and dynamic responses to endogenous and exogenous shocks. The latter one demands high level of social capital of the country. Therefore, it sounds like utopia.

References

Alesina, A., & Ardagna, S. (1998). Tales of fiscal adjustment. *Economic Policy, 13*(27), 489–517.

Alesina, A., & Perotti, R. (1997). Fiscal adjustments in OECD countries: Composition and macroeconomic effects. *IMF Staff Papers, 44*, 210–248.

Ardagna, S. (2004). Fiscal stabilisations: When do they work and why? *European Economic Review, 48*(5), 1047–1074.

Bađun, M. (2011). Odnos političke korupcije i javnih investicije – slučaj hrvatske. *Društvena istraživanja, 20*(2), 295–316.

Družić, I. (2012). Oportunitetni troškovi stabilizacije 1980–2010. Politička ekonomija ekonomske krize u Hrvatskoj, Zbornik radova, Iz krize u depresiju, HAZU, Zagreb, 143–166

Eichegreen, B., & Wyplosz, C. (1998). The stability pact: More than a minor nuisance? *Economic Policy, 13*(26), 66–113.

European Commission (2013). Assessment of the 2013 economic programme for Croatia. Commission Staff Working Document 361.

Favero, C., & Giavazzi, F. (2007). *Debt and the effects of fiscal policy* (NBER Working Paper 12822). http://www.nber.org/papers/w12822.

Giavazzi, F., & Pagano, M. (1990). Can severe fiscal contractions be expansionary? Tales of two small European countries. In O. J. Blanchard & S. Fischer (Eds.), *NBER macroeconomics annual* (pp. 76–110). Cambridge, MA: MIT Press.

Giavazzi, F., & Pagano, M. (1996). Non-Keynesian effects of fiscal policy changes: International evidence and the Swedish experience. *Swedish Economic Policy Review, 3*, 67–103.

Grdešić, M. (2006). Tranzicija, sindikati i političke elite u sloveniji i hrvatskoj. *Politička misao, XLIII*(4), 121–141.

Gross, D., & Alcidi, C. (2010, September). *Fiscal policy coordination and competitiveness surveillance: What solutions to what problems?. The Centre for European Policy Studies* (CEPS Policy Brief, 213). http://www.ceps.be/book/fiscal-policy-coordination-and-competitiveness-surveillance-what-solutions-what-problems

Guaijardo, J. et al. (2011). *Expansionary austerity: New international evidence* (IMF Working Paper, 158). http://www.imf.org/external/pubs/ft/wp/2011/wp11158.pdf

Gupta, S., et al. (2003). *What sustains fiscal consolidations in emerging market countries?. IMF* (IMF Working Paper, 224). https://www.imf.org/external/pubs/ft/wp/2003/wp03224.pdf

IMF. (2012). *The republic of Croatia, 2012 Article IV consultation. IMF* (IMF Country Report No. 12/302). http://www.imf.org/external/pubs/ft/scr/2012/cr12302.pdf

Levit, M., & Lord, C. (2000). *The political economy of monetary union*. London: Macmillan Press.

Perotti, R. (1999). Fiscal policy in good times and bad. *The Quarterly Journal of Economics, 114*(4), 1399–1436.

Radošević, D. (2012). Politička ekonomija ekonomske krize u Hrvatskoj, Zbornik radova, Iz krize u depresiju, HAZU: Zagreb, 33–59

Rajković, D. (2011). *Kako je Ivo Sanader ukrao Hrvatsku?* Zagreb: Jesenski i Turk.

Ravlić, S. (2007). Transformacija predstavničke funkcije političkih stranaka. *Zbornik Pravnog fakulteta Zagreb, 57*(6), 979–1004. Zagreb.

Ravlic, S. (2010). Izvori političke korupcije u demokratskom poretku: o stranačkoj korupciji. *Zbornik Pravnog fakulteta Zagreb, 60*(3), 1241–1264.

Roubini, N., & Sachs, J. D. (1989, April). *Government spending and budget deficits in the industrial economies* (NBER Working Paper No. w2919). http://ssrn.com/abstract=459425

Rukelj, D. (2010). *Modelling fiscal and monetary policy interactions in Croatia using structural vector error correction model. Privredna kretanja i ekonomska politika. EIZG* (Research Paper, No 121). http://www.econbiz.de/Record/modelling-fiscal-and-monetary-policy-interactions-in-croatia-using-structural-vector-error-correction-model-rukelj-dario/10003941668

Sever, I., et al. (2009). The starting point of new economic policy in conditions of recession. Proceedings of Rijeka Faculty of Economics. *Journal of Economics and Business, 27*(2), 217–262.

Sever, I., Drezgić, S., & Blažić, H. (2011). Budget spending and economic growth in Croatia: Dynamics and relationship over the two past decades. Proceedings of Rijeka Faculty of Economics. *Journal of Economics and Business, 29*(2), 291–331.

Spillimbergo, A., et al. (2008). *Fiscal policy for the crisis. IMF staff position note*. Washington, DC: IMF.

Tornell, A., & Lane, P. R. (1999). The voracity effect. *The American Economic Review, 89*(1), 22–46.

Transparency international (2012). 2012 corruption perception index. http://www.transparency.org/cpi2012/results.

Uhlig, H., & Janagawa, N. (1996). Increasing the capital income tax may lead to faster growth. *European Economic Review, 40*(8), 1521–1540.

World Bank. (2012). *Doing business 2013. Smarter regulations for small and medium-size enterprises*. Washington, DC: The World Bank. http://www.doingbusiness.org/~/media/GIAWB/Doing%20Business/Documents/Annual-Reports/English/DB13-full-report.pdf

World Economic Forum. (2012). *The global competitiveness report 2012–2013*. Geneva: World Economic Forum. http://www.weforum.org/gcr

World Economic Forum. (2013). *The global competitiveness report 2013–2014*. Geneva: World Economic Forum. http://www.weforum.org/gcr

Chapter 4
Building Competitiveness and Increasing Trade Potential in the Western Balkans: Policy Making in Preparing for European Integration

Predrag Bjelić

1 Introduction

The Western Balkans[1] comprises the economies of Albania, Bosnia and Herzegovina, Croatia, Macedonia, Montenegro, Serbia and Kosovo.[2] These economies largely share a common heritage and were once part of Yugoslavia—except for Albania. Despite being a Socialist Republic, the former Yugoslavia maintained some unique features including elements of a market-based economy. Thus, it was expected that the transition to a full market economy would be easier than in other East European countries. However, the breakup of Yugoslavia proved to be complex, marked by conflict and lengthy resulting in a difficult and messy transition for the economies that subsequently emerged. Albania's path to transition was separate but similar in many respects. As the individual states emerged from the conflict, there was no regional cooperation or evidence of regional trade integration. A clear, strategic foreign policy objective of all Western Balkan countries was to join the European Union (EU) and significant portions of their respective citizenry similarly aspired to the benefits of EU membership. The attractions of EU membership include a better standard of living and higher economic growth. However, as noted by Kaminski and de la Rocha (2003), the EU Stabilization and Association Agreements signed by aspiring EU neighbourhood countries in the Balkans commits them "to upgrading institutions and policies to European standards and governance" while motivating "public support and, thereby, facilitating implementation of structural reforms." So while many of the institutional and economic policy reforms in the Western Balkans result from political pressures from the EU, the policy of conditionality for EU

[1] As defined in European Union policy documents.

[2] Separate customs territory, as defined under UNSCR 1244.

P. Bjelić (✉)
Faculty of Economics, University of Belgrade, Belgrade, Serbia
e-mail: bjelic@ekof.bg.ac.rs

M. Thomas, V. Bojicic-Dzelilovic (eds.), *Public Policy Making in the Western Balkans*, DOI 10.1007/978-94-017-9346-9_4

Table 4.1 Affiliation of Western Balkan economies with CEFTA 2006, EU and the World Trade Organization (2014)

	CEFTA 2006	European Union	WTO
Albania	Contracting party	Candidate	Member
Bosnia and Herzegovina	Contracting party	Potential candidate	Observer
Croatia	Contracting party	Member	Member
Macedonia	Contracting party	Candidate	Member
Moldova	Contracting party	Neighbourhood policy	Member
Montenegro	Contracting party	Candidate	Member
Kosovo[a]	Contracting party	Special tracking mechanism	–
Serbia	Contracting party	Candidate	Observer

Source: Author compilation based on data from CEFTA, EU and WTO Web portals

[a]As a separate customs territory defined under UNSCR 1244, and the original contracting party in CEFTA 2006 singed in the name of customs territory of Kosovo by UN Mission in Kosovo (UNMIK)

membership has limited results because there is a large gap between introduction of policies in the Western Balkans and their implementation in this region.

One condition for all Balkan countries for EU membership was regional cooperation. Regional trade integration was initiated by the EU, and in 2000 the Memorandum on Liberalisation of Trade in South East Europe was concluded by all Western Balkan economies. Regional trade integration was achieved in phases starting with bilateral trade agreements and the creation of a network of 32 bilateral trade agreements among the Western Balkan economies. In 2006, the 1993 Central European Free Trade Agreement (CEFTA) was revised to support the establishment of a regional trade association in the Western Balkans. Even though this was a single agreement, trade preferences were included from bilateral agreements and were arranged on a bilateral level. The CEFTA 2006 agreement included provisions for creating a free trade zone for industrial goods by the end of 2010. The Republic of Moldova is not geographically positioned in Western Balkans region but is a contracting party of the CEFTA 2006 integration even though the volume of trade between Moldova and the rest of CEFTA 2006 members is very low.

The Western Balkan economies are also trying to integrate into the world economy. An important step in this direction is gaining World Trade Organization (WTO) membership. As shown in Table 4.1, five of the Western Balkan economies are WTO members two are in the process of accession and have observer status. Kosovo has not applied for WTO membership. The WTO oversees the specific multilateral trade regime that must be followed by all WTO members.

The objective of this chapter is to examine the trade policy process in selected Western Balkan economies, taking into account the roles of key domestic, regional and international actors, and the influence of global, bi-lateral, and regional trade regimes on key policy episodes. With rapid globalisation and the importance of international trade and investment for economic growth, countries are under increasing pressure from trade partners and institutions such as the International Monetary Fund (IMF) and WTO to liberalise, and harmonize policies in order to compete and tap into global value chains. Some have argues that smaller and less developed economies are under greater competitiveness pressures compared with the large, developed ones. By accepting membership in relevant international organizations the Western Balkan economies are similarly under pressure to significantly liberalise their trade regimes and implement significant tariff cuts.

When considering trade policy reforms, the Western Balkan economies have to take into account three main trade regimes: CEFTA 2006; the EU; and WTO. Obligations derived from the membership of Western Balkan economies in all these set the conditions for trade policy adjustment since member countries are not completely autonomous in trade policy creation. Sometimes trade regimes can be conflicting, and their effect on countries competitiveness on international markets can be significant. But these trade regimes set the framework for the operation of domestic and foreign businesses and have significant impact on their competitiveness in both the regional and the global market. In trade policy creation, the Western Balkan economies are also influenced by these companies' efforts to secure better operating conditions for themselves.

Western Balkan economies have not finished the process of transition to a fully functioning market economies and do not have fully developed economic systems, as demonstrated by European Bank for Reconstruction and Development (EBRD) research. Their competitiveness on the world market is very weak with no prospect of rapid recovery, demonstrated by World Economic Forum data shown in Fig. 4.1. These economies are becoming severely indebted, and the problem of domestic and international liquidity is an issue. Western Balkan economies are relatively small and highly dependent on exports to international markets and on the inflow of foreign private investments. Specifically Bjelić and Dragutinović-Mitrović (2012) demonstrated on the case of Serbia how conflicting trade regimes influence trade flows, and show that significant trade preference cannot divert trade from traditional trade partners in a long run. The companies operating in these economies while not

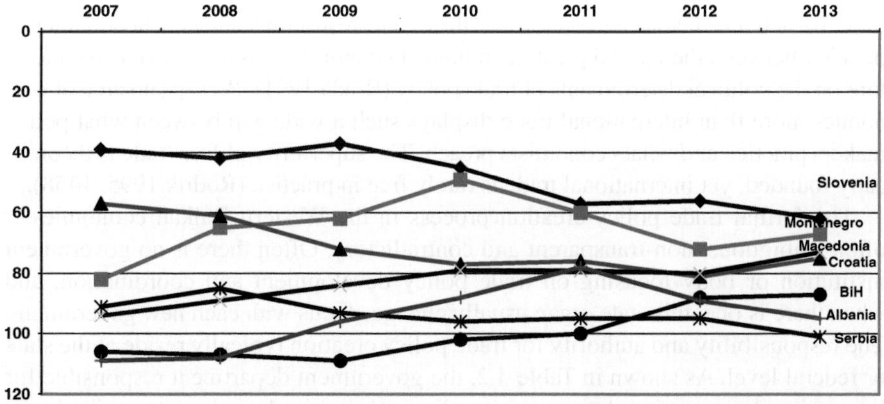

Fig. 4.1 Western Balkan economies and Slovenia competitiveness ranked by the World Economic Forum (Source: World Economic Forum, 'Global Competitiveness Report', 2008–2014, Davos)

internationally competitive are highly competitive in the domestic and regional markets. Western Balkan economies have been benefiting from EU asymmetrical trade preferences but as the EU trade regime becomes symmetrical the competitiveness of Western Balkan economies and companies operating in this countries started to decrease (Dragutinović-Mitrović and Bjelić 2013). Generally speaking, the interest of foreign-owned companies operating in the Western Balkans is greater liberalisation, while domestic companies tend to be more protectionist-oriented.

Foreign direct investment (FDI) in the Western Balkans is only from those willing to operate in a corrupt and unstable political and economic environment, as illustrated by Perez et al. (2012). But the foreign-controlled enterprises operating in the Western Balkans also exert some informal influence on trade policy creation in the region to provide a better business environment for themselves in the CEFTA 2006 area, and require significant subvention in order to starts its operations.

2 Formal Trade Policy Creation in the Western Balkans

Trade policies embody the strategies pursued by countries in order to regulate its foreign trade and to keep it in line with societal interests. 'Trade policies refer to all policies that have a direct impact on the domestic prices of tradeables, that is, goods and services traded across national boundaries as imports and/or exports' (Milner 1999, 93). An economy can regulate international trade with unilateral actions, passing laws on trade matters like customs law, customs tariff law and laws on foreign trade. But as international trade is a transnational business activity, to fully regulate this activity, economies must cooperate between themselves. The main instruments in their joint regulation of international trade are trade agreements (Cooper 1973). It is often mistakenly felt that it is only in state-planned economies that the state has a large impact on trade and the trade regime. In both market and planned economies politicians have designed institutions and implemented policies that interfere with free trade by actively favouring some trade flows and restricting others. This conflict or paradox between theory and practice in market economies has led to extensive literature on the political determinants of trade policy (Brada 1991). Perhaps no area of economics more than international trade displays such a wide gap between what policy makers practice and what economists preach. The superiority of free trade is theoretically founded, yet international trade is rarely free in practice (Rodrik 1995, 1458).

The formal trade policy-creation process in the Western Balkan economies is often ambiguous, non-transparent and contradictory. Often there is no government institution or body focusing on trade policy development and coordination, and when there is one, this state organ usually changes focus with each new government. The responsibility and authority for trade policy creation typically reside at the state or federal level. As shown in Table 4.2, the government department responsible for international economic relations are usually not organised as separate ministries or entities but as a part of ministries responsible for economic affairs. The exceptions in the region are Bosnia and Herzegovina, where the Ministry for Foreign Trade and

Table 4.2 Bodies responsible for trade policy in Western Balkan economies (2013)

Economy	Focus state institution
Albania	Ministry of economy, trade and energy[a]
Bosnia and Herzegovina	Ministry of foreign trade and economic relations (state level)[b]
Croatia	State office for trade in the ministry of economy[c]
Macedonia	Sector for international trade cooperation in the ministry of economy;[d]
Montenegro	Sector for multilateral and regional trade cooperation and international economic relations in the ministry of economy[e]
Serbia	Ministry of domestic and foreign trade and telecommunications[f]
Kosovo[g]	Ministry of trade and industry[h]

[a]Internet, www.mete.gov.al
[b]Internet, www.mvteo.gov.ba
[c]Internet, www.mingo.hr
[d]Internet, www.economy.gov.mk
[e]Internet, www.mek.gov.me
[f]Internet, http://mtt.gov.rs
[g]The customs territory of Kosovo is a specific situation since trade policy creation and execution is under United Nations Security Council Resolution 1244 vested in UNMIK but since 2008 and the declaration of political independence of Kosovo from Serbia, the Ministry of Economy and Finance took over the trade policy–creation role unilaterally. The countries that had recognised Kosovo as a state accept this situation while Serbia and other countries not recognising Kosovo as a state insist on UNMIK's role in this matter
[h]Source: www.mti-ks.org

Economic Relations still exists as a separate ministry at the state government level. Our opinion is that all Western Balkan economies, as small and open economies, should have a separate ministry focusing on external economic relations, especially foreign trade.

Typically trade policy initiatives emanate from the government through laws and by-laws covering trade and draft trade agreements and are subject to parliamentary review and adoption. As standard procedure for most laws, draft legislation is first debated in the responsible parliamentary committee and require a majority vote before being sent to the General Assembly for a decision. Trade-related legislation and agreements are usually debated in parliamentary committees that responsible for economic matters. Sometimes important trade-related legislation is directed to different committees. For example in the case of Serbia, foreign trade law is debated in the foreign affairs rather than the economics parliamentary committee. Increasingly parliaments in the region are adopting the practices of Western Democracies by soliciting the testimony of experts and holding public hearings on proposed legislation to arrive at better informed decisions about technical and policy issues that require specialized knowledge.

Most often, after parliament passes a certain trade-related legislation or agreement, it is the government that executes that legislation. The government is responsible for the implementing regulations based on the law passed by the parliament—directives, regulations and procedures—which provide detailed instruction for complying with the law. Although the ministry that is responsible for trade-related matters (e.g., the Ministry of Foreign Trade or the Ministry of Economy) had responsibility for implementation and compliance, trade policy execution demands cooperation among many different ministries in the government facilitated by special technical bodies including commissions and working groups. For example, the ministry that covers agriculture is in charge of application of sanitary and phyto-sanitary measures in international trade, and their inspectors are present at the border with other border control agencies.

To explain this process, we can illustrate it with an example of the WTO accession process. When a government sends a letter to the Director General of the WTO, expressing its wish to join the Organisation, the process of accession is initiated. For each individual country, the ministry in charge of trade policy plays the main role in the accession process. Usually a subsidiary coordinating organ is established as a commission to focus all efforts towards WTO accession. This subsidiary organ coordinates the efforts of several ministries, but the elected negotiators represent the government at negotiations held in WTO headquarters in Geneva. When the Draft List of Concessions is adopted, the Draft Protocol of Accession is forwarded to the state parliament to be adopted. When the parliament ratifies the accession package, the Director General of the WTO is notified, and the country becomes a WTO member in 30 days from this notification. It is apparent that the national government bears the heaviest burden in the WTO accession process.

Although national trade regimes are unilaterally established with laws and regulations determining tariff schedule and the regulations spelling out non-tariff measures, in today's world, countries tend to set the conditions of foreign trade in cooperation with other countries—their trade partners. This can be achieved in processes of bilateral, regional or multilateral trade cooperation. The most important instrument of trade cooperation until the nineteenth century was bilateral trade agreements that countries concluded setting the customs duties in their mutual trade at a lower level than the general level of tariff regime defined in tariff schedules. These preferential trade agreements were the cornerstones of the international trade system since they included the most favoured nation (MFN) clause, lowering tariffs from the general tariff regime; thus, this is referred to as the MFN regime. In this way a country lowers its tariffs for trade partners, and these new tariffs are known as conventional tariffs since they are introduced by international agreements (conventions).

In the first part of the following table (Table 4.3), we have presented the trade regime applied by Western Balkan economies; this is set unilaterally by these countries by adopting national tariff schedules. We can observe that nominally Serbia and Macedonia have the most restrictive tariff regimes, measured by the average tariff rate.[3] This average tariff rate, in the first line of the table, represents the average for tariffs for all products in the tariff schedule. The other two rows represent average tariff rates separately for agricultural products and industrial products. Usually countries have more restrictive tariff regimes for agricultural products than for industrial ones. Apart from Serbia and Macedonia, we see that Montenegro and

[3] It represents simple average tariff rate.

Table 4.3 Tariff regimes of West Balkan economies (percentages)

	Albania	Bosnia-H	Croatia	Macedonia	Montenegro	Serbia
Applied tariff regime (MFN)						
Average tariff rate—all products	**3.8**	**6.6**	**5.0**	**6.9**	**4.3**	**7.3**
Agricultural goods	7.7	11.0	10.3	13.0	10.4	14.2
Industrial goods	3.2	5.9	4.1	5.9	3.3	6.3
Trade weighted average tariff rate—all products	**4.7**	**7.4**	**4.7**	**6.2**	**7.8**	**5.9**
Agricultural goods	6.9	16.2	12.9	16.4	18.6	16.5
Industrial goods	4.3	5.4	3.7	4.9	4.5	5.1
Tariffs >15 %	0	2.6	3.9	11.5	4.6	13.7
Max tariff	15.0	595.0	55.0	65.0	60.0	30.0
Non ad valorem duties	0.0	3.2	1.9	1.5	1.0	0.0
WTO-bound regime						
Bound tariff average—all products	7.0	–	6.2	7.2	5.1	–
Agricultural goods	9.5	–	11.0	13.0	10.8	–
Industrial goods	6.6	–	5.5	6.3	4.3	–
% bounded	100.0	–	100.0	100.0	100.0	–

Source: WTO 2013, ITC and UNCTAD 'World Tariff Profiles 2013', Geneva 2013

Bosnia and Herzegovina have significant average tariff rates for agricultural products. Bosnia and Herzegovina has a significant average tariff rate even for industrial goods.

But if we observe a tariff regime using the weighted average tariff rate, where we use trade in specific products at certain tariff rates as weights, we can see that Bosnia and Herzegovina and Montenegro have the most restrictive tariff regimes, especially for industrial products. This is even more obvious if we observe the data on the maximum tariff that countries apply, which in the case of Bosnia and Herzegovina goes up to 595 %, knowing that this country has around 3 % of all tariffs expressed in non ad valorem form.[4] Serbia has a very restrictive regime for agricultural products, measured by a weighted average tariff rate, and a significant number of products with tariff rates above 15 %, around 13 % of products in Serbia tariff schedule.

Liberalisation from a general tariff regime—today usually the MFN regime that the country unilaterally adopts—can be achieved in two dimensions: regional trade liberalisation and multilateral trade liberalisation. Regional trade liberalisation is more usual and comprehensive since similar economies are bound in the trade integration processes. Countries in the region are similar not only economically but also culturally, linguistically and consumption-wise. For these reasons regional trade integration sometimes tends to be deeper and wider than multilateral trade liberalisation. Today every region in the world has its regional trade integration; in some

[4] Not in the form that is calculated from a percentage of the value of the good that is traded but rather in some specific form.

regions there are several regional trade integrations. But one integration always dominates, and there is some initiative that links entire continents in trade integration.

In the Western Balkans, regional trade integration commenced with the signing of the CEFTA 2006 agreement. The revised CEFTA agreement from 2006 included all trade preferences negotiated on a bilateral basis between Western Balkan economies in the framework of the Memorandum on Trade Liberalisation in South East Europe, signed in 2000. CEFTA 2006 integration regulates only intra-regional trade since it represents a free trade area for industrial goods and agricultural products. Services will soon also be included in the CEFTA 2006 framework. There has been some discussion that CEFTA 2006 may become a customs union, meaning that member economies adopt a common external tariff to be applied in trade with all countries outside CEFTA 2006. This would mean the deepening of trade integration in CEFTA 2006, but in practice this is not realistic as CEFTA 2006 is only a provisional integration as all members tend to be EU members.

Trade relations of individual CEFTA 2006 economies with non-members are not regulated by the CEFTA 2006 agreement so these economies regulate these relations on their own by creating different regimes. A country can become a member of different regional trade integrations if this integration is at a lower level—like the free trade area. But the dominant trade integration in Europe is the EU, and countries of the Western Balkans are set to become members. When a country joins the EU, it has to relinquish all other trade regimes; it especially has to discontinue membership in all other preferential regional trade integrations since EU is a trade block integrated at a higher level of regional trade integration with a common trade policy. This was the case for the majority of Eastern European economies in 2004, for Romania and Bulgaria in 2007 and Croatia in 2013.

The countries of the Western Balkans can now regulate their trade relations with CEFTA 2006 non-members on their own, but once a part of EU, they must follow a common EU trade policy and apply an external EU tariff schedule. The trade agreement that Serbia has with the Russian Federation, which is quite generous in trade preferences, will be terminated when Serbia joins the EU; this is an example of the sacrifice that countries must make to become EU members. Serbia will, from that day forward, apply the EU trade regime towards the Russian Federation. The EU is a regional trade integration that has a joint external trade regime, and it is the important element that defines the layers of trade policy that EU members apply. There is some discussion that the Western Balkan economies could adopt the EU customs union for trade in industrial products even before they achieve formal membership, since their individual tariff schedules are very diverse (Kathuria 2008, 67), but this could obstruct trade between Western Balkan economies with third countries especially if EU membership does not come in the foreseeable future, as in the case of Turkey.

Apart from regional trade liberalisation, the other very important process in the world economy is multilateral trade liberalisation, within the World Trade Organization framework. When a country becomes a member of this global body, it effectively relinquishes aspects of its trade sovereignty in order to receive the collective benefits of membership. One basic obligation of membership is defining a list of trade preferences for other WTO members. These preferences establish the bounded tariff rates which are the maximum tariffs a country can set in its trade relation with other WTO members. In this way defined market access for all WTO members is guaranteed by the WTO, and a specific multilateral trade regime is created (a WTO-bounded trade regime). WTO has two mechanisms to ensure the application of its rules: Trade Policy Review Mechanism and Dispute Settlement Mechanism. The former is a method of surveillance by the organisation of its members' trade policy. The members have to incorporate all WTO rules in their trade systems, and their tariff schedules (applied tariff regime) must be in compliance with their WTO-bounded trade regime. If some members feel that their trade interests are jeopardised by actions of other WTO members, they can instigate a Dispute Settlement Process in the WTO that examines whether there was a breach of WTO obligations.

In this way more conventional tariffs are applied than the autonomous tariffs set unilaterally by each country. This demonstrates the influence of international organisations on international trade policy of their members. The WTO-bounded trade regime is usually set during the country accession process and further liberalised during the rounds of multilateral trade negotiations. Western Balkan countries have recently joined WTO or are in the process of WTO accession. During this process, the key phase is negotiations on market access where the acceding country must bind its tariffs. There are no clear rules of accession, so each country must negotiate its own 'entrance ticket'. WTO membership brings certain costs linked to modernisation and harmonisation of various institutions directly involved in the conduct of foreign trade policy. But the impetus to join WTO lies in the benefits of membership. The main draw is improved market access for export products due to the WTO multilateral trade regime. But some researchers have discovered that there are limits to how far and how much the agreements help. WTO membership cannot address problems originating in poor domestic supply response, terms of trade changes or exogenous shocks. The accession itself may not even open up new markets for the acceding countries as incumbents are not expected to provide new concessions to them (Drabek and Bacchetta 2004, 1122).

The Western Balkan countries that are WTO members like Albania, Croatia, Macedonia and recently Montenegro have bound their tariffs in the WTO framework. Average bounded tariff is around 5–7 %. The regime is more restrictive for agricultural products, especially in Macedonia and Croatia, where the tariffs are 13 % and 11 %, respectively. The average tariff for industrial products is in the 4.3–6.6 % interval. All Western Balkan economies have bounded all products in its tariff schedule, as shown in Table 4.3. Even Western Balkan countries that are in the process of accession to the WTO are observing the multilateral trade regime and are influenced by it. Serbia's 2009 Law on Foreign Trade Business, Article 1 stipulates that 'this law regulates foreign trade business in accordance with WTO rules and EU regulations'.[5] It is a rule that countries acceding to WTO cannot make significant changes in their trade regimes, but this rule is not observed in all Western Balkan economies.

[5] Zakon o spoljnotrgovinskom poslovanju, Službeni glasnik RS br. 36/2009.

3 Competitiveness of Western Balkan Economies and Informal Trade Policy Creation

The unilateral, regional and multilateral trade liberalisation often creates different trade regimes. Sometimes these regimes can diverge, and countries have to work actively to align them. For companies, these regimes represent the frameworks in which they operate and can significantly impact their international as well as domestic competitiveness. In the global arena, companies are becoming more influential actors as their economic grip on international trade is rising. Large transnational companies (TNCs) are main actors in international trade and the biggest sources of private capital that moves across borders. With this economic power they are able to exercise greater political power and to influence policy creation in many countries. Thus the formal process of trade policy creation is not completely relevant as trade policy creation globally, but especially in the Western Balkans, is deeply influenced by informal actors such as foreign companies and local pressure groups. This leads to the creation of a framework of trade policy, which is biased to the interests of certain pressure groups. In a sense, trade policy in the Western Balkan countries is shaped more by economic interests of large capital than by the state institutions in charge for this process.

The concept of country competitiveness, or macroeconomic competitiveness—although at times disputed—is now accepted by the majority of economists. This concept was developed from a microeconomic concept that shows the rivalry of companies on the market. We have to acknowledge that countries today compete for resources, markets and investments. These economic rivalries on international markets create their geostrategic dimension. The theoretical background for macroeconomic competitiveness was developed by American business economist Michael Porter. One important postulate of his theory of competitive advantage was that competitiveness of companies operating in one country significantly influences the competitiveness of that country and vice versa—the macroeconomic competitiveness of a country influences competitiveness of its companies (Porter 1990).

Western Balkans economies are in the bottom tier of the global competitiveness league compared to most other economies in the world, according to the analysis by the World Economic Forum (WEF). One of the most competitive countries in the region is Slovenia, which has been an EU member since 2004. The majority of Western Balkan economies have recorded decline in their global competitiveness rankings in the observed period 2007–2011. Most of them fell below the 70th position among 130 observed economies in 2011 in a World Economic Forum sample. Only Montenegro and Macedonia show rising ranks in the period 2007–2011. With rapid growth, Montenegro became the most competitive economy in the Western Balkans in 2011, well before Croatia, the economy set to become the newest EU member. The Croatian and Serbian economies experienced the largest fall in competitiveness in the last years. Serbia and Bosnia and Herzegovina are at the bottom of the regional competitiveness list.

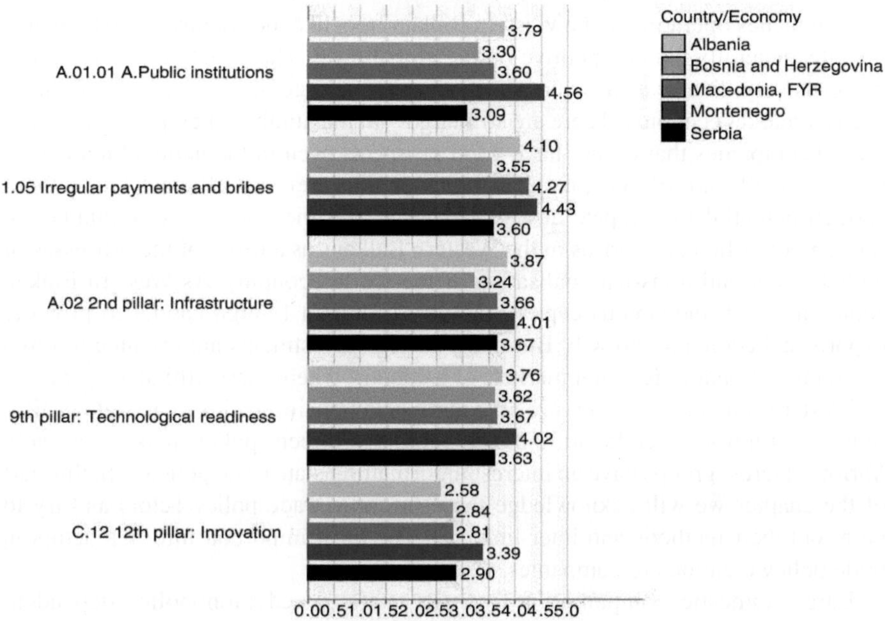

Fig. 4.2 Competitiveness factors for Western Balkan economies in 2011 (Source: World Economic Forum, Internet, http://gcr.weforum.org/gcr2011/)

The causes of low competitiveness of Western Balkans economies lie not only in low economic performance but also in the political, social and legal frameworks in these countries. The WEF has pointed out that countries in the Western Balkans have weak and undeveloped state institutions and that the performance of these institutions is one of the main factors for low competitiveness. Institutions in these countries are wracked by corruption. All Western Balkans countries show weak results by WEF ranks, which represent a subjective estimation of managers in these countries, but similar results are indicated in the objective statistical data by organisations researching corruption, such as Transparency International (Fig. 4.2).

One of the lower ranked competitiveness factors is infrastructure—testimony that infrastructure in the Western Balkans is underdeveloped—and this significantly influences economic growth and trade perspectives. Infrastructure is a prerequisite for improved economic development. There have been some moves to improve infrastructure, especially in the larger economies of the Western Balkans, like Croatia and Serbia. But sustained economic development is dependent today on the improvement and application of technology in business processes. The development of technology is connected to innovation, which is very low in these economies. Without investment in technology and stimulation of innovation, Western Balkan economies cannot improve their international competitiveness in the long run.

Companies operating in the Western Balkans are, like the countries in which they operate, generally not competitive on the global level. The structure of these companies is very diverse as their host countries are undergoing a process of transition to a full market economy. There are still large—in the number of employees—state-owned companies that do not have good prospects even in the national market, as well as small and vibrant private companies that are very efficient but without enough potential to compete at a global level. But there are a rising number of foreign-controlled enterprises in the Western Balkans as a result of the processes of globalisation and trans-nationalisation of the world economy. As Western Balkan economies lack indigenous capital, they try to attract foreign capital to promote exports and economic growth. But many foreign investments are oriented towards servicing national or regional markets of a country where these affiliates operate.

Western Balkan economies are all countries in transition with weak state institutions. Corruption is endemic and very possibly affects policy makers as well. Various interest groups have an interest in formatting state trade policies. In this part of the chapter we will acknowledge these informal trade policy actors and try to point out their methods and inter-linkages. The most important informal actors in trade policy creation are companies.

Large domestic companies are usually state-owned monopolies dependent exclusively on a national market; they tend to pressure the government to adopt protectionist policies—restrict imports and limit competition in the domestic market. The main instrument of pressure is the large number of their employees, who are also the voters in elections. One example of this is the Serbian steel producing company, which was taken over by the Serbian government last year before the national elections, when a US steel company drew back from its Serbian investment. In large state-owned companies that fall into the category of public state enterprise, the politicians are usually also the managers appointed by the national government. They also put pressure on the government to raise tariffs to protect these companies. Even if these companies are natural monopolies, they operate with a loss since they serve as unofficial sources of political party funding.

Even private companies that operate solely on the national market since they are not competitive abroad can pressure the government to restrict international trade because they only supply consumers in this market. These restrictions are hard to introduce with a tariff rise, since they cannot be justified on the world scene, so today they use nontariff barriers. An example from our survey of opinions in Serbia was the adoption of the Law on Genetically Modified Organisms (GMOs).[6] Although there are many conflicting views on GMOs, the WTO principle is that country members cannot obstruct trade in these organisms since there is still no sound scientific proof that they may be dangerous for human health. Serbia adopted a law in June 2009 banning production and trade in GMOs. This law was in conflict with WTO rules, and Serbia as a country in accession had an obligation not to change its trade regime significantly while acceding to the WTO. There are some indications in a US demarche to the Serbian Ministry of Agriculture from June 29, 2009, that the law

[6] Zakon o genetićki modifikovanim organizmima, Službeni glasnik RS br. 41/2009.

was adopted under the influence of Serbian producers of soya and soya products to guarantee the consumption of locally produced soya,[7] which is also produced in a significant degree from GMO seeds. The main instrument of pressure on the government concerning trade policy is in the form of donations that these companies give to political parties.

On the other side, there are many domestic companies that are in the trade business—usually imports for domestic consumption—and they push for a more liberal import policy. Since their influence on trade policy tends to be very strong, they are often referred to as the 'import lobby'. But this liberalisation is limited to only these companies since even with the liberal import regime in some sectors, they obstruct the entrance of competitors into their market. Lack of competition even in the import business creates high prices that Serbian customers are obliged to pay for foreign goods; these goods can be a few times more expensive than in their market of origin. These extremely high prices are specific to the clothing sector and are not influenced by customs and tax duties but rather by a high wholesaler's margin. The government is reluctant to deal with these monopolies—by liberalising total imports of monopolised products, for instance—since these companies are often connected to government officials, or else, owners of these companies pay a premium to politicians to be 'protected' on the market.

Since the Western Balkan economies by and large lack dedicated institutions tasked with the creation and coordination of trade policy, in this void informal actors, including foreign companies and special interests, exert considerable influence. One can posit that the economic interests of large capital in fact define the trade policy of these countries with consequences in the prospects for improving competitiveness and stimulating growth. Foreign companies using foreign direct investment establish a company that is incorporated and functions under the law of the host country, but it is economically dependent on its parent company. The region is becoming especially interesting for big international companies as it approaches membership of the European Union. These companies bring fresh capital and new technologies but can also influence state institutions. They would like to profile the trade policy of host economies to have greater profit-making ability.

Concerning the inflow of FDI, Western Balkan economies have been active in buyer-driven production chains but have not yet managed to make a significant transition towards producer-driven supply chains. During the initial phase of the transition, most Western Balkan countries relied on unskilled labour–intensive exports associated with buyer-driven production chains in clothing and furniture, in which global buyers create a supply base without direct ownership (Kathuria 2008, 42). This has a small impact on value-added in Western Balkan economies and does not represent significant integration into the global economy. Exports are all about transferring more of the local value-added abroad. However, the business environment is not favourable for attracting respectable foreign investments; rather, the capital that enters these countries is for speculative purposes.

[7] According to Novi Standard Magazine, Internet, http://www.standard.rs/ivan-ninic-kako-je-dinkic-pokusao-da-ucini-amerikancima-da-se-legalizuju-mutanti-gmo.html

The question that remains is how companies—domestic or foreign—exert influence on trade policy creators, that is, the government? One main channel of influence is the political parties with representatives in parliament or the government. Usually large companies finance the activities of the parties, especially during the election campaigns. This finance can go through official or unofficial channels, and is known as 'soft money'. Usually domestic firms (including companies incorporated in one country but under foreign control) employing a substantial number of people can use these jobs as a pressuring instrument—big layoffs create political pressure, as workers are also potential voters. Sometimes companies use bribes to influence trade policy creation. In the Western Balkans it is not rare for companies to bribe a civil servant to act in they interest. These instruments of influence tend to restrict the trade regime through escalation of tariffs, but since these escalations are limited by WTO international obligations, the restrictions are made through nontariff barriers. In the global economy countries compete for market access and access to resources, and they take actions that favour their companies at home—through public procurement preferences, and abroad—through subventions and other aids. In literature, these government actions are known as strategic trade policy.

A main characteristic of the world economy today is the monopolisation of global markets through capital concentration and the appearance of large global companies known as transnational corporations. These companies have higher yearly sales than the GDP of many countries in the world. These companies can influence not only countries where they are registered (home countries), but also countries where they have established their affiliate companies (host countries). TNCs tend to influence trade policy creation in these countries to create greater possibilities for profit generation. The target of their influence can also be international intergovernmental organisations where significant global trade rules are passed. Their interests are also protected and communicated by their global organisation, the International Chamber of Commerce (ICC) and some informal groups such as the World Economic Forum, which serve as instruments of influence to countries and international intergovernmental organisations (Bjelić 2003, 84–88) (Fig. 4.3).

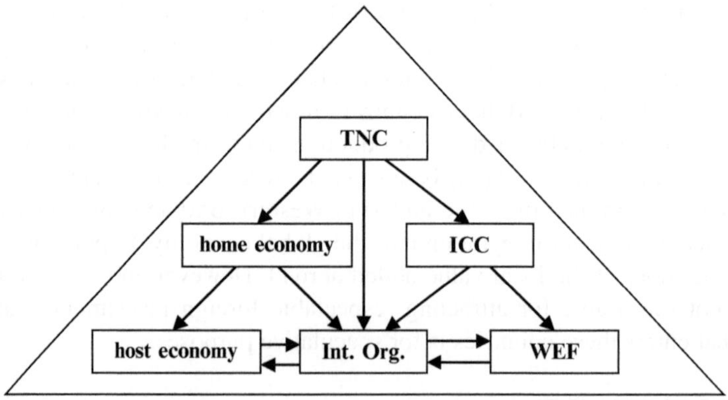

Fig. 4.3 Transnational corporations' trade policy influence pyramid (Source: Bjelić 2003, 84)

Some authors have defined contemporary international relations through the model of triangular diplomacy consisting of three factors: competition of companies for market share, negotiations between companies and states, and competition between states with trade policy as a main instrument. In this way global companies can even influence international politics (Stopford and Strange 1991).

These companies can also influence government at lower levels—as in the functioning of government agencies—and in international trade where the customs procedures are specific. Usually trade preferences are connected to the domestic origin of the export products. To prove the domestic origin, a company must provide a certificate of origin from the exporting country's customs. Only with this document can the company benefit from a preferential tariff regime. But in countries where the system of rules of origin is not significantly developed and where there is endemic corruption, companies can obtain these certificates for products that do not have local origin. An example is the re-export of sugar from Cuba through Serbia to the European Union. A Serbian company obtained a certificate of origin for cane sugar even though in Serbia sugar is produced from beet. The certificate was a pass to use the preferential tariff rates given to Serbia by the EU based on the bilateral agreement. When EU customs established there had been a breach of rules of origin, the export of sugar from Serbia to the EU was banned.

Citizens of Western Balkan countries favour a liberal trade policy since they are customers and prefer a larger variety of goods and lower prices that only foreign competition can ensure. But as employees, they would like their jobs and salaries to be secure, and from that angle they fear foreign competition for their domestic employers. Economic theory suggests that if an imported good is produced in a labour-intensive manner, a worker in an economy facing fixed international terms of trade will favour an import duty, while a capitalist will favour free trade (Baldwin 1989, 120). The social concerns model explains trade policies mainly by the government's concern for the welfare of certain social and economic groups and by its desire to promote various national and international goals (Baldwin 1989, 126). Some authors argue that trade bureaucrats lead in trade policy creation (Finger 1984, 745). All these interests must be considered when a country defines its trade policy. Any changes in the present trade regime can significantly affect the interests of diverse stakeholders. Policy implementation is frequently fragmented and interrupted, and policy change often requires difficult adjustments in the supporting stakeholder coalition, changes in the structures and rules of familiar institutions, and new patterns of interaction (Crosby 1996, 1405). Free trade does not exist today; rather, there are different trade regimes. These regimes need to be stable over a longer time so companies can make proper long-term investment decisions. However, one trade regime that will persist in the longer run is the EU trade regime.

4 EU Membership of Western Balkan Economies and Trade Policy Reform

The biggest change in trade policy for Western Balkans economies will come with EU membership. Many changes in economic policies have already resulted from the economic and political influence of the EU, in some cases through conditionality and other requirements. This 'pull or push' policy has had limited effect since there is often a considerable gap between the introduction of policies in the Western Balkans and their implementation.

The EU's trade policy powers are vested in its institutions. Member countries cannot set its trade rules but rather have to follow the common EU external trade regime. The Common Trade Policy of the European Union was created in 1957 with the signing of the agreement establishing the European Economic Community. The main institutions in the EU common trade policy-creation process are the Council of the EU and the European Parliament. But all the legal initiatives in trade policy come from the European Commission, which, after these initiatives are adopted by the council and the parliament, also implements the rules. The focus organ that coordinates all the activities in the EU concerning trade policy is the 133 Committee (Bjelić 2003, 129). Even though this committee is a body of the council, some researchers feel that it has significant influence on common trade policy creation in the EU without transparent procedure, especially after the adoption of the Lisbon Treaty (Woolcock 2010, 7). There are some, even in the EU, who say the 133 Committee is the real power and decision-making centre for the European Union's commercial policy.[8] The members of the 133 Committee are trade experts who prepare decisions for the council, which adopts them without much debate. European policy making is not a depoliticised process wherein the exchange of functional expertise and information stands central; political cleavages considerably affect the day-to-day policy network among Euro-level bureaucrats, politicians and societal interests. In the European Parliament, for example, three groups can be identified in connection to trade policy creation: Prosocial Europe Coalition, Proecology Coalition and Progrowth Coalition (Beyers and Kerremans 2004, 1146).

One of the basic conditions for EU membership is the candidate country's ability to cope with the competitive pressures of the single European market. Given that the countries in the Western Balkans are at a lower level of global competitiveness, the EU has designed a transitory process for all Western Balkan countries to lower their tariff regime towards the EU. Since 2000 the EU has unilaterally granted a special trade regime to these economies in the form of Autonomous Trade Measures (ATMs), which are asymmetrically biased towards Western Balkan economies. Also these countries must use the period before EU accession to significantly improve their competitiveness.

---

[8] Bart Staes, Written Question E-4037/00 to the Council (2001/C 261 E/021), January 3, 2001, EN *Official Journal of the European Communities* C 261, September 18, 2001.

Regional trade integration in the Western Balkans created by a revised Central European Free Trade Agreement from 2006 (CEFTA 2006) is a transitory integration since all countries in the Western Balkans are moving towards EU membership. But CEFTA 2006 can be an effective framework for these economies to build competitiveness—individual as well as regional—and to prepare them for future EU membership. Western Balkan economies are at a similar level of economic development, with similar economic and political legacies and with many cultural affinities. In the policy arena, the area needs regional coordination of trade policy with formal frameworks and institutions that can improve competitiveness at the regional level. Therefore, the CEFTA 2006 trade regime could not only stimulate intraregional trade but also allow member economies to use their trade potential in relation to the EU—the EU has a very favourable trade regime towards Western Balkan countries, as well as the diagonal accumulation of origin to prepare for their integration into the single market.

But the economic cooperation of Western Balkan countries has some political boundaries. Greater economic cooperation sometimes requires greater regional coordination of policies, and some groups see this process as a new political reunification in this region. Regional trade integration in the Western Balkans has been initiated by the EU; sometimes the only impetus for this regional cooperation is the prospect of EU membership.

While Western Balkan economies hesitate to cooperate further, illegitimate businesses and representatives of large capital have good regional cooperation. Western Balkan economies have a large share of GDP from the so-called grey zone. Many employees are not officially registered, so not all turnover is reported for tax evasion purposes, and many goods are imported unofficially. The trade between Western Balkan economies still occurs in unregulated channels while crime organisations cooperate at the regional level. This is due to the low level of political cooperation of Western Balkan countries and the lack of coordination of different national policies in combating smuggling and illegal cross-border trade in the region. This is the area where traditional trade policy has no effect and where there are other actors and stakeholders. Trade is still largely influenced by political factors in the Balkans. A typical example is the trade relations between Serbia and Kosovo, which are complicated by Kosovo's unilateral declaration of independence and Serbia's refusal to engage in dialogue on trade matters with institutions in Priština (Bjelić et al. 2012).

The EU is a heterogeneous mix of economies at different levels of development and with diverse competitive advantages, but operating within the EU common trade regime, is something the Western Balkan countries will have to adopt as part of the EU membership package. These economies will have to find their trade niche within the single European market and learn how to increase competitiveness as EU members and contribute to EU competitiveness. Free trade does not exist in the global economy; it is all about regulated trade and the understanding of trade regimes. The EU is a global trade player that resorts to a large number of protectionist measures, which distort global trade flows. A typical example is EU's Common Agriculture Policy (CAP), which was set primarily to ensure high prices to European producers of agricultural products. The European agricultural market was protected against the large influx of foreign agricultural products by tariffs and nontariff barriers that offset the difference between European and world prices. Due to subventions, which are one of the main instruments of CAP, instead that EU import most agricultural products, if there were free trade, the EU produced more agricultural products than consumers at home and abroad needed and EU was left with the surplus. Subsidized prices in the EU are higher than both world prices and prices that would be set in the European market without imports. But CAP has significant influence not only on the EU agricultural market but also on international trade in agricultural products. Subsidized European prices push down world prices whereby claims on higher subsidies grow because of the increase in the gap between world and European prices. There is no logical economics-based explanation for this since costs for European consumers and taxpayers surpass benefits for agricultural producers (Krugman and Obsfeld 2003, 198–99).

One trade regime that influences the Western Balkan economies' competitiveness on the global market is the WTO multilateral trade regime, which should be in accordance with Western Balkans' future EU trade obligations. The precondition for EU membership is membership in the WTO, which is not important just because of the international trade regime that WTO sets and oversees but because of the sets of technical agreements that lay down basic trade principles. Institutions like WTO have another function that has been largely ignored by researchers—reduced volatility in trade policy and trade flows. Exposure to global markets increases terms-of-trade volatility, and governments seek to insulate their economies from such instability through membership in international trade institutions and even regional trade integrations (Mansfield and Reinhardt 2008). But in WTO accession negotiations, Western Balkan economies can be asked to commit to greater trade liberalisation than the EU trade regime envisages. An example of this was Estonia's accession to the WTO, which resulted in new trade concessions that EU had to give in the WTO framework when Estonia joined EU. Aligning the two processes of EU and WTO accession is of paramount importance in building competitiveness of the Western Balkan economies; the role of policy makers is vital to that end.

The process of WTO and EU accession should be compatible for Western Balkan countries. Western Balkan companies should be able to envisage future trade regimes enforced by these economies so they can position themselves better on a single European and global market. So, the question is not, what are the comparative advantages for Western Balkans economies in international trade under a free trade regime? But rather, what are the competitive advantages for Western Balkans economies on the single European market at the moment they join this integration? The trade regime applied by the Western Balkans will determine their competitiveness. When Serbia joins the EU, it will not be important whether it is globally competitive in fruit production but rather if it is competitive compared to other EU members.

Policy makers in the region must be able to create a stable and predictable framework for the locally operating companies. At present, various trade regimes influence the competitiveness of the Western Balkan economies and companies operating in these economies—CEFTA 2006 trade regime, EU preferences trade regime, WTO multilateral trade regime and many others that regulate trade with other countries in the world on a more preferential basis than MFN and WTO trade regimes. Companies must be able to predict the applicable trade regimes, and there must be some stability and time horizon of application of certain regimes (Bjelić 2013). The dominant trade regime for the Western Balkan economies as they approach EU membership will be the EU common trade regime. But even this could soon change with the multilateral trade negotiations round in the WTO—the Doha trade round—which can significantly liberalise the trade regimes of WTO members including the EU, especially for trade in agricultural products.

Trade policy makers in the Western Balkans must explore the ability of these economies to take an active role in the Common EU Trade Policy so they can create a stable framework of operations for the companies operating in this region. This means that rules of doing business must be the same for all companies—big or small, foreign or domestic. Apart from this, many institutional mechanisms must be in place to ensure the fair and legal operation of companies that go under functional market economy condition for EU membership. Then the competitiveness of the Western Balkan economies will depend on the competitiveness of the companies that operate there, leaving aside the strategic trade policy of global trade powers.

The Western Balkans trade policy will be shaped significantly by the EU common trade regime towards non-member countries, but this trade reform in the Western Balkans will not only include the application of a new tariff schedule and regulations connected to the application of nontariff measures, but will be more focused on the development of trade infrastructure and institutions that can take all EU membership obligations and apply them in practice.

5 Conclusions

The Western Balkans is a region diverse in ethnic and cultural heritage but similar in economic structure, trade interests and the taste of local consumers. The formal trade policy–creation process in this region is often ambiguous, non-transparent and contradictory since there is no focus organ for trade policy coordination, and usually the trade regime changes significantly over short periods of time. The trade regime of the Western Balkan countries is fairly liberal, but it is far from the tariff levels of the EU. Trade policy creation is now significantly influenced by international organisations like EU and WTO, to which these economies belong or seek membership.

Apart from the formal actors who shape trade policy, this process is largely influenced by informal actors such as large domestic and foreign companies. Every group has its own specific interest and lobby and pushes for a specific trade policy outcome, which will result in profit maximisation. Informal actors use bribes and layoffs of large number of employees as the main instruments of influence. Their final aim is protection in the local market from foreign competitors with higher tariff rates or application of nontariff barriers. Transnational corporations are very important in international trade today and can wield significant influence on trade policy creation in the home country as well as in host countries of their foreign affiliates.

Globally, the countries of the Western Balkans are at lower levels of trade competitiveness. One of the causes for this low level of competitiveness is the performance of weak and underdeveloped state institutions, which is often exacerbated by endemic corruption. The Western Balkan economies have underdeveloped state institutions and are not fully functioning market economies; thus corrupt practices and monopolistic behaviour of companies is widespread. The state in this region must be able to set a fair and sustainable market system and to empower the state institutions to function properly. This will minimise the influence of informal actors on trade policy creation in this region. All this is a precondition for joining the EU, and some positive benefits from EU membership for Western Balkans lie in this area.

The Western Balkans are faced with three trade regimes—trade regimes for CEFTA 2006 members, the EU common trade regime and the multilateral WTO trade regimes. Trade creators must be clear which trade regime will prevail in the future to provide a stable framework for company operations. Free trade today is still an unreachable goal, and the question of a nation's competitiveness is discussed not in the global context but rather in the framework of specific trade regimes. The competitiveness of Western Balkan economies will depend on their ability to specialise and sell on the single EU market shielded from outside competition by the EU common trade regime. But the changes in this regime can also be foreseen in the ongoing round of multilateral trade negotiations in the WTO.

References

Baldwin, R. E. (1989). The political economy of trade policy. *The Journal of Economic Perspectives, 3*(4), 119–135.

Beyers, J., & Kerremans, B. (2004). Bureaucrats, politicians, and societal interests: How is European policy making politicized? *Comparative Political Studies, 37*(10), 1119–1150.

Bjelić, P. (2003). *Ekonomika međunarodnih odnosa*. Belgrade: Prometej.

Bjelić, P. (2013). World trade organization and the global risks. In A. Alemanno, F. den Butter, A. Nijsen, & J. Torriti (Eds.), *Better business regulation in a risk society* (pp. 193–206). New York: Springer.

Bjelić, P., & Dragutinović Mitrović, R. (2012). The effects of competing trade regimes on bilateral trade flows: Case of Serbia. *Proceedings of Rijeka Faculty of Economics – Journal of Economics and Business, 30*(2), 267–294.

Bjelić, P., & Jaćimović, D. (2012). Impact of the world economic crisis on trade and foreign investments in the West Balkans. In: B. Boričič & M. Jovičić (Eds.), *Factor markets and the effects of the world crisis* (Conference proceedings of selected papers, Vol. 2. pp. 45–62). Belgrade: Faculty of Economics Publishing House (CIDEF).

Bjelić, P., Šećeragić, B., Čeku, H., Petronijević, V., Jelačić, M., & Vinca, D. (2012). *Freedom of movement of people and goods between Kosovo and Serbia in the context of regional co-operation: Scientific research study*. Novi Sad: Centar za regionalizam.

Brada, J. C. (1991). The political economy of communist foreign trade institutions and policies. *Journal of Comparative Economics, 15*, 211–381.

Cooper, R. N. (1973). Trade policy is foreign policy. *Foreign Policy, 9*(Winter), 18–36.

Crosby, B. L. (1996). Policy implementation: The organizational challenge. *World Development, 24*(9), 1403–1415.

Drabek, Z., & Bacchetta, M. (2004). Tracing the effects of WTO accession on policy-making in sovereign states: Preliminary lessons from the recent experience of transition countries. *World Economy, 27*(7), 1083–1125.

Dragutinović-Mitrović, R., & Bjelić, P. (2013). International competitiveness and asymmetry in trade regime in the EU integration: Evidence from Western Balkans'. In *The tenth international conference: Challenges of Europe: The quest for new competitiveness proceedings, 2013*, Faculty of Economics, Split.

Finger, J. M. (1984). The political economy of trade policy. *Cato Journal, 3*(Winter), 743–755.

Kaminski, B., & de la Rocha, M. (2003). *Stabilization and association process in the Balkans: Integration options and their assessment* (World Bank Policy Research Working Paper No. 3108). Washington, DC: World Bank.

Kathuria, S. (Ed.). (2008). *Western Balkan integration and the EU: An agenda for trade and growth*. Washington, DC: World Bank.

Krugman, P. R., & Obsfeld, M. (2003). *International economics: Theory and policy* (6th ed.). New York: Addison-Wesley.

Mansfield, E. D., & Reinhardt, E. (2008). International institutions and the volatility of international trade. *International Organization, 62*, 621–652. doi:10.1017/S0020818308080223.

Milner, H. V. (1999). The political economy of international trade. *Review of Political Science, 2*, 91–114.

Perez, M. F., Brada, J. C., & Drabek, Z. (2012). Illicit money flows as motives for FDI. *Journal of Comparative Economics, 40*(1), 108–126.

Porter, M. E. (1990). *The competitive advantage of nations*. New York: Free Press.

Rodrik, D. (1995). Political economy of trade policy. In: G. M. Grossman & K. Rogoff (Eds.), *Handbook of international economics* (Vol. 31, pp.457–494). Elsevier.

Stopford, J. M., & Strange, S. (1991). *Rival states, rival firms*. Cambridge, UK: Cambridge University Press.

Woolcock, S. (2010). *The treaty of Lisbon and the European Union as an actor in international trade* (European Centre for International Policy Economy (ECIPE) Working Paper, No. 01/2010). Brussels: ECIPE.

World Trade Organization (WTO), International Trade Centre (ITC), United Nations Conference on Trade and Development (UNCTAD). (2013). *World tariff profiles 2013*. Geneva.

Chapter 5
The Political Economy of Economic Liberalisation and Competitiveness in Bosnia and Herzegovina

Fikret Čaušević

1 Introduction

The main goal of this chapter is to examine the interaction of local political actors and the international community in Bosnia and Herzegovina (BiH) in the implementation of economic reforms based on trade liberalisation, financial liberalisation and privatisation, and their impact on the competitiveness and sustainable growth of BiH economy. Considering that BiH is a small, open post-conflict economy whose political future for hystorical reasons and specifically recent episode of war is closely linked to the political economy of neighbouring countries, the hypothesis of this chapter is that the key barrier to the country's sustainable economic growth since the end of 1992–1995 war has been a questionable politico-economic program of transition applied in the context whereby the effective management of economic policy has been lodged with sub-national bodies. This division of economic power between the two Entities[1] representing three (politicised) ethnicities in BiH has disrupted the agglomerations, productive capacity and business clusters developed in the prewar period and has undermined the country's competitiveness.

An economy's competitiveness[2] depends on a number of factors including the ability of its institutions to support the development of business clusters and the microeconomic foundations of competitiveness, allowing economies of scale and increased productivity. The single most important factor for competitiveness is the capacity to increase productivity and pave the way for sustainable economic growth. Michael Porter has written very clearly about this, pointing out:

[1] According to the BiH constitution, BiH is comprised of two Entities, the Federation of Bosnia and Herzegovina (the FBiH) and the Republika Srpska (the RS).

[2] Michael Porter 2005.

F. Čaušević (✉)
Department of Economics, University of Sarajevo, Sarajevo, Bosnia and Herzegovina
e-mail: fikret.causevic@efsa.unsa.ba

M. Thomas, V. Bojicic-Dzelilovic (eds.), *Public Policy Making in the Western Balkans*, DOI 10.1007/978-94-017-9346-9_5

> The world economy is not a zero-sum game. Many nations can improve their prosperity if they can improve their productivity. There are unlimited human needs to be met if productivity drives down the cost of products and productive work supports higher wages. Thus, the central challenge in economic development is how to create the conditions for rapid and sustained productivity growth. Microeconomic competitiveness should be the central item on the economic policy agenda of every nation.[3]

The institutional set up in BiH has created administrative and political barriers which have facilitated the concentration of economic power within the three dominant ethnic groups by splitting up production clusters created before the war, effectively dividing up the economy and productive capacity along ethnic lines. This process has negatively impacted productivity and diminished BiH's potential for achieving sustainable export-oriented growth over the long-term.

The chapter sets out to examine the complex administrative and political institutional set up in the post-war Bosnia and Herzegovina, assess the implementation of economic liberalization measures and the outcomes in terms of BiH's competitiveness and economic sustainability.

2 Bosnia and Herzegovina in the International Context

BiH is a small open economy with a 0.035 % share in world GDP over the past 5 years and a 0.048 % share in world population.[4] There are three constituent peoples in BiH: Bosniaks, Serbs, and Croats and none has an outright majority. The country lies at the heart of the Balkan Peninsula so that its geographic position makes it a natural cross road linking Central Europe with the Adriatic, and Western Europe with the East. The country has been historically linked with Western Europe since its transfer to the Austro-Hungarian government by decision of the Berlin Congress (1878), with comparatively strong economic ties, particularly to Germany, Austria and Italy.

Economic connections established with Western European companies, most prominently from Germany, under the second Yugoslavia (1945–1990) were particularly significant in the growth of the metal processing and wood processing industries and in the development of the relevant engineering expertise. This accumulated human capital stock in manufacturing has played a major role in the post-war economic recovery of Bosnian enterprises.[5] In addition to the human capital,

---

[3] Ibid.

[4] The author's calculation based on the World Bank data; http://data.worldbank.org/country/bosnia-and-herzegovina.

[5] Three of the five largest exporters in the former Yugoslavia were from BiH, and two of them took turns as best performers during the final 10 years of the country's existence: Energoinvest Sarajevo (production of electrical equipment; engineering; oil refining and the production of petroleum derivatives, metallurgy, clay and aluminium) and Unis Sarajevo (the auto-industry, metallurgy, military industry). In the 1980s the largest car factory in the Balkans was located in Sarajevo (in 1990, annual production was 32,000 Golf cars) as a result of a joint venture by Volkswagen and

BiH's potential for electricity generation from both nonrenewable and renewable sources is another significant resource, of relevance for the Western Balkans and even for Western Europe.

The war that marked the rise of BiH as an independent state from the breakup of former Yugoslavia in 1992, attracted an unprecedented attention among political establishments worldwide. Major world powers, spearheaded by the United States of America (USA) intervened with an intention to stop the fighting and human suffering unseen in the Western World since the end of the WWII. During his first election campaign for the president, Bill Clinton made a promise that dealing with the crisis in the former Yugoslavia and ending the war would be his administration's top foreign policy priority. Subsequently, the USA mediated among the warrying parties and eventually an agreement was brokered between the Bosniaks and the Croats, the so called Washington agreement signed in 1994. Under the terms of the Washington agreement, a Federation of Bosnia and Herzegovina (FBiH) was created as that part of BiH in which Croats and Bosniaks were the constitutive peoples. This agreement constituted the FBiH as an Entity that included ten cantons. The first Prime Minister of the BiH government set up after the signing of the Washington agreement was Haris Silajdzic, the then member of the majority Bosniak Party of Democratic Action (SDA) who from 1990 to 1994 served as Minister of Foreign Affairs of BiH.

Keeping the focus on BiH, the United States' next direct intervention was to cooperate with France and Great Britain to end the conflict throughout the territory of BiH which required addressing Bosnian Serb demands. When the Bosnian Serb leadership refused the USA's proposals for ending the war, military intervention followed with the combined military forces of the United States, France and Britain bombing military targets on the territory under the control of the Bosnian Serbs. Following this intervention (August 1995), the political leaders from BiH, Croatia and Serbia agreed to start peace negotiations and peace agreement (Dayton Peace Agreement) was signed in December 1995 in Paris. The parties to this Agreement agreed to end the armed conflict in BiH and to establish BiH as an internationally recognised state comprising the two Entities: the Federation of Bosnia and Herzegovina (FBiH) and the Republic of Srpska (RS). The chain of events during this period made it clear that the war in BiH would not have ended without the direct involvement of the United States. The political and military involvement of external actors was matched by their prominent role in assisting the countries in economic reconstruction and development. Already as part of the process to negotiate peace agreement, the discussions including the key international financial institutions World Bank and the International Monetary Fund, were underway to prepare the

Unis (TAS — The Sarajevo Car Factory). Between 1970 and 1991 the contribution of manufacturing, particularly metal processing, the car industry, electricity, wood processing, and chemicals to gross domestic product (GDP) in BiH increased markedly. The increasing role of middle and higher value-added products in GDP led to significant economic progress and an increase in the standard of living in BiH between 1970 and 1991. The Sarajevo Tobacco Company produced one of the best cigarettes in Europe, in cooperation with the American Philiph Morris Company (the well-known "Sarajevo Marlboro").

economic reconstruction programme. Unlike in other countries in the Western Balkans, in BiH the international community has played a direct role in implementing economic and political reforms. The Dayton Peace Accords (DPA) and the Paris Peace Agreement, authorised a leading role for the international community in the BiH political system through the Office of the High Representative (OHR) and the role of the High Representative himself in implementing reforms, which over time made him the de facto the highest executive authority in the country.

3 The Role of the International Community in Political and Economic Reforms

The international community played a pivotal role in BiH in setting priorities for political and economic reforms which were explicitly incorporated into the constitutional order based on the Dayton Agreement. The role of the OHR and the High Representatives was particularly important, most pronouncedly in the period 1996–2005. The most far reaching in their importance were the reforms in the area of financial and trade liberalisation, and privatisation as an integral part of the transition to a market economy, which was interrupted by the onset of war. During the first four postwar years, the Priority Reconstruction Program was directly implemented and coordinated by the World Bank resident mission to BiH. Transport infrastructure, schools and hospitals were reconstructed, while a substantial number of small- and medium-size businesses were helped to restore production[6].

To expediate economic reconstruction, a Quick Start Package for BiH was adopted under the patronage of High Representative Carlos Westendorp y Cabeza[7], laying the ground work for the establishment of the core institutions responsible for economic reform at the national level.[8] The Central Bank of Bosnia and Herzegovina (the CBBiH) would not have been established had it not been for direct engagement by the international community, including the High Representative and the USAID in parallel providing technical assistance. The extent of international involvement is perhaps best illustrated by the fact that the first two governors of the CBBiH were foreign bankers. The single BiH currency (the KM—the convertible mark) was also introduced through direct international action. USAID financed technical support for the internal payment system reform in early 2001, making BiH the first successor state of former-Yugoslavia to adopt such a reform which transferred control from Entity-controlled payment bureaus to the CBBiH and commercial banks. This

[6] Total investment under the programme was approximately USD 5.1 billion.

[7] Carlos Westerndorp y Cabeza served as the High Representative from June, 1997 to August, 1999.

[8] The Quick Start Package, imposed by the High Representative against RS opposition in 1997, comprised five laws aimed at integrating the BiH economy: the Law on the Central Bank of Bosnia and Herzegovina, the Law on a Single Basis for Customs Policy of BiH, the Law on Foreign Trade Policy of BiH, the Law on Foreign Direct Investment Policy and the Law on Tariffs.

was one of the key, successfully implemented reforms, which besides creating effective instruments for the control of money flows across the country[9] also freed the money flows from the grip of local political structures.

The United States and the United Kingdom's Department for International Development (DFID) provided technical assistance for public finance reform, especially the preparation of laws, regulations and institutions for privatisation. The necessary laws and bylaws for privatisation were adopted at Entity level (in the FBiH in 1997, and in the RS in 2001), and parallel institutions were established in both entities. However, as of 2014, these institutions have not yet been unified at national level. The financial and technical support from USAID and the UK Department for International Development also played a role in establishing the institutions for implementing privatisation, including the—privatisation agencies, securities and exchange commissions, registers of securities, and stock exchanges. The arrival of Austrian High Representative Wolfgang Petritsch[10] marked a certain shift in the international community's engagement in that he explicitly supported a coalition of mainly left-of-center opposition parties – that is an opposition to the ruling nationalist parties that were the same ones that took the country into the war-gathered in an Alliance for Change. The Alliance for Change won the 2,000 general elections[11] and Mr Petritsch worked closely with its representatives from the Social Democratic Party (SDP), the Independent Croat Initiative (NHI), the Party for Bosnia and Herzegovina (SBiH) and the Party of Democratic Progress (PDP) to implement economic and political reforms and break the deadlock generated by the nationalist parties' obstructions. Under the coalition government and with Mr Petritsch's direct involvement, BiH signed free trade agreements with the countries of the former Yugoslavia, and became a member of the Council of Europe, while each Entity parliament separately ratified the Law on Foreign Direct Investment (FDI) in BiH, enabling its smooth implementation. The law was adopted at the national level in 1998, and it was ratified in the FBiH Parliament in 2001, and in the RS National Assembly in 2002.[12] During this period, the Raiffeisen Bank became the first major Western European bank to enter the BiH banking market, heralding a string of takeovers by the Western European banks that would in a space of only few years transfer over 90 % of the bank assets to foreign ownership[13].

The High Representative and the international community were directly engaged in building key institutions for effective control of cross-border transport of goods and people. From 1995 to 2000 the entities controlled the state border and it was only in late 2000 that a State Border Service was established with the support by the

[9] Keefer writes: "The higher priority given to governance and the greater involvement in Bosnia's postwar political affairs also reflect greater donor willingness to address the difficult issues of postconflict government accountability when they have committed military forces."See Philip Keefer 2009.

[10] Served as High Representative from August, 1999 to September, 2002.

[11] See: Janez Kovac January 2001.

[12] See: Bosnia and Herzegovina, Ministry of Foreign Trade and Economic Relations 2013.

[13] The Raiffeisen Bank after more than 10 years of operations in BiH has become the market leader.

Office of the High Representative (OHR) and the EU, one of the major milestones in setting up the customs structures. Another High Representative, a British diplomat Paddy Ashdown during his period in office (May, 2002–January, 2006) played a prominent role in driving the reform agenda under the slogan 'jobs and justice' which had business environment improvement to promote exports and job creation as its main focus. Mr. Ashdown, working with the Chair of the Council of Ministers (Adnan Terzic of the Party for Democratic Action—(SDA[14])) and other ministers, exerted direct pressure to accelerate tax reforms, establish a state level Indirect Tax Authority (ITA), and introduce value-added tax (VAT). In pushing for the business environment reforms, Mr Ashdown launched a programme in cooperation with the Council of Ministers named Bulldozer Initiative, which involved the application of 50 reforms in 150 days. This initiative drew on and complemented the World Bank/ Foreign Investment Advisory Service (FIAS) review of the administrative barriers to local and foreign investment that produced recommendations for deeper and systemic reforms in the business enabling environment. Important headways were made in removing barriers to business operations, thanks to the reforms backed by support from the World Bank and USAID. This period saw the arrival of some of highly export-oriented foreign investors, including Arcelor Mittal Zenica (steel), CIMOS TMD Gradacac (auto industry), MAN Hummel Tesanj (machinery) and Kastamonu Entegre Maglaj (wood).

In parallel with economic reform process, the US administration and the US ambassadors to BiH were directly and intensely involved in preparing proposals for constitutional reform in BiH during early 2006 by which time it became clear that the Dayton institutional set up was a straight jacket both politically as well as in terms of economic development prospects. After the failure of this package of constitutional reforms caused by the intransigence of the local political leadership, the American administration's interest in reforms was significantly reduced. And overall, the international community's influence on economic and political reform has substantially weakened since 2006, while the assertiveness of local political actors has risen. A sort of poisonous vicious cycle has been created through which economic competition between the entities and deteriorating political relations have fed one another. And when the global economic crisis triggered a recession in 2009, there was no political or economic common ground and resolve to formulate a meaningful program to cope with the crisis; consequently, the road to economic recovery has been a slow one, with some modest improvement recorded in 2013.

A strong, and in many ways unique mode of international engagement in Bosnia-Herzegovina because of the war, and akin to Kosovo only, saw Russia and Turkey playing an increasing role in BiH politics and economic development starting in 2000 with their respective economic resurgence. Serious political and economic problems in Russia in the 1990s were reflected in a relatively weak Russian presence in the Balkans, especially in Serbia and BiH. In contrast, Russia's rapid

[14] It is important to note that the SDA is a strong advocate of strengthening central state and its institutions, hence the support for this particular reform.

economic expansion during the period 2002–2008[15], have strengthened Russia's political position and fostered expansion of its economic interests through FDI in the energy sector in Serbia and BiH. Russian influence in BiH is reflected through its strong links to the RS government and FDI in the RS energy sector. The Oil Refinery in Brod, in northern BiH was, during the prewar period, an integral part of one of the Yugoslavia's largest exporters—Energoinvest. After the war in BiH, the assets of Energoinvest company were split between the entities; thus the Oil Refinery in Brod was owned by the RS government from 1995 to 2007, when the RS government decided to sell its majority stake to the Russian Zarubezhneft Company.

Turkey's economic expansion in the first decade of this century has resulted in a gradual strengthening of its political significance in the Balkans and in Europe generally. Historical ties due to Turkey's presence in the Balkans for many centuries have been very important. They are most visible in the links between Turkish business circles and business circles in which Bosniaks are dominant or significant partners. Trade with Turkey has intensified since the signing of the free trade agreement in 2003 as has Turkish investment in BiH the largest of which to date has been by the Kastamonu Entegre in the Natron-Hayat Maglaj (pulp production).

This review of the economic impact of external actors on the BiH economy has aimed to highlight that not only overall FDI in BiH has been modest but that relatively small amounts of the total has been invested in export-oriented production capacities, even though these businesses are of greatest importance for increasing the productivity, competitiveness, exports and solvency of the country.

4 The Major Political Players and the Structure of Economic Power in BiH

Given the relatively weak position of the national government, political and economic power in BiH is concentrated in the political parties and leaders governing the entities. Importantly, fiscal policy, as the only active segment of economic policy, was completely dominated by the entities between 1996 and 2005. Thereafter, the responsibility for the collection and allocation of indirect tax was transferred to the national level and mandated to the Indirect Tax Authority. But given that the main trust of economic policy making rests with the entities, this has been a source of inter-entity competition such as in the area of labour market policy. The entities determine the minimum cost of labour on the basis of labour laws. Contribution rates for pension, medical and unemployment insurance are also determined at the entity level, as are personal income and corporate income taxes. The total (cumulative) fiscal burden[16] of labour differs between the entities, and it is on average approximately 18 % of the net wage lower in the RS than in the FBiH. The party in

[15] See: Global Finance Country Report..

[16] The total fiscal burden of labour is the sum of personal income tax, and contributions for pension, health and unemployment insurance.

power in the RS-the Association of Independent Social Democrats—(SNSD) claims a better investment climate in the RS than in the FBiH due to this lower fiscal burden, but this inter-entity tax competition eventually caused the RS government to abandon promised tax cuts after the 2010 election and to increase the pension contribution rate to close a growing imbalance in the RS Pension Fund.

While it is a fact that the constitutional set up of BiH which endows the entities with primary responsibility for economic policy making and is hence conducive to a possible divergence in policy design, this has been reinforced by the local political dynamic. For a number of years in the immediate aftermath of the 1992–1995 war, the political scene in the FBiH was dominated by the SDA (the Party of Democratic Action) and the HDZ BiH (the Croat Democratic Union of BiH), and the RS government was under majority control of the SDS (the Serb Democratic Party). The frictions and outright obstructions held the pace of reforms, the pattern which was broken for a short span under the SDP-led Alliance for Change (2000 and 2002). The period from 2002 to 2006 saw the return to power of the SDA and its splinter party the SBiH (the Party for BiH), alongside the HDZ BiH as an-all time strongest Bosnian Croat party in the FBiH; in the RS, the SDS and the PDP (the Party of Democratic Progress) shared power. There was major political change in the RS in March 2006 when the SNSD forced early elections and replaced the SDS and the PDP in government. These changes had an impact on the political-party scene in BiH, given a strong antagonism between the leader of the SNSD Milorad Dodik and Haris Silajdzic, the SBiH head. As already mentioned, the 2006 April package of constitutional reforms failed in the Parliamentary Assembly blocked by the SBiH with support of two SDA representatives. The SNSD and the SBiH, both of which rallied on ethnic-based sentiment in the follow up of the constitutional reform fiasco, emerged victorious from the October 2006 elections. These two parties and their respective leaders became the most influential political forces in economic reform (in the FBiH the power was shared with the SDA, which filled the post of prime minister in the FBiH government), notorious for their intransigence towards international efforts at mediation.

Thus Milorad Dodik, thanks to his electoral triumph in the RS, controlled all the levers of power in the RS and could carry out reforms, in accordance with his party's plan. In the FBiH, due to the election results, Haris Silajdzic was forced to share power with the SDA with whose leadership Mr Silajdzic's relationship had by that time gone sour, particularly with Mr Sulejman Tihic, who succeeded Alija Izetbegovic, the founder of the party. There were major differences on the economic policy front between two parties, and the policy making was additionally complicated by most of the time protracted and problematic negotiations with the Bosnian Croat counterparts. The position of minister of industry, energy and mining belonged to the SBiH, however, and it was through this ministry that the SBiH attempted to carry out its economic programme, largely based on investment in the energy sector of the FBiH. This plan was blocked by the FBiH prime minister, other ministers from the SDA, and ministers from the Croatian Democratic Union BiH (HDZBiH). The second half of the FBiH coalition government's term (2008–2010) was marked by the negative effects of the global economic crisis and the recession of 2009, followed by a very modest economic recovery in 2010.

The SNSD leader Milorad Dodik, who served as prime minister in the RS from 2006 to 2010, took advantage of the complicated political structure in the FBiH to forge ahead with a set of reforms aimed primarily at improving business environment in order to attract foreign investors. Promoting the RS government, his party and himself, Mr Dodik has spent his time in power creating an image of the RS as the more advanced part of BiH, successfully tackling legal reforms, simplifying procedures for doing business and, in particular, attracting foreign direct investors. One of the hallmarks of RS economic policy under Dodik's leadership was a foray into privatisation which began in 2006 with a 'great privatisation deal'—selling the 65 % government stake in Telekom Srpske (the telecommunications company) to a strategic partner—Telecom Srbije, a state-owned company from the Republic of Serbia. The deal represented the largest amount realised from the sale of a major public asset in BiH. It was followed by another strategic sale of the Oil Refinery in Brod and the Motor Oil Factory in Modrica, including a chain of petrol stations to the Russian OAO-Zarubezhneft. The third major deal was a joint venture between a Czech company CEZ and Elektroprivreda RS to build a power plant in Gacko. The RS government also concluded an agreement with a partner from Slovenia to extend the capacity of the power plant in Ugljevik. These last two deals failed, however and subsequently became a subject of heated political battle between the SNSD, Mr Dodik and the opposition parties in the RS. The Czech partner sued the RS government for failing to meet its contractual obligations, while the Slovenian partners withdrew from their investment in Ugljevik. Russian FDI in Brod and Modrica gave the OAO-Zarubezhneft a dominant market position in the RS market, and the rapid expansion of imports from Russia for oil on the domestic market for domestic needs meant BiH's trade deficit with Russia increased sharply. None of these investments, with the exception of the factory in Modrica, helped increase the export capacity of enterprises in the RS. Nor did the investments dominated by foreign investors from Serbia and Russia create basis for export-led growth in BiH, which would help BiH and the RS to remain solvent and to service the external debt.

Because of the political and economic fragmentation and the political voluntarism of the local authorities, the entity governments have continued to enjoy exclusive authority over privatisation transactions with foreign investors, although the Law on Foreign Direct Investment was adopted at the State level in 1998. Despite an overall dearth of foreign investment compared to regional peers, there have been some major foreign direct investments in the last 15 years in production which have been pivotal in recovering the country's industrial production and export capacity. Those include, besides ArcelorMittal Zenica, Kastamonu Entegre and CIMOS TMD Gradacac, ASA Prevent (automotive industry), Heidelberg Cement (cement production), Alas International (cement production), and Global Ispat (coke production). The largest FDI in the RS manufacturing sector was the aforementioned Russian investment partner in oil refining and motor oil, and investments by Lithuanian partners in alumina production at Birac Zvornik and the metal pipe factory in Derventa. After almost 13 years of operations in Zvornik, in 2013

Lithuanian investors decided to leave BiH, and the Birac Company facing a huge accumulated loss. In order to save Zvornik region from economic collapse, the RS government was forced to re-nationalize Birac Zvornik and to save from bankruptcy a bank that was owned by Lithuanian partners—the Balkan Investment Bank.

An important consequence of the exclusive right of the entities to implement FDI policy and privatisation, the two most effective economic policy instruments, is that BiH economic policy and policy making thus lacks the necessary focus on the creation and development of production units based on natural and geographical links. Business clusters developed before the war in the field of agro-industrial production, chemicals, wood processing and the metal sector were broken up after the war into a number of smaller and medium-size manufacturers without functional links. This destruction of existing business chains based on clusters took place primarily because of the entity-based FDI policy and, in particular, the ethnic exclusivity of the privatisation process. Synergy effects of cluster development and economies of scale have been blocked by the administrative structure of BiH, based on economic irrationality due to the constant tendency to create parallel systems from the production and distribution of electricity through very ineffective management of natural resources, to totally irrational capital market division at the entity level. The consequences for the country's competiveness have been severe.

A particularly significant factor behind the economic fragmentation of the country were the entity company privatisation laws, particularly for so-called small privatisation and for privatisation based on mass distribution of certificates exchangeable for shares in companies or in privatisation investment funds (large-scale privatisation was strongly supported by the representatives of the international community in BiH in the first phase of economic reforms). These laws in effect created the legal basis for ethnicised privatisation that concerns only or predominantly a single ethnic group, which effectively cemented economic division of the country.

In the FBiH the so-called mass privatisation was carried out for the most part on the ethnic principle, as the cantonal privatisation agencies were the agents for sale of companies whose property was connected to the territory of the canton. In the RS, privatisation also facilitated ethnic exclusivity, with at that time only one group considered constitutive in that part of BiH.[17] The management of the companies which remained in a majority-state ownership (including telecommunications, the generation and distribution of electrical energy, metal production, and mining) has been divided along tripartite ethnic lines, that is, on the principle that each people controls one company active in its area.

Thus, in BiH there exist three electricity distributors: Elektroprivreda BiH d.d. Sarajevo (majority Bosniak control), Elektroprivreda HZ HB d.d. Mostar (Croat control) and Elektroprivreda RS a.d. Trebinje (Serb control). Similarly, in the telecommunication sector there are three operators: BH Telecom d.d. Sarajevo (Bosniak majority control), HT d.d. Mostar (Croat majority control) and Telekom RS a.d.

[17] A detailed analysis of the techniques of privatisation in two entities (FBiH and RS) can be found in Bojicic-Dzelilovic et al. 2004, pp. 11–15, available at www.wiiw.ac.at/balkan/2ndphase.html.

Banja Luka (Serb majority control). The RS government sold 65 % of Telekom RS to a strategic partner, Telecom Srbije but this deal in fact illustrates deeply politicised nature of the economic policy making process by demonstrating foreign direct investment can be exploited successfully in the process of creating ethnic elites in particular sectors by drawing them from neighbouring ethnic kin countries.

Privatisation in BiH was also a channel for investing the capital accumulated during the war, landing the assets within the circles of the economic and political elites who took part in the illegal dealings. Select circles existed in all three ethnic groups who controlled the flow of basic commodities and fuel (including part of humanitarian aid), particularly in areas under siege (Sarajevo, Mostar, Tuzla, Zenica, Bihac, Gorazde, Travnik), at very high prices. The second significant source of quick access to cash between 1994 and 1999, as preparation to participation in the privatisation process, was domination of trade. This dominance was based on the creation of large numbers of mostly small, but also medium-size retail businesses connected to ethnic elite circles, which had for the most part accumulated the cash to create such firms during the war. The intensive promotion and interpretation by foreign experts of the number of newly created small and medium-size companies as indicators of the dynamic of economic growth, the flowering of the private sector and the BiH economy in general provided a fertile environment for the creation of such companies. Furthermore, the large number of small and medium-size trading companies, combined with the number of small banks between 1995 and 1999 were also conducive to avoidance of tax payments and the accelerated concentration of ownership. BiH had no common currency for cash transactions until June 1998 or for noncash until September 1999 (four currencies had been used), and nearly every proposal for the creation of state-level institutions to control goods or money was considered an infringement of ethnic interests, which also contributed to the expansion in various corrupt practices damaging economic recovery.

5 Political Stability, Growth and Competitiveness of Bosnia and Herzegovina

The turbulent post-war politics in BiH has been intrinsically connected to the developments in its immediate neighbourhood, namely Croatia and Serbia. After all, the two countries have been the co-signatories of the Dayton peace agreement and party to an array of regional initiatives aimed at economic and political cooperation. Not only these countries have had a very considerable political clout, but therefore their economic influence through the two-entity administrative structure has been equally influential. Under the provisions of the Dayton peace agreement, the two entities are allowed to establish special and parallel relations with their kin states; thus special economic relationships were created between the RS and Serbia, and part of the FBiH (primarily Western Herzegovina) and Croatia. While these links have been important economically, and culturally, their political repercussions have overall been adverse in so far that they have fed inter-ethnic tensions within BiH. In some instances, such as in implementing trade liberalisation, special relations between the entities and their ethnic kin states have been harmful to the interests of BiH and indeed have been a stumbling stone in adopting more effective measures. There is also an open question as to what extent has this type of ethnically motivated economic links contributed to the improvement in the productive base of the respective BiH entities given that most FDI from Croatia and Serbia was channeled to telecommunications and trade, thus focusing on exploiting the potential of the domestic market rather than increasing the manufacturing productivity or export capacity of BiH.

A problem of a weak production base and export capacity has been at the core of BiH macroeconomic imbalances that have been the permanent feature since the end of the 1992–1995 war. The following section takes a closer look at some of the main trends in the country's economic performance since 1996.

5.1 *Bosnia and Herzegovina's Trade Balance Before and After the 2009 Economic Crisis*

BiH's trade since the war has been characterised by a high deficit, initially due to wartime damage to and loss of human and physical capital.[18] This was especially true between 1996 and 2000 and between 2002 and 2005.[19] The average trade deficit during this period was approximately 50 % of GDP. These trends were primarily due to the low competitiveness of domestic producers, combined with high interest rates to finance manufacturing companies that were technologically obsolete due to the war, which had excluded all the domestic companies from European markets from 1992 to 1996.

After changes to the privatisation laws in both entities to favour the tender privatisation of enterprises, as opposed to the mass privatisation based on certificates, there was an increase in foreign investments in the processing industry (metal processing industry, automotive industry, wood processing industry) between 2002 and 2007. A growth of domestic investments in certain strategically important companies (electricity production), combined with FDI from Germany, Austria, Slovenia and Luxembourg, produced an increase in the export potential of the BiH economy. The result was a significant drop in the trade deficit, especially sharp during the crisis (2009–2010). This reduced trade deficit was, however, due primarily to a sharp drop in foreign demand. In the 2006–2010 period, exports grew by 107 % (from EUR 1.75 billion to EUR 3.63 billion) while imports increased by 81 % (from

---

[18] See Zupcevic and Causevic (2009, p. 13).

[19] For a detailed study of the impact of foreign trade policy and trade liberalisation in Bosnia and Herzegovina on the trade and current account balance see Causevic 2006.

EUR 3.84 billion to EUR 6.96 billion). As a result, the trade deficit increased from EUR 2.19 billion to EUR 3.33 billion (by 52 %).[20]

The trade deficit grew fastest between 2006 and 2008 (the 2 years preceding the recession), however. During this period it increased from EUR 2.19 billion to EUR 4.90 billion (by 123.7 %). BiH's largest trade deficit was with the largest trading partner—neighbouring Croatia. The deficit increased from EUR 333 million to EUR 831 million (by 149 %), over those 2 years, while growing 102 % with Germany, the second largest trading partner, and by 172 % with Serbia, the third. Over the same period, BiH's trade deficit with Italy and Slovenia increased by 234 % and 127.5 %, respectively. The largest percentage increase in trade deficit with a single country in those 2 years, was with Turkey (310 %).

Special trade relations between Croats from BiH (FBiH) and Croatia, Serbs from BiH (RS) and Serbia, and Bosniaks from FBiH with Turkey represent additional sources of fairly rapid turnover of capital related to attempts to concentrate wealth within the context of the ethnic elite groups. These special trading interests do not serve the interests of producers in BiH, who are after all the major creators of growth in export capacity and competitiveness, or promote the import substitution. The paradoxes of inappropriate liberalisation of foreign trade are clear in the very poorly defined bases and capacity for control of fair trade, combined with inefficient excise policy for high tariff goods from neighbouring countries.

A further paradox is apparent in the inappropriate liberalisation of the import of certain groups of goods. The main benefits of trade liberalisation for a country recovering from war should be looked for in the reduction or removal of customs on imports of goods which represent a basis for increased competitiveness and for building export-oriented manufacturing. Instead, trade liberalisation in BiH was established so as to remove customs on final consumer products, but maintain them on capital goods. Thus, the import of equipment, a key segment for increasing productivity and competitiveness, remained subject to customs levies (like the import of materials destined for the production of export goods), while foreign cigarettes cost the same or less than domestic ones.

In the period of global economic crisis (2008–2010), BiH succeeded in significantly reducing its trade deficit—from EUR 4.90 billion to EUR 3.33 billion (by 32 %). This was mainly due to a reduction of the trade deficit with the five most important trading partners: with Croatia by 39.0 %, Germany by 66.5 %, Serbia by 32.0 %, Italy by 48.7 % and Slovenia by 43.4 %. BiH also sharply reduced its trade deficit with Turkey (by 64.7 %). The only country with which BiH's trade deficit continued to grow rapidly was Russia. As a result of the foreign direct investment in the Brod oil refinery, Bosnia's trade deficit with Russia increased by 250 % in 2008–2010.[21] (Fig. 5.1.)

[20] Based on data published by the Central Bank of Bosnia and Herzegovina (2011). (http://www.cbbh.ba/files/godisnji_izvjestaji/2010/GI_2010_en.pdf) and the Agency for Statistics of Bosnia and Herzegovina, 2011. (http://www.bhas.ba/tematskibilteni/ETS_2010_001_01-bh.pdf)

[21] Ibid.

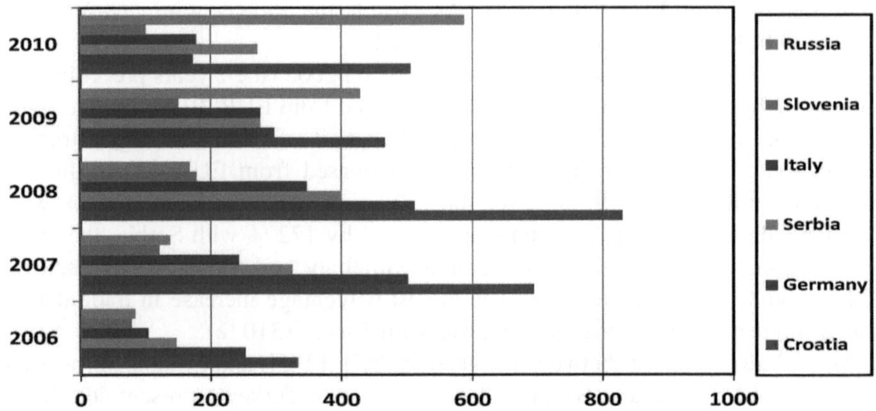

Fig. 5.1 Largest trade deficits of Bosnia and Herzegovina in merchandise trade—millions of EUR (Source: Based on data of the Agency for Statistics of Bosnia and Herzegovina 2011, and the Central Bank of Bosnia and Herzegovina 2011)

Over the last 5 years the most important export partners have been EU countries (55.8 %), Croatia (17.3 %) and Serbia (13.2 %), while the most important countries of origin for imported goods were EU countries (47.7 %), Croatia (16.4 %) and Serbia (10.3 %).[22] In the same period, the most important Bosnian trade partners from the EU were Germany (second largest trade partner after Croatia) with an average share in the BiH total trade of 13.1 %, Italy (11.1 %) and Slovenia (8.2 %). In 2009–2010 Russia's share in Bosnian imports increased to 8.7 % (from 2.2 % in 2006), but in the 2 years Russia's share in BiH's exports was only 0.5 % on average (Fig. 5.2).

It is almost impossible to explain the relatively high growth rates in BiH's foreign trade and trade deficit without taking into account credit activity in the banking sector. The growth in trade (and the trade deficit) in 2004–2008 was strongly supported by rapid credit expansion due to FDI in the BiH banking sector from Austria, Italy and Slovenia. From 2004 to 2010 total banking sector assets grew by 124 %, credit to enterprises by 143 %, and credit to households by 136 %. This credit expansion and the increase in banking assets were even more remarkable between 2005 and 2008. In that period, the average rate of growth of credit to enterprises was 23.6 %, while credit to households and total assets grew by 26.4 % and 22.7 %, respectively.[23]

[22] World Economic Forum (2009a, b, p. 128).

[23] The author's calculations based on the Central Bank of Bosnia and Herzegovina data;http://www.cbbh.ba/index.php?id=33&lang=en&sub=mon&table=konsolidovani_bilans_komercijalnih_banaka_bihh

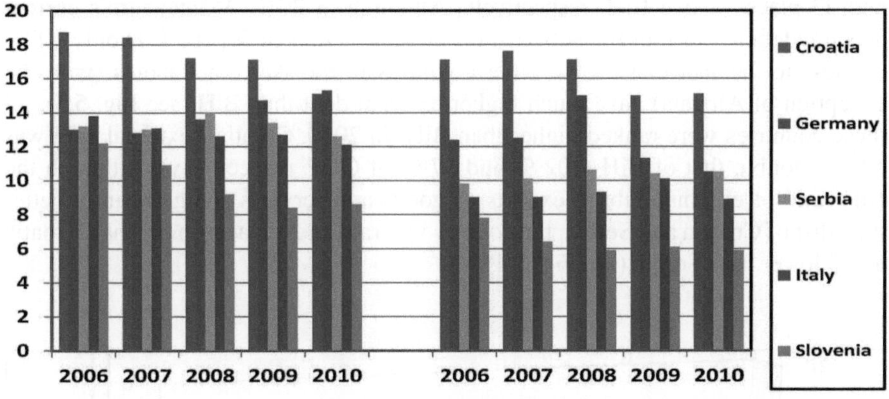

Fig. 5.2 Shares of the largest Bosnian trade partners in exports (*left* side) and imports (*right* side) of goods (in percent) (Source: The author's calculation based on data of the Agency for Statistics of Bosnia and Herzegovina 2011 and the Central Bank of Bosnia and Herzegovina 2011)

5.2 Competitiveness and Economic Growth

According to the *Economist,* BiH was the 17th fastest growing economy in the world between 1997 and 2007. The average growth rate for the period was 11.2 % in real terms.[24] From 1996 to 2000, the average growth rate was above 25 %. This was mainly due to the very low baseline (in 1991 BiH GDP was USD 10.2 billion, while in 1996 it was only USD 2.2 billion). Although in the 2008–2010 period BiH succeeded in cutting its current account and trade deficits from 40.8 % to 26.0 % and from 26.0 % to 6.6 %, respectively, in the Global Competitiveness Report 2011–12 (the GCR), BiH is ranked 100 out of the 142 countries included in the report.[25] The other countries of South East Europe are ranked as follows: Albania (78), Bulgaria (74), Croatia (76), the FYR Macedonia (79), Montenegro (60), Romania (77) and Serbia (95).[26]

The major differences in ranking between the countries in the region cannot be explained by any major difference in export capabilities. In 2004 and 2008 the ratio of external debt to export of goods and services was the following: Albania (119 %; 94 %), BiH (173 %; 117 %), Bulgaria (124 %; 166 %), Croatia (161 %; 181 %), FYR Macedonia (98 %; 70 %), Romania (110 %; 138 %) and Serbia (254 %; 222 %).[27] Bulgaria and Romania are the most obvious examples. In spite of the clear decline in export capacity (and competitiveness in the original sense of the word), these two countries achieved a better ranking in the GCR than BiH, being ranked 26

[24] Economist (2009, p. 32).

[25] The World Economic Forum (2011).

[26] Ibid.

[27] EBRD. 2008. Transition Report 2008 — Growth in Transition. London The first number in parentheses is for 2004; the second is for 2008.

and 23 places above BiH, respectively. Although in 2010, Montenegro's current account deficit was four times BiH's, the country is ranked 60, and BiH only 100.

Despite the fact that all the other countries in the Western Balkans (with the exception of Albania) have much higher external debt than BiH (see Fig. 5.3), all these countries were ranked higher than BiH. In 2010, Croatia's external debt was almost double that of BiH (102 % and 57 % of GDP, respectively). Although the BiH ratio of external debt to exports of goods and services is significantly better than that of Croatia and Serbia, the country was ranked 24 places lower than Croatia and 5 lower than Serbia (see Fig. 5.4).

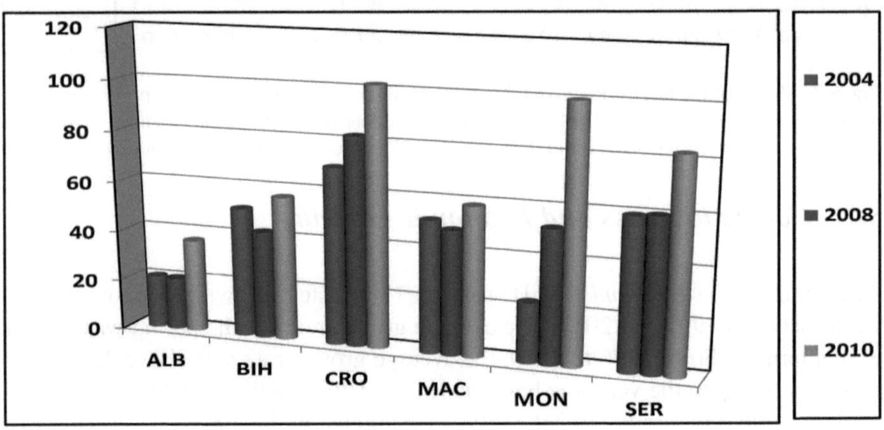

Fig. 5.3 External debt to GDP in the Western Balkans 2004–2010 (in % of GDP) (Sources: EBRD 2005, 2009, 2011)

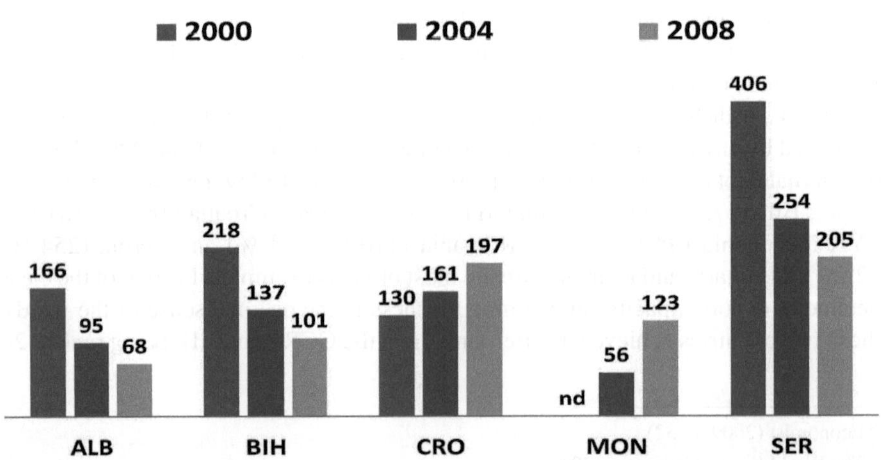

Fig. 5.4 External debt to exports of goods and services in the Western Balkans: 2000–2008 (index numbers) (Sources: EBRD 2005, 2009)

It is necessary to review the above data to arrive at a more objective understanding of the potential for economic growth and the actual economic results achieved by BiH in comparison to these countries. Presenting BiH as the most economically backward country in South East Europe, as well as the least competitive economy, is simply not consistent with basic economic indicators. Moreover, given the scale of the losses the BiH economy suffered between 1992 and 1995, particularly with regard to human capital, but also in the form of physical capital (equipment and infrastructure), on the one hand, and the actual rate of economic growth achieved with a below-average level of foreign debt, on the other hand, BiH has achieved relatively good results. Still, and in spite of these results, it must be admitted that the BiH economy has not made optimal use of its arguably generous potentials for economic growth. The basic question is why has this happened, and why is it continuing to happen?

The answer to this question, again, somewhat paradoxically, can be deduced from the GCR and *Doing Business 2010*[28] report of the World Bank. According to *Global Competitiveness Reports* from 2008 to 2012, the main barriers to economic development and competitiveness in BiH have been government and political instability, inefficient government bureaucracy, poor access to financing, unfavourable tax rates, and corruption. According to *Doing Business,* the lowest rankings received by BiH have been related to complicated procedures for starting a business, for issuing operational licenses and for paying taxes, and for inefficient registration of ownership. Of these barriers to the development of business and the national economy, only the tax rates and access to financing represent barriers deriving mainly from the economic system. The other barriers are of an institutional and political nature.

5.3 The Global Economic Crisis and Its Impact on Economic Growth

The global economic crisis, which spilled over into BiH in the last quarter of 2008, caused a recession in 2009, with a fall of 3.2 % in real GDP. The recession revealed the political weaknesses of the governments in both entities, as well as their inability to implement adequate countercyclical measures to fight the recession. The crisis was, in effect, important in that it demonstrated the emptiness of the governments' political rhetoric. This was particularly true of the former prime minister of the RS and his alleged ability to attract FDI. In fact, both major foreign direct investments in the RS were results of his attempt to create strategic political alliances based on FDI. In fact, the economic effect of FDI in the oil industry in RS with the Russian partner has caused a sharp increase in BiH's trade deficit with the Russian Federation since 2007, as already mentioned.

[28] The IBRD/The World Bank (2009).

The ruling political coalition in the FBiH (SBiH, SDA, HDZ) from 2006 to 2010 was completely unprepared for the recession. With unrealistically projected budget expenditures and with a sharp decline in budget revenues in the first quarter of 2009, the FBiH government ran short of money and was forced to borrow from two commercial banks. In June 2009, the then prime minister of the FBiH was forced to step down and a new prime minister was appointed. Thanks to BiH's Stand-By Arrangement (SBA) with the IMF (in July of 2009),[29] the FBiH government was able to repay its debt to the commercial banks. The FBiH's government's financial instability was manipulated by certain politicians in an attempt to prove the political unsustainability of the FBiH and call for a third entity. In actual fact, the government of the FBiH has EUR 2.2 billion in equity as a stakeholder in the four largest infrastructural companies in the FBiH and has significant borrowing capacity on the basis of that ownership.[30]

On the other hand, the new RS government, despite promises of major economic successes between 2006 and 2010, now faces a budget deficit of above EUR500 million. This budget deficit has forced the government to propose an increase in the income tax rate and social insurance contributions. This move has shown that fiscal competition at the inter-entity level has been unsustainable and a wrong-headed economic policy. The entities' economic policy based on tax competition has proved harmful for both entities and for BiH society as a whole.

6 Conclusions

In the period between the end of the war and the global economic crisis of 2008, Bosnia and Herzegovina achieved high rates of economic growth, placing it among the twenty fastest growing economies in the world. According to the Economist, BiH was the seventeenth fastest growing economy in the world between 1997 and 2007, while according to the World Bank its GNI per capita increased by 60 % between 2005 and 2010. Exports of goods increased fourfold from 2002 to 2008. Export expansion in the metal, automotive and wood processing industry was fueled by the arrival of foreign investors from Western Europe. Investments in the power sector increased electricity generation and created possibilities for export. Natural resources and technical knowledge inherited from the prewar period provide a reasonable basis for further economic growth and sustainable development, despite the losses in human and physical capital that BiH, unlike any other European country, suffered in the first half of the 1990s.

Although the above data suggest that BiH has the potential to improve economic performance results in the future, the main factors contributing to its economic

[29] The International Monetary Fund (2010).

[30] For more details about ownership in the utility sector see Causevic (2012). http://www.sant.ox.ac.uk/seesox/opinionpieces/Causevic-Economicperspectives.pdf

recovery and significant growth after the war were the Priority Reconstruction Program, implemented under the guidance of the World Bank (1996–2000) and the reactivation of production capacity due to export-oriented FDI, largely from Germany, Austria, Slovenia and Luxembourg. Such export-oriented FDI in production has not dominated overall investment in BiH, however. In the initial ten postwar years, the dominant forms tended to promote import dependency rather than an export orientation. Although BiH is one of the least indebted countries in South East Europe, the growth of import dependency has contributed to illiquidity and a need for new borrowing, leading finally to the signing of the standby agreement with the IMF in June 2009 and October 2012.

Since the end of the war in BiH, the international community has had a very significant impact on the implementation of economic reforms in BiH, including trade liberalisation, financial liberalisation and privatisation. Its direct involvement in the reconstruction and reform of the economic sector was based on the provisions of the Dayton Peace Accords. While trade liberalisation was conducted at national level, most other economic policy has been left to the entity governments or even the cantonal governments in the FBiH. Insofar as an economy's export capacity and competitiveness depend on its ability to increase productivity and chains of production that enable economies of scale, BiH has failed to create the preconditions for growth in productivity and competitiveness or unemployment reduction. The main reason for the import dependence, high unemployment and low productivity of the BiH economy is the political-administrative division of such a small country. This division, without a sufficiently strong coordinating role for national government, has laid the ground for irrational economic policies aimed at promoting the interests of ethnic political elites in their entity fiefdoms, while at the same time keeping the country's import dependence. All the production chains built by BiH in the prewar period have been divided along ethnic lines in the postwar period, which has led to irrational economic management and weakened competitiveness.

Over the last two decades, economic growth in BiH and in neighbouring countries has been based on domestic demand-led growth. A sustainable economic strategy for BiH and its entities relies on the development of export-oriented investment which requires tax incentives, and coordination of entity economic policies. BiH and its entities should redefine their strategies to attract foreign direct investors by providing significant tax relief for investors with a long-term export orientation that can integrate the entity economies and local businesses with international production chains. BiH also needs stronger financial institutions to finance export-oriented projects. These two measures, combined with tax incentives for domestic investors with export potential, could help change the dominant development model practiced in BiH and other Western Balkan countries over the past two decades.

Because of the extremely important role played by neighbouring countries Croatia and Serbia in the political and economic future of BiH, and having in mind that all three countries have low competitiveness rankings, even in the latest Global Competitiveness Report 2013–2014, a redefinition of investment strategies and economic cooperation between companies in the three countries would be a very welcome move forward. Better cooperation, based on reciprocal foreign direct investment in manufacturing with an export orientation towards other regions in the world would be a win-win strategy, instead of the zero-sum strategy pursued through "beggar-thy-neighbour" policies.

References

Agency for Statistics of Bosnia and Herzegovina. (2011). Foreign trade. *Thematic Bulletin 06*, Sarajevo. http://www.bhas.ba/tematskibilteni/ETS_2010_001_01-bh.pdf

Bojicic-Dzelilovic, V., Causevic, F., & Tomas, R. (2004). *Understanding reforms in Bosnia and Herzegovina*. Vienna: The World Bank project in cooperation with the Vienna Institute for International Studies. http://balkan-observatory.net/wp/2004%2006%20wiiw%20bo%20wp%20046.pdf.

Bosnia and Herzegovina, Ministry of Foreign Trade and Economic Relations. (2013). Izvjestaj o procjeni regulative na Zakon o politici direktnih stranih ulaganja u Bosni i Hercegovini/ The Report on assessment of the regulatory impact on the Law on Foreign Direct Investment in Bosnia and Herzegovina, available at: http://www.mvteo.gov.ba/linkovi/RIA%20na%20Zakon%20o%20politici%20DSU%20-%20april%202013%20PDF.pdf.

Causevic, F. (2006). *Foreign trade policy and trade balance of Bosnia and Herzegovina*. Sarajevo: Economics Institute Sarajevo.

Causevic, F. (2012). *Economic perspectives on Bosnia and Herzegovina in the period of global crisis*. Oxford: SEESOX, St Antony's College, University of Oxford. http://www.sant.ox.ac.uk/seesox/opinionpieces/Causevic-Economicperspectives.pdf.

Central Bank of Bosnia and Herzegovina. (2011). *Annual report 2010, Sarajevo*. http://www.cbbh.ba/files/godisnji_izvjestaji/2010/GI_2010_en.pdf.

EBRD (European Bank for Reconstruction and Development). (2005). *Transition report 2005 — business in transition*. London.

EBRD (European Bank for Reconstruction and Development). (2008). *Transition report 2008 — growth in transition*. London.

EBRD (European Bank for Reconstruction and Development). (2009). *Transition report 2009 — transition in crisis*. London.

EBRD (European Bank for Reconstruction and Development). (2011).*Transition report 2011 – crisis and transition: The peoples' perspective*. London.

Economist. (2009). *The pocket world in figures 2010*. London: Profile Books.

Global Finance, Russia Country Report. http://www.gfmag.com/gdp-data-country-reports/193-russia-gdp-country-report.html#axzz2qZfK8hD2

IBRD (The International Bank for Reconstruction and Development)/The World Bank. (2009). *Doing business 2010 – reforming through difficult times*. Washington, DC. http://www.doingbusiness.org/~/media/fpdkm/doing%20business/documents/annual-reports/english/db10-fullreport.pdf. Accessed 20 Apr 2012.

IMF (The International Monetary Fund). (2010). IMF Executive Board Concludes Article IV Consultation with Bosnia and Herzegovina. Public Information Notice(PIN) no..10/154, Washington, December 3, http://www.imf.org/external/np/sec/pn/2010/pn10154.htm

Keefer, P. (2009). Foreign assistance and political market imperfections in post-conflict countries. *Foresight, 2*(2), 1–14.

Kovac, J.(2001, January). Bosnian moderates oust nationalists. Balkans: Regional reporting & sustainable training, BCR Issue 211. http://iwpr.net/report-news/bosnian-moderates-oust-nationalists.

Porter, M.(2005, January–April). *What is competitiveness?*, IESE Business School. http://www.iese.edu/en/ad/AnselmoRubiralta/Apuntes/Competitividad_en.html

The World Economic Forum. (2009a).The global competitiveness report 2009–10. Geneva.

The World Economic Forum. (2009b). The global enabling trade report 2009. Geneva. http://www.weforum.org/pdf/getr09_dev/GETR09_Fullreport.pdf. Accessed 8 Nov 2009.

The World Economic Forum.(2011). The global competitiveness report 2011 12. Geneva.http://www.weforum.org/documents/GCR12/index.html. Accessed 19 Apr 2012.

The World Economic Forum. (2013). The global competitiveness report 2013–14. Geneva. http://www3.weforum.org/docs/WEF_GlobalCompetitivenessReport_2013-14.pdf. Accessed 15 Jan 2014.

Zupcevic, M., & Causevic, F. (2009). *Case study: Bosnia and Herzegovina", Centre for developing area studies*. Montreal: McGill University. http://www.mcgill.ca/isid/sites/mcgill.ca.isid/files/peace_and_development_case_studies.pdf.

Part II
Policy Making and Governance: Building Markets and Competitiveness in the Western Balkans

Chapter 6
Strengthening Regulatory Governance: The Case of Serbia

Andreja Marušić and Slavica Penev

1 Introduction

Regulatory policy may be broadly defined as an explicit, dynamic, and consistent 'whole-of-government' policy to pursue high-quality regulation. It is a relatively young discipline, designed to maximize the efficiency, transparency and accountability of regulations based on an integrated rule-making approach and the application of regulatory tools and institutions. Regulatory policy refers to the way policy makers draft, update, apply and enforce regulations and foster public understanding of these processes. Regulatory policy addresses the permanent need to ensure that regulations and regulatory frameworks are justified, of high quality and achieve policy objectives. The objective of regulatory policy is to ensure that regulations support economic growth and development, achieve broader societal objectives such as social welfare and environmental sustainability, and strengthen the rule of law. Regulatory policy helps policy makers reach informed decisions about what to regulate, whom to regulate, and how to regulate (OECD 2011).

The OECD has played a fundamental role in stimulating the diffusion of regulatory policies at the international level. The *Recommendation for Improving the Quality of Government Regulation* (OECD 1995) was the first-ever international statement of regulatory principles common to OECD member countries. Based on the 1995 principles, in 2005 the OECD adopted a new set of Guiding Principles for Regulatory Quality and P erformance (OECD 2005b), which set out: (i) the importance of political commitment to regulatory reform, (ii) the desirable characteristics of good regulation,

A. Marušić (✉)
International Finance Corporation (Formerly with the Balkan Center for Regulatory Reform), Belgrade, Serbia
e-mail: AMarusic@ifc.org

S. Penev, Ph.D.
Institute of Economic Sciences, Belgrade, Serbia
e-mail: slavica.penev@ien.bg.ac.rs

M. Thomas, V. Bojicic-Dzelilovic (eds.), *Public Policy Making in the Western Balkans*, DOI 10.1007/978-94-017-9346-9_6

and (iii) the links with competition and the elimination of barriers to trade and investment. These principles emphasise effective and continuous regulatory management to secure high-quality regulation. Even though the OECD 2005 principles still remain relevant, the OECD member countries recognized the need to expand their coverage in light of more recent experience, including the global financial and economic crisis (OECD 2010, 2011).

Regulatory policy started life as deregulation[1] in the 1970s and 1980s, following the rapid growth of regulation through most of the twentieth century and the dawning realization that the accumulation of this regulatory stock was harmful to business, and stifling entrepreneurship and innovation. With policies to increase competition in markets in the 1980s and 1990s, deregulation evolved to more systemic regulatory reform, involving a mixture of deregulation and reregulation and overall improvement in the effectiveness of regulations, and became a regulatory reform (see Malyshev 2006). Regulatory reform refers to changes that improve regulatory quality to enhance economic performance, cost-effectiveness or legal quality of regulations and related government formalities (OECD 2005a, 4).

In the early 2000s, regulatory reform started evolving to regulatory governance, which covers both the design and implementation of instruments and the methods for assessing the impact of regulation and governance principles such as transparency, accountability, efficiency, adaptability and coherence. In this sense, both the outcome and process dimensions are important in regulatory governance. According to OECD (2002), regulatory reform to improve regulatory governance involves three elements: regulatory policies, tools and institutions.

Regulatory governance is grounded in the principles of democratic governance and engages a wider range of players including the legislature, the judiciary, subnational and supranational levels of government and standard setting activities of the private sector. Effective regulatory governance maximizes the influence of regulatory policy to deliver regulations that will have a positive impact on the economy and society, and that meet underlying public policy objectives. It implies an integrated approach to the deployment of regulatory institutions, tools and processes (OECD 2011, 8).

Effective regulation to meet the challenges facing governments will only be achieved through stronger regulatory governance, closing the loop between regulatory design and evaluation of outcomes. This draws attention to a range of issues, including a renewed emphasis on consultation, communication, cooperation and coordination across all levels of government and beyond, including not least the international arena; and strengthening capacities for regulatory management within the public service.

The regulatory governance cycle. A core challenge for effective regulatory governance is the coordination of regulatory actions from the design and development of regulations to their implementation and enforcement, closing the cycle with monitoring and evaluation, which informs the development of new regulations and the adjustment of existing ones.

[1] Deregulation is a subset of regulatory reform and refers to complete or partial elimination of regulation in a sector to improve economic performance.

A number of studies support the view that efficiency and quality of regulation affect private investment and economic performance. Djankov et al. (2002), (2006) argue that the quality of institutions and excessive regulation can have a significant negative impact on investment. Jalilian et al. (2007) and Djankov et al. (2005) have shown that there is a strong causal link between regulatory quality and economic growth, and confirm that the standard of regulation matters for economic performance. Busse and Groizard (2008) claim that countries need a sound business environment in the form of good government regulations to be able to benefit from foreign direct investment (FDI). These findings confirm the importance of a favourable legal and regulatory environment for economic growth and efficient investment in the Western Balkan countries. Serbia was selected for this case study as it has been active in developing and implementing a comprehensive regulatory reform agenda. The objective of the study is to draw out lessons for future policy design and implementation of regulatory reform in transition countries with similar challenges in this area.

The case study examines policy making in Serbia and the policy issues being addressed, including the political, economic and social context and drivers of the reform, the stakeholders and policy actors involved in designing, implementing and evaluating the impact of the policy, as well as the linkage of regulatory policy to overall public policy goals and the government's overall reform agenda. More specifically, the case study includes analysis of the specific roles of the stakeholders and policy actors, the collaboration and eventual competition that occurred during the policy design process, the networks and coalitions that occurred and how they influenced the scope, timing and pace of reforms, and the leaders and their spheres of influence and special interests.

The findings of the case study are based on available strategic and other documents related to the regulatory reform initiatives in Serbia, interviews and questionnaires with policy makers, policy implementers, private businesses and other relevant stakeholders involved in the creation and the assessment of the regulatory policy implementation. In addition, available international datasets, which attempt to measure the quality of regulations and their implementation, were used as a relevant benchmark of the quality of the regulatory environment in the country.

2 Regulatory Reform in Serbia

Regulatory reform has been one of the key reforms in Serbia 'since the renewal of the transition process' that followed the democratic changes from October 2000. In the early years of its implementation, the reform was ad hoc and fragmented, and focused mostly on creating market-friendly laws to foster the functioning of a market economy. It has been closely correlated with and strongly influenced by (i) the transition process from a socialist to a market economy, and (ii) the EU accession process.

Regulatory reform was identified as a priority for private sector development in the analyses of relevant organisations, competent institutions and expert consultants. The major supporting donors at the beginning were the World Bank, the IMF, the EU and other relevant donors. The reform proceeded through several sequences from idea formation to reform organisation, legal drafting and stakeholder management.

In the period starting from the democratic changes in October 2000 up to the present, the development of regulatory reform can be divided into four separate phases (see also Table 6.1):

Phase 1: Ad hoc approach to regulatory reform, 2000–2004
Phase 2: First steps towards a more systemic approach to regulatory reform, 2004–2007
Phase 3: Systemic approach to regulatory reform—adoption and implementation of a Regulatory Reform Strategy, 2008–2011
Phase 4: Formally institutionalized regulatory reform, 2011 to present

The objective of regulatory reform was to reduce regulatory risk and improve Serbia's competitiveness by undertaking a series of reforms to simplify the existing regulatory framework and introduce quality control in the adoption of new regulation.

2.1 First Phase: Ad Hoc Approach to Regulatory Reform, 2000–2004

After the democratic changes in 2000, Serbia initiated the reform process with an inherited legal system, which was a mixture of French and German legal institutions from the first half of the twentieth century and a centralized, socialist state administration. The complexity of the system was exacerbated by the existence of institutions specific for former Yugoslavia, such as social ownership and self-management.

In this phase, regulatory reform was ad hoc and fragmented and focused mostly on privatisation and the elimination of social ownership, deregulation and the creation of market-friendly laws, with the aim to eliminate socialist-era laws and foster a functioning market economy.

The main actors of reform were individual ministries—in particular, the Ministry of Economy and the Ministry of International Economic Relations. The donor community, in particular the World Bank, the IMF and the EU, played a very important role in driving forward the reform agenda. Most of the legislative reforms were implemented with donor assistance, and the working groups established for drafting new laws or amendments to existing laws regularly comprised external local and foreign experts. In this phase of reform, there was practically no inter-ministerial coordination of ongoing reforms, and the government was more focused on 'putting out fires' and resolving particular urgent problems rather than establishing a systemic, coordinated and strategic approach to reforms. There was scarce use of relevant regulatory tools in the process of drafting and adoption of laws.

Public consultation was limited, due to the Government Rules of Procedure, which prescribed that draft laws were confidential until their adoption by the government, unless the government decided on public consultation. However, despite this limitation in the Government Rules of Procedure, some ministries in charge of economic areas started introducing informal consultation, mostly by inviting

Table 6.1 The sequence of regulatory reform in Serbia

Institutional framework	Actors-stakeholders	Tools implemented
Phase 1: ad hoc approach to regulatory reform, 2000–2004		
Established temporary institutional framework for regulatory reform: *Interministerial Working Group on Deregulation*, headed by deputy minister of economy	Ministry of Economy	Ad hoc deregulation: initiation and implementation of business registration reform
Established advisory body: *The Business Advisory Council to the Ministry of Economy*	Ministry of International Economic Relations	RIA pilot on business registration
	Associations and NGOs	Study and action plan on the elimination of administrative barriers
	Donor community (World Bank, IMF, EAR and other donor organisations)	
Phase 2: first steps towards a more systemic approach to regulatory reform, 2004–2007		
Council for Regulatory Reform, headed by minister of economy; replaced the previous institutional structure	Ministry of Economy	Introduction of mandatory public consultation for systemic laws
	Associations and NGOs	Introduction of mandatory RIA; Institutionalized RIA expert-led oversight as a temporary function
	Donor community (World Bank, IMF, EU and other donor organisations)	Drafting of a Regulatory Reform Strategy
		Training of civil servants for regulatory reform tools and RIA

(continued)

Table 6.1 (continued)

Institutional framework	Actors-stakeholders	Tools implemented
Phase 3: systemic approach to regulatory reform—adoption and implementation of a Regulatory Reform Strategy, 2008 to December 2011		
Council for Regulatory Reform, headed by the vice prime minister	The government of Serbia	Adoption and implementation of the Regulatory Reform Strategy (2008–2011)
	Ministry of Economy	Implementation of RIA
	All ministries and regulatory agencies	Implementation of a comprehensive review of all business-related legislation
	Businesses, i.e., the private sector	Training of civil servants for regulatory reform tools and RIA
	Associations and NGOs	Introduction of forward planning of legislative activities related to EU harmonisation process
	Donor community (SIDA, EU, World Bank, IMF, EBRD and other donor organisations)	
Phase 4: formally institutionalized regulatory reform, December 2011 to present		
Established formal/permanent institutional framework for regulatory reform: *Office for Regulatory Reform and RIA* at the level of the Prime Minister's Office, replacing the previous temporary institutional framework	The government of Serbia	Drafting of a Regulatory Reform Strategy (2012–2014)
	All ministries and regulatory agencies	Institutionalized RIA oversight as a permanent function led by civil servants
	Businesses, i.e., the private sector	
	Associations and NGOs	
	Donor community (EU, World Bank and other donor organisations)	

experts, lawyers, donors and foreign investor representatives to participate in draft legislation. Foreign investors had significant influence on the legislative process through their association—the Foreign Investors Council (FIC), which started publishing its White Book in 2002 with recommendations and concrete proposals to the government for improvement of the business climate, including a set of priorities in economic policy as seen by foreign investors, but additionally, revealing suggestions for ease of doing business in specific business areas.

Forward planning of legislation was informal and in a rudimentary phase. It was largely based on segments of forward-planning activities in different ministries or government bodies. Due to the lack of coordination and communication of such fragmentary legislative plans, overlap of legislative activities occurred leading sometimes to parallel draft legislation prepared in different ministries. The first attempt to coordinate regulatory reform activities and establish an institutional structure for regulatory reform was made in 2001 when the Ministry of Economy and Privatisation established a temporary Inter-ministerial Working Group on Deregulation (established in 2001) with the aim of 'deregulating' and simplifying the business environment. This inter-ministerial working group was headed by the Assistant Minister of Economy, and its members were either assistant ministers or other public officials of other relevant line ministries. The working group faced significant challenges in its operation, considering that its members were members of numerous other working groups established by the line ministries or the government, and did not have sufficient time to devote to this agenda.

An additional problem was lack of any technical support for its operation. Therefore, in its first 2 years, this working group did not achieve any significant results. An attempt to revive the regulatory reform agenda was made in 2003, when the Ministry of Economy established a Business Advisory Council (comprising private sector representatives) with the objective to provide input and proposals for simplifying the business environment to the Inter-ministerial Working Group. This was one of the first efforts to establish a dialogue between the public and private sector with respect to regulatory reform and the business environment. Creation of the Inter-ministerial Working Group on Deregulation in the Ministry of Economy was a good step towards recognizing the need for a coordinated, government-wide strategy to reduce business barriers, but the working group's mandate was focused only on deregulation and not on a broader view to speed up activity and stimulate private sector development, which would have real impact on the ground for the business community.

In 2002, the working group initiated the reform of business registration, recognized by businesses as one of the most significant barriers to entry. The reform was initiated by performing a regulatory impact assessment (RIA); this was the first reform in Serbia, in which an *RIA* was performed to evaluate the costs and benefits as well as the preferred reform alternatives. The piloted RIA proposed that business registration should be taken out of the commercial courts, and that a new administrative business registration institution should be established. This proposal met with significant opposition. The biggest opponents to this reform were the commercial courts and the Ministry of Justice. In fact, in an attempt to prevent this reform, the Ministry of Justice undertook a parallel initiative aimed at improving the business registration system within the commercial courts by focusing on technical solutions, that is, the development of a business registration system with the court system. This opposition was caused mainly by the fear of losing competences, control and sources of funding. However, after several attempts, the government adopted a set of principles that governed the business registration reform, including the principle that the new business register would be administered by an independent administrative agency rather than through the commercial courts and municipalities. The reform was implemented through the establishment of the Serbian Business Registers Agency, and resulted in a significant simplification of business registration procedures, increase of transparency and reduction of registration costs.

The RIA that was piloted in business registration was important for the further development of systemic regulatory reform in Serbia. It was not only useful in proving the need to reform business registration, but due to the significant success of this reform, served as the basis for introduction of mandatory RIA in the legislative process (see Sect. 2.2).

In this period, to support the efforts of the government to simplify the business environment, IFC initiated an Administrative Barriers Study, which was implemented in cooperation with the Ministry of International Economic Relations. The Administrative Barriers Study identified several areas that were limited by significant administrative barriers in all areas of business operations. Based on this study, the government adopted an action plan for reduction of administrative barriers, with a main focus on the elimination of administrative barriers related to starting business, reduction of business licenses and simplification of the process for obtaining construction permits. However, the action plan was only partially implemented, with some improvements in the areas of business registration and simplification of the construction permits procedures.

In parallel, the donor community also attempted to coordinate commercial law reforms among themselves and with the government, for which purpose it established in 2001 a Donors Law in Transition Working Group, comprising all relevant donors operating in Serbia at the time—the World Bank, European Agency for Reconstruction, Deutsche Gesellschaft für Internationale Zusammenarbeit (GIZ), United States Agency for International Development (USAID), United Nations Development Programme (UNDP), European Bank for Reconstruction and Development (EBRD) and other bilateral donors. The working group met on a regular basis to exchange information about ongoing projects and coordinate activities. Representatives of the Ministry of International Economic Relations were regularly invited to attend and participate in these meetings. One of the activities that achieved most visibility and success was undertaken after the change of government in 2003, when significant reforms initiated by the previous government were still pending, with the danger that these reforms would not be taken over and implemented by the new government. The Law in Transition donor group prepared a list of 10 priority laws to be enacted by the new government, and officially presented this list to the new government. This activity was highly publicized and most of the laws on the priority list were in fact thereafter adopted by the new government.

In spite of the above progress in regulatory reforms and the elimination of administrative barriers in Serbia, a more systematic approach in this area was a precondition for eliminating the still significant burden of barriers to businesses.

2.2 Second Phase: First Steps Towards a More Systemic Approach to Regulatory Reform, 2004–2007

Based on the progress achieved, and strongly supported by the international community, the Serbian government shifted from an ad hoc to a more strategic approach in regulatory reform.

The Inter-ministerial Working Group on Deregulation was transformed into the Council for Regulatory Reform, with the objective to broaden its agenda from activities aimed at purely deregulation of the regulatory environment to a more systemic approach to regulatory reform in general. Stronger political support for this agenda was demonstrated by the fact that the Council for Regulatory Reform was in this period chaired by the minister of economy, instead of the deputy minister as in the previous period.

Introduction of mandatory RIA (introduced in 2004) was one of the reform activities agreed on between the government and the World Bank within the World Bank's Structural Adjustment Credit for Serbia (SAC II). As a result, at the joint proposal of the Ministry of Economy and Privatisation and Ministry of Finance, the government adopted amendments to the Rules of Operation of the Government on October 14, 2004 (published in the *Official Gazette of the Republic of Serbia*, no. 113/04), which provide that for each new law, and other regulatory instruments such as decrees and orders, the responsible ministry will prepare a justification statement containing the answers or analysis to a set of questions developed in accordance with the OECD RIA recommendations. More specifically, for each new law and other regulatory instrument such as decrees and orders, the responsible ministry will be required to prepare a justification statement, which will answer the following key questions:

- What is the problem being addressed?
- Why is government action needed to correct the problem?
- What are the objectives of government action?
- Which options for dealing with the problem are being considered? Why is the proposed option the best approach?
- Do the benefits justify the costs? Who is affected by the problem, and who is likely to be affected by its proposed solutions? What are the likely costs for consumers and businesses, including SMEs? What are the impacts on market entry and exit, and on market competition? (In this section, identify the expected benefits and costs of the proposal. Determine which groups are likely to experience these benefits and costs, and the size of these impacts.)
- Have all interested parties had the chance to present their views?
- How will the proposal be implemented?

The introduction of RIA in the legislative process was championed by the Ministry of Economy and Privatisation, and it did not face any opposition within the government, even though at the time there were no capacities at the level of the ministries to perform proper RIA.

To facilitate the implementation of RIA, the Ministry of Economy and Privatisation established a RIA Secretariat as the provisional technical advisory unit of the Council for Regulatory Reform (Decision of the Ministry of Economy, November 12, 2004). The RIA Secretariat was comprised exclusively of external experts, rather than government officials, and support for its operation was provided by the World Bank through a number of grants.

The Council for Regulatory Reform had the mandate to issue opinions to all proposed draft legislation from the perspective of RIA implementation. Considering that public consultation is an essential cross-cutting activity within RIA, the provision from the Government Rules of Procedure that prescribed confidentiality of draft bills until their adoption by the government was eliminated. However, this was just an initial step towards securing transparency of the legislative process, as public consultation was still not required for all laws.

In this phase, the drafting of a Regulatory Reform Strategy was initiated, with the objective to introduce a wider range of regulatory reform tools, in addition to RIA implementation, and to secure a systemic approach to regulatory reform. In addition, the business community started playing a more active role, which increased awareness of the importance of public consultation. In practice, public consultation often goes beyond the requirements of the legal system.

As a result of the implementation of the business registration reform (see Sect. 2.2) and several other reforms in key areas, Serbia was identified as 'top reformer' in the World Bank's Doing Business report of 2006. This recognition of the reforms undertaken in this phase was a significant achievement.

The leading actor in the implementation of reforms in this phase was the Ministry of Economy and Privatisation. Within the government structure, the main opposition, in particular against RIA implementation came from the Ministry of Justice. Even though RIA was mandatory, the Ministry of Justice did not comply with these provisions and neglected to perform RIA even for extremely significant legislative proposals such as the Enforcement Law.

In the implementation of regulatory reform a significant ally for the Council for Regulatory Reform was the Foreign Investors Council FIC, which published the so-called White Book every year, offering a set of priorities in economic policy as seen by foreign investors, and suggestions for ease of doing business in specific business areas.

Considering the constraints in implementation of the regulatory reform agenda, in particular the lack of capacities both at the level of the Council for Regulatory Reform and its Secretariat as well as at the level of the line ministries, donor funds in the amount of approximately EUR 2.4 million were secured from Swedish International Development Cooperation Agency (SIDA), for the implementation of regulatory reform in Serbia in the following 4 years. The projects' objectives were to build the capacity of public administration to implement effective legal and regulatory reforms and thereby to comply with the overall government strategy to strengthen accountability and transparency of the public sector and assist in the private sector development through sound regulation.

2.3 *Third Phase: Systemic Approach to Regulatory Reform: Adoption and Implementation of a Regulatory Reform Strategy, 2008–2011*

As a consequence of the growing awareness of the importance of a strategic approach in regulatory reform, the Serbian government adopted an overall strategic document, a Comprehensive Regulatory Reform Strategy (2008–2011) that encompassed the entire regulatory reform agenda. The Comprehensive Regulatory Reform

Strategy was prepared by the Council for Regulatory Reform and its Secretariat; it was in this period that the regulatory reform agenda gained prominent place within the overall government agenda. The Council for Regulatory Reform gained stronger political support in this phase, since the chair was given to the Deputy Prime Minister in 2008. The council continued to be supported by a technical Secretariat staffed with independent regulatory reform experts backed by the international donor community. This structure ensured that the political support and championship of the Ministry of Economy. Also, since the chair of the Council for Regulatory Reform was now the deputy prime minister, this provided a direct channel through which the activities undertaken were promoted and discussed to a much greater extent in government sessions.

For the first time, this strategy introduced explicit standards for regulating quality through the introduction of principles of good regulatory practice (including the principles of necessity, cost-effectiveness and transparency) and envisaged implementation of the following reform activities:

- One-time elimination of redundant and unnecessary regulations—Comprehensive Regulatory Reform (CRR), a regulatory guillotine—and establishment of the Regulatory Review Unit to coordinate this process;
- Introduction of all-important regulatory tools for drafting and adopting laws, including: (i) strengthening of the existing ex ante regulatory quality control system (RIA); (ii) creation of a system of forward planning for new laws and regulations; (iii) enhancing the transparency of laws and regulations through consultation; (iv) establishing the tools for maintaining the quality of the regulatory environment both at national and local levels; (v) establishing the tool for coordinating regulatory activities;
- Strengthening the institutional capacity for regulatory reform implementation by the transformation of the Council for Regulatory Reform into a permanent government Office for Regulatory Reform and RIA.

As for the implementation of the CRR, the principal goal of this reform was to reduce administrative costs for businesses by 25 % by 2011, by abolishing or amending outdated regulations, which create unnecessary administrative costs or are not being applied. The aim of this reform was not focused so much on the specific number of legislations abolished as on the elimination of unnecessary administrative procedures, decreasing costs and overall regulatory risk, and increasing the competitiveness of the Serbian economy. This reform was conducted in four main phases: (i) inventory; (ii) analysis; (iii) recommendations; and, (iv) implementation.

The inventory phase catalogued approximately 6,000 regulations in force in Serbia, reported by 24 ministries and 76 regulatory bodies. This electronic database could serve as the basis for the creation of an electronic register of regulations, which is to be established in the final phase of the guillotine implementation.

In the analysis phase, approximately 2,000 regulations that affect business were reviewed and analysed. Direct communication between the government and the business community resulted in approximately 800 proposals aimed at simplifying business operations and reducing administrative costs in the country.

Table 6.2 Results of implementation of one-time elimination of redundant and unnecessary regulations—comprehensive Regulatory Reform

Recommendation status	Number	Estimated savings in million Euros old/new assessment
Implemented	196	121.0
Implementation in process	36	25.8
Not implemented	72	36.2
Recommendations abandoned	36	–
Total	340	183.0

Source: Regulatory Reform Strategy of Serbia 2012–2014 (www.ria.gov.rs)

Businesses actively participated in proposing measures to simplify the regulatory environment, and their proposals were incorporated in the recommendations presented to the government by the Regulatory Review Unit. Participants in this process included the government, the Council for Regulatory Reform and its Secretariat, business associations (including FIC, the American Chamber of Commerce and the Chamber of Commerce of Serbia and Belgrade), and the international community (the World Bank, the EU) (Table 6.2).

The implementation of this reform was the first time the government asked the private sector to actively participate and suggest proposals for the regulations and administrative procedures that prove a burden for their operation. The CRR technical team comprised approximately 20 team members, mostly lawyers and economists. The process involved coordination with 100 regulatory authorities (24 ministries and 76 other regulatory bodies). A web portal and software were developed whereby the private sector could access all information about the reform and give their proposals online. In addition, several working groups were established in relevant areas (tax, customs, trade, transport and tourism), which were coordinated by NGOs and private sector associations such as the FIC, the National Alliance for Local Economic Development (NALED) and the Chamber of Commerce of Belgrade and Serbia. Even though, the entire government was unified in supporting this reform, once the recommendations were given, implementation was slow mainly because of the opposition from mid-level civil servants. The strongest opposition against the implementation of CRR recommendations came from the Ministry of Finance and the Tax Administration, as most of the constraints were identified in that area. In addition, the Secretariat for Legislation of the Government significantly impaired the efficiency of the reform by not agreeing to implement CRR recommendations through an omnibus law, insisting on particular laws for each of the recommendations of the CRR.

To accelerate implementation as well as to identify problems in implementation, the CRR relied on the private sector as well as the media as allies through whom it had actively promoted the reform. However, even today, several recommendations remain unimplemented due to opposition from the line ministries and regulatory authorities.

In this phase, significant progress has been achieved in RIA implementation and capacity building, followed by the results achieved in simplification and reduction

Table 6.3 RIA implementation: Opinions issued by the Council for Regulatory Reform, 2006–2011

Year	Opinion positive	Opinion negative	Opinion partial RIA	RIA not required	Total
2006	10 (25 %)	4 (10 %)	16 (40 %)	10 (25 %)	40
2007	27 (47.4 %)	3 (5 %)	8 (14 %)	19 (33.3 %)	57
2008	35 (46.1 %)	11 (14.5 %)	12 (15.8 %)	18 (23.7 %)	76
2009	45 (40.5 %)	13 (17.7 %)	32 (28.8 %)	21 (18.9 %)	111
2010	34 (41.5 %)	8 (9.7 %)	29 (35.4 %)	11 (13.4 %)	82
2011	2 (33.3 %)	7 (10.2 %)	33 (47.8 %)	6 (8.7 %)	69
Total	151	39	97	79	366

Source: www.ria.gov.rs

Table 6.4 Perception of respondents on transparency, predictability and burden of regulations, 2011

	Statement	Disagree	Agree in part	Agree
1.	Transparency and predictability for doing business in Serbia has increased in the last 12 months (in percent)	77	19	4
2.	The burden of laws and regulations affecting my business has decreased in the last 12 months (in percent)	83	15	2

Source: Business Survey—Serbia 2011, Centar za slobodne izbore i demokratiju (*CESID*)

of administrative barriers, while the progress has been less evident in the area of public consultation and the creation of a system of forward planning for new laws and regulations (Table 6.3).

In this period, several detailed pilot RIAs were performed as a way of further raising civil servant capacity to perform RIAs; this included important framework laws such as the Bankruptcy Law and the Company Law. A detailed RIA manual was drafted and is publicly available. During this phase, RIA trainings became part of the official government training agenda for civil servants, and over 100 civil servants were trained to perform RIA. However, as in the previous phase, the main champion of RIA implementation remained the Ministry of Economy while some of the ministries, such as the Ministry of Justice as well as the Ministry of Public Administration and Local Self-Government still refused to comply with this obligation, and performed hardly any RIAs for the laws they were proposing.

One of the principal benefits of implementing the Regulatory Reform Strategy is the establishment of an active channel of communication between the government and the business community. However, when it comes to the perception of businesses about the reforms implemented, the results are still very negative. In 2011 a business survey was carried out on a sample of 913 legal entities; the overall perception of respondents with respect to the policy, legal and regulatory environment for doing business in Serbia remained negative (see Table 6.4).

In this phase, the strategy was not fully implemented, and the measures that were foreseen and but not implemented include the following: (i) enactment of RIA regulation that would enumerate criteria for performing basic or detailed RIAs; (ii) regulating in more detail the process of informal and formal consultation, including setting minimum consultation standards; (iii) introducing the obligation to perform ex post RIA, that is, monitor the implementation of legislation to see whether it is producing the impacts foreseen in the ex ante RIA.

Forward planning of legislative activities has partially been made transparent through the publication of the EU National Integration Plan. However this plan does not include laws and regulations that are not part of the EU harmonisation agenda. The complete legislative plans are gathered at the level of the General Secretariat of the government and are not publicly available.

The institutional framework for regulatory reform achieved its final shape with the transformation of the Council for Regulatory Reform into a permanent government Office for Regulatory Reform and RIA in December 2010, as envisaged in the Regulatory Reform Strategy.

2.4 Fourth Phase: Formally Institutionalized Regulatory Reform, 2011 to Present

The Office for Regulatory Reform and RIA was established by Decree of the Government in November 2010, as a permanent unit at the level of the Prime Minister's Office with the mandate to deal with quality control of RIA as well as with the reduction of administrative burdens on a permanent basis. Technical assistance to the office was still provided by outside expertise, while staffing of the office with civil servants only started in mid-2011.

The Office for RIA and Regulatory Reform has drafted a new Regulatory Reform Strategy for the period 2013–2016, which is in the process of being adopted by the government. The new strategy foresees the following measures:

- Improving transparency of forward planning of legislative activities and transparency during the process of drafting and enacting legislation
- Full implementation of the principles of good regulatory practice
- Further improvement of RIA implementation
- Capacity building of the Office for Regulatory Reform and RIA
- Introduction of the SME test within RIA
- Establishment of a forum for business initiatives by the Office for Regulatory Reform and RIA
- Following the impact of regulation during their implementation (ex post RIA)
- Regular measurement of administrative costs of businesses at the national level
- Identification and prioritization of measures to improve the international rating of the Republic of Serbia
- Improving transparency of implementation of regulations by state authorities
- Establishment of a publicly available electronic register of legislation at the national level, with positive legal security, accessible free of charge

The Office for Regulatory Reform and RIA faces significant challenges in its operation. The main role of the Council for Regulatory Reform and the deputy prime minister chairing it was to provide political support for the implementation of regulatory reform. Now that the Office for Regulatory Reform and RIA is a purely technical office of the government, the challenge is whether it will be able to establish itself as a meaningful operation with the authority to secure continued compliance of ministries and regulatory authorities with good regulatory practices. In addition, now the Office for Regulatory Reform and RIA is staffed exclusively by civil servants, with the additional challenge of securing the same quality of work as in the previous period.

2.5 The Impact of Regulatory Reform in Serbia on the Quality of Regulations and their Implementation

The intensification of Serbia's comprehensive regulatory reform agenda and the intensification of its EU accession and EU approximation process resulted in the permanent improvement of the quality of laws and their implementation. These findings are confirmed by the World Bank Governance Indicators, which measure the quality of laws (Figs. 6.1 and 6.2).

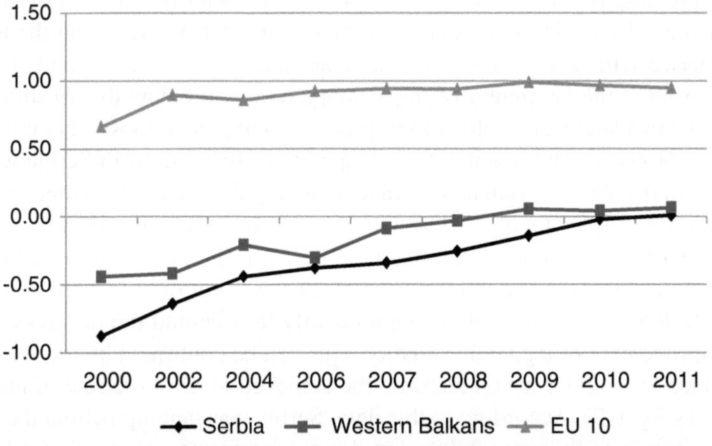

Fig. 6.1 World Bank Worldwide Governance Indicators: Regulatory Quality, 2000–2011 (Source: World Bank Governance Indicators Database; *Note*: The values of indicators range from –2.5 to 2.5, with higher scores corresponding to better outcomes. *The Western Balkans refers to Albania, Bosnia and Herzegovina, Macedonia, Montenegro, Serbia and Kosovo (According to the EU-mediated agreement between Serbia and Kosovo—reached in Brussels on February 24, 2012—Kosovo will be represented under the name 'Kosovo*', with a footnote referring both to UN Resolution 1244 and the opinion of the International Court of Justice (ICJ) on Kosovo's declaration of independence). **The EU 10 refers to the new EU member states excluding Malta and Cyprus (Bulgaria, the Czech Republic, Estonia, Hungary, Latvia, Lithuania, Poland, Romania, the Slovak Republic and Slovenia))

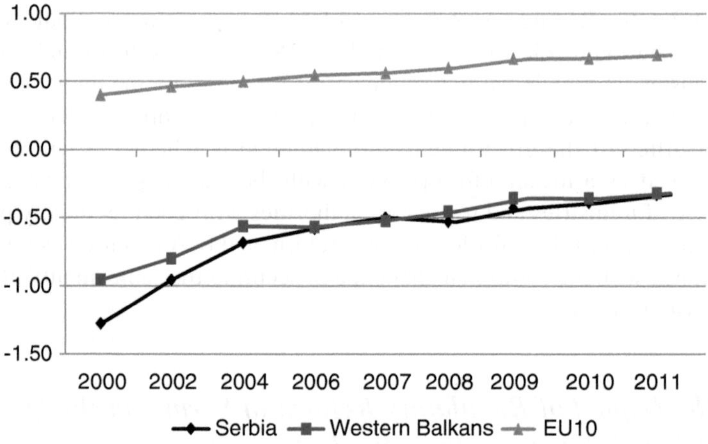

Fig. 6.2 World Bank Worldwide Governance Indicators: Rule of law, 2000–2011 (Source: World Bank Governance Indicators Database; *Note*: The values of indicators range from −2.5 to 2.5, with higher scores corresponding to better outcomes. *The Western Balkans refers to Albania, Bosnia and Herzegovina, Macedonia, Montenegro, Serbia and Kosovo*. (Ibid.) **The EU 10 refers to the new EU member states excluding Malta and Cyprus (Bulgaria, the Czech Republic, Estonia, Hungary, Latvia, Lithuania, Poland, Romania, the Slovak Republic and Slovenia))

In the previous decade, not only Serbia but all the countries of the Western Balkans region achieved notable improvement in the quality of laws, reducing the huge difference between them and the new EU member states (EU 10). The quality of legislation in Serbia at the beginning of this century was well below the Western Balkan average due to a later start in the reform process compared to most other countries of the region. However, improvement of the quality of regulations in Serbia was faster compared to the Western Balkans average, reaching the regional average in 2011.

In addition to reforms of the legislative framework, building institutional infrastructure is of utmost importance for the efficient implementation of laws and the rule of law. Progress in the implementation of laws, not only in Serbia, but in the Western Balkan region as a whole, significantly lags behind the progress achieved in the improvement of legislative quality. This can be confirmed by the World Bank Governance Indicators, which measure the achieved level of the rule of law implementation (Fig. 6.2). According to this data, Serbia was lagging behind the Western Balkans average in the early 2000s, but due to its progress in securing rule of law, Serbia reached the Western Balkans average in 2011.

Despite this positive trend, Serbia and the whole Western Balkan region are far behind in the quality of legislations and their implementation compared to the EU 10. There is huge scope for improvement. In this context, continuation of regulatory reform implementation and acceleration of the EU approximation process are of utmost importance for the improvement of the legal environment in Serbia, and in the region as a whole.

The improvement of the quality of legislation and its implementation positively influenced economic growth and the inflow of FDI to Serbia in the precrisis period.

These positive trends were interrupted by the devastating effects of the global crisis on the Serbian economy, only confirming the importance of the improvement of the legal environment in the country in ensuring economic recovery and sustainable growth of the Serbian economy.

3 Conclusion

In the past decade, regulatory reform in Serbia became one of the most successful reform areas of the government reform agenda. The main motive for this reform was improvement of competitiveness and economic growth of Serbia's economy through the improvement of its legal and regulatory environment. The approximation of its legal systems with the EU Acquis Communautaire was an additional motive for the implementation of this comprehensive reform.

After a period of ad hoc regulatory reforms, the adoption of the Regulatory Reform Strategy 2008–2011 initiated a new approach in regulatory reform in line with the OECD Guiding Principles for Regulatory Quality and Performance, which state that an effective regulatory policy should be adopted at the highest political levels, contain explicit and measurable regulatory quality standards, and provide for continued regulatory management capacity. The level of implementation of this strategy varied from significant progress in RIA implementation to less evident progress in other segments of regulatory reform, especially in public consultation and forward planning for new regulations.

Throughout the period covered by this case study, the Ministry of Economy was the main driver of regulatory reform, while some of the ministries (such as the Ministry of Justice) remained passive throughout. The process was significantly influenced by international organisations and donor support. The involvement of the private sector gradually increased, reaching a significant level in the implementation of the CRR; it remains a significant factor in pushing for further reforms.

With respect to the institutional structure for regulatory reform, the transformation of the Council for Regulatory Reform and its Secretariat from a temporary into a permanent function was the main objective, aimed at securing sustainability of regulatory reform in Serbia. This objective was realized through the establishment of the Office for Regulatory Reform and RIA as a permanent office of the government. However, this transformation also represents a significant challenge for future implementation of regulatory reform. Now that the Office for Regulatory Reform and RIA is a purely technical office of the government, staffed exclusively with civil servants, the challenge is whether it will be able to establish itself as a meaningful enterprise with proper authority to secure continued compliance of the ministries and regulatory authorities with good regulatory practices.

The improvement of the legal environment positively influenced the economic growth in the pre-crisis period. However, further improvement of the quality of legislation and its implementation gained even more importance in the period of financial and economic crisis to ensure the economic recovery and sustainable growth of Serbian economy.

The adoption of a new Regulatory Reform Strategy (2012–2014), which is underway, confirms the readiness of the government, similar to the EU and its member states, to continue with a strategic approach to regulatory reform in Serbia and to articulate that regulatory reform as a dynamic, ongoing process. Despite visible results, very little effort has been put into its promotion, which would increase awareness among stakeholders of its importance.

The global financial and economic crisis sheds new light on the importance of a regulatory reform agenda in the context of fostering economic growth of the Serbian economy. In that context, the implementation of the new Regulatory Reform Strategy will help overcome the negative effects of the economic crisis and improve the competitiveness of Serbia's economy.

References

Busse, M., & Groizard, L. (2008). *Foreign direct investment, regulations and growth* (World Bank Policy Research Working Paper Series No. 3882). Washington, DC: World Bank.

Djankov, S., La Porta, R., Lopez-de-Silanes, F., & Shleifer, A. (2002). The regulation of entry. *Quarterly Journal of Economics, 117*(1), 1–37.

Djankov, S., La Porta, McLiesh, C., & Ramalho, R. (2005). *Regulation and growth* (Working Papers Series, pp. 1–9). Washington, DC: World Bank.

Djankov, S., McLiesh, C., & Ramalho, R. (2006). Regulation and growth. *Economic Letters, 92*(3), 395–401. Washington, DC: World Bank.

European Commission (2001). Mandelkern group on better regulation final report. http://ec.europa.eu/governance/better_regulation/documents/mandelkern_report.pdf

Jalilian, H., Kirkpatrick, C., & Parker, D. (2007). The impact of regulation on economic growth in developing countries: A cross-country analysis. *World Development, 35*(1), 87–103.

Organisation for Economic Co-operation and Development (OECD). (1995). *Recommendation of the Council of the OECD on improving the quality of government regulations*. Paris: OECD.

OECD. (2002). *Regulatory policies in OECD countries: From interventionism to regulatory governance*. Paris: Organization for Economic Cooperation and Development.

Organisation for Economic Co-operation and Development (OECD). (2005a). *APEC-OECD integrated checklist on regulatory reform*. Paris: OECD.

Organisation for Economic Co-operation and Development (OECD). (2005b). *OECD guiding principles for regulatory quality and performance*. Paris: OECD.

Organisation for Economic Co-operation and Development (OECD). (2010). *Regulatory policy and the road to sustainable growth*. Paris: OECD.

Organisation for Economic Co-operation and Development (OECD). (2011). *Regulatory policy and governance, supporting economic growth and serving the public interest*. Paris: OECD.

Chapter 7
Investment Policy Design, Process and Implementation in Kosovo

Dita Dobranja

1 Introduction

The scope of this chapter is to evaluate the policies adopted by countries in the Western Balkans to ensure regulation and attract foreign investment, and to examine the actors behind these policies. The chapter will be focused particularly on the role of different groups of policy actors in Kosovo in designing investment policies and the impact this has had in the country's economic development. Investment policies set the basis for a strong legislative framework, which in turn provides the best environment for investments, both local and foreign.

While foreign direct investment (FDI) encompasses a wide range of investments, it is often divided into two categories: investments in privatized or existing non-state owned enterprises and direct investments in new ventures, known as greenfield investments. Matija Rojec (2005) identifies three different levels of FDI deriving from privatization, '(i) partial or full acquisition of a state-owned company; (ii) additional investment in a state-owned company; and (iii) joint venture with a state-owned company'. In such terms, for transition economies with significant state-owned assets, privatization constitutes an important channel for FDI. As these state-owned assets are privatized, they are often a major attraction for foreign investors.

Following the reforms undergone by Central and East European countries in establishing a market economy, the privatization of state-owned enterprises is a step towards both increasing efficiency of the respective industries as well as establishing the economy as potentially attractive for other forms of investment. Conversely, greenfield investments in the countries of South East Europe (SEE) have been relatively low. The 2010 OECD Investment Report Index, focusing on SEE countries, identifies the lack of greenfield investments as one of the most concerning issues for the region (OECD 2010).

D. Dobranja (✉)
Good Governance and Economic Policy Program, Institute for Development Policy, Pristina, Kosovo
e-mail: dobranja.dita@gmail.com

M. Thomas, V. Bojicic-Dzelilovic (eds.), *Public Policy Making in the Western Balkans*, DOI 10.1007/978-94-017-9346-9_7

A major concern is that FDI through privatization may, at least in the short run, lead to employee retrenchment as assets are restructured for increased efficiency. This poses a political and economic problem in transitioning countries with high structural unemployment levels. Botrić and Skuflic (2005) argue that changes caused by privatization in the managing and operating structure of the enterprises may result in layoffs as means of increasing productivity and profitability (Botrić and Škuflić 2005). Another concern, pointed out by Botric, is the dependence on privatization as a source of FDI in the Western Balkans and the implications for projected FDI inflows as privatizations taper off (Botrić 2010). These countries must enhance their competitiveness as locations for FDI to attract greenfield investments and benefit from job creation, market access and new technologies.

The social and political unrest, which has been a significant part of the transition narrative of the Western Balkan economies over the past few decades, has had a negative impact on the reputation of the region as a destination for FDI as reflected in the relatively low levels of greenfield FDI.

While there is an extensive body of work on the various determinants and trends of private investment flows to Central and Eastern Europe following the first wave of economic transition that led to the accession of the EU Ten, relatively little work has been done on private investment in the Western Balkans. The following section provides a brief survey of the literature on investment flows to the Western Balkans.

Estrin and Uvalic (2013) have examined whether the Western Balkans are *sui generis* in terms of investment in transitioning and developing economies and found that there are three sets of factors influencing the level of FDI in the region. These factors are size of the domestic economy (all relatively small with the exception of Romania); distance from investor source countries and 'remoteness' from the EU and other trading blocs—the announcement of potential EU accession has a significant positive effect for some countries in the region; and finally, institutional quality, or lack thereof. Penev and Rojec (2011)—in examining the competitiveness of a subset of Western Balkan countries for FDI—noted a number of weaknesses that overlap with the findings of Estrin and Uvalic. These include small domestic markets with low per capita income, relatively high country risk, slow progress in structural and institutional reforms, underdeveloped infrastructure, inefficient government bureaucracy and high administrative barriers.

Demekas et al. (2005) further examine the impact of FDI policies, while considering specific factors impacting the level of FDI in the Western Balkans. However, this analysis does not include data from Kosovo; thus, this chapter will only reference the theory of the Demekas et al. paper and use it as a basis to built new comparisons with the recent data and policies in the region. This chapter will focus more on the existing legislation of the countries in the Western Balkans and the opportunities that this legislation offers for potential investors. Furthermore, the dedication of governments of the region to improve the business environment will be examined and compared. One of the indicators that will be looked at is the Doing Business Rankings (DBRs) of the World Bank, which, though it may not serve as a basis for decision making for most investors, serves as a good starting point for policy and business environment reform in the Western Balkan countries.

Finally, this chapter attempts to highlight the policy-making procedures for attracting investments and the key players designing these procedures. Moreover, it will look into identifying cooperation areas in the countries of the Western Balkans to learn from the best practices of policy making.

2 Factors Influencing Investment Policy Making

Politics provides the context for policy making and often determines policy outcomes. Although objective policy making is the ideal, particularly for developing and transition economies, the reality is that politics influences policy. As a result, policies designed during the governance of a certain political party or coalition often reflect the ideologies of the ruling party. Moreover, policy design and implementation remains highly dependent on the electoral cycle, especially in the developing countries. As noted by Haggard and Webb (1993), developing countries lack a clear system of accountability due to the paucity and limitations of independent media to investigate the relationship between the interests of the electorate, political interests and public policy. It has been observed that electoral business cycles often drive the timing of policy reforms with most policy reforms and the launch of policy initiatives concentrated closer to upcoming elections to suit personal agendas of politicians rather than the economic exigencies of the country.

Sound investment policies and the related legal and regulatory framework are critical for economies seeking FDI to drive economic growth. There are differing theories about the main drivers of FDI, especially in developing and transition economies, ranging from the most basic factors identified by the gravity model of trade such as the relative size of the host and source economies and the distance between the two (Carr et al. 2001), to factors such as governance, the rule of law and policy frameworks.

Since the size of the economy and the proximity of the host and investing economy cannot be changed, we must look at other factors that determine FDI—those directly influenced and determined by policy actors. Recognizing that the policy environment is an important factor in attracting or deterring investments in a country, the examination of investment policies from the perspective of the policy environment by Demekas et al. (2005) concluded that the policy environment represents a major problem, especially in the Western Balkans. This conclusion is based on the fragile state of the institutions in these countries as well as a high level of corruption and organized crime, which directly influence the policy actors and the policies to be implemented.

This chapter examines the role of policy actors and coalitions in developing and implementing the investment policy framework for FDI, drawing on the experience of Kosovo. Kosovo is a transition economy for which FDI in privatizing entities and greenfield investment is a critical driver of economic growth and employment creation. In view of the ongoing policy-making process, Kosovo provides a good prism for examining the role of policy actors and institutions in developing and implementing policies aimed at enhancing the competitiveness of Kosovo as a location for investment.

3 Designing Investment Policies in the Western Balkans

While the global economic situation has contributed greatly to a decrease in FDI, not only in Kosovo, but in the Balkan region in general, the legal framework that regulates foreign investments in the countries of the region largely aims at ensuring an environment that is most suitable for attracting investors. Mateev and Tsekovb (2012) have conducted a study, which, apart from explanatory factors known as gravity factors (proximity, market size and factor endowments), also cites infrastructure and human capital and identifies trade openness, labour cost, regional integration, and tax policies and incentives as important in determining FDI. In the Western Balkans, regional integration plays an especially important role, considering the market size of each Western Balkan country. There are several important areas of the legal framework, which differ from country to country, that can affect the level of investment a country receives, and the following comparative analysis will highlight them.

4 FDI Legislation in the Region

Policies regarding investment regulation, with special focus on foreign investment, differ from one country to another, depending on a number of factors ranging from the governmental development plans, and social and economic structure of the country, to specific industrial sectors to be developed. Based on a comparative analysis of the legal framework regulating foreign investments in countries of the Western Balkans, it is clear that there are certain areas that continue to require regulation through legislation. The following sections discuss the most important fields to be regulated by investment legislative framework and relate issues that differ among countries in the Western Balkans. This part of the chapter will compare specific issues regulated by laws on investments in the countries of the Western Balkan, as identified by a careful analysis of these laws (Table 7.1).

4.1 Investment Policies and Their Impact on Private Investment Levels

Countries of the Western Balkans region have employed different strategies and different policies for attracting foreign investment and encouraging domestic investment. Although differences in legislation remain negligible, strategies to ensure a better business environment for investment have differed between countries. Looking at the World Bank data on the indicators of Doing Business, it is easy to see that Macedonia has been most dedicated in improving policies and legislation that, if implemented, lead to a better business environment. Below are the data for the

Table 7.1 Specific issues in the foreign investment law

Definition of foreign investor	The main problem with this definition has been whether to include the diaspora as foreign investors. In the Western Balkans, where the diaspora represent a substantial part of investments, this inclusion is crucial. While all other Western Balkan countries include diaspora as foreign investors, in Kosovo this remained a challenge until the final 2013 draft of the law, when diaspora were included in the definition
Treatment of investors	While laws of all countries call for compliance with international legislation and regulations, there are still questions about how foreign investors are treated, especially in comparison to domestic investors. In the Western Balkans foreign investors are expected to be given preferential treatment. The first draft of the new Law on Foreign Investments in Kosovo contained a debated article, which outlined that foreign investors will not be treated any less favourably than domestic investors. This, however, has been addressed in the latest draft of the law, to state that foreign investors and investments will have the same and equal treatments as domestic ones. Therefore, apart from the application of international legislation and norms, countries in the Western Balkans, through their legislation, ensure equality of treatment of foreign and domestic investments
Standardized procedures of investment legislation	Mechanisms for resolving disputes—all countries in the Western Balkans, by law must apply the standard resolving of disputes; this includes respecting all agreements on foreign investments agreed upon by the government and investor, national judiciary branch, as well as international courts and international courts of arbitrage
	Expropriation and compensation—this is to be done in a fair and timely manner, and interest must be paid to investors to whom payment is delayed
	Transfer of financial capital—investors are permitted by law to transfer the capital out of the investment country. However, this must be done in accordance with the taxation requirements of the receiving country, the Law on Foreign Investments in the country, as well as all secondary legislation

Doing Business Rankings of the countries as reported by the World Bank Doing Business Report 2008–2013 (Fig. 7.1).

However, to have a clearer view of the relation between legislation improvement and investment we look at the changes in both the Doing Business ranking and the changes in the level of investment in these countries, in the past 5 years, starting from 2008 (Fig. 7.2).

It is clear that foreign direct investment is influenced by more than just the policies, which are considered in formulating the rankings in the Doing Business Report of the World Bank. However, there is no clear correlation between FDI and the DBR rankings to conclude whether the impact is negative or positive. When looking closely at the data, we find that Macedonia, despite all the improvements in its DBR rankings, has not gained significantly in attracting foreign investors. On the other hand, Croatia, which made a number of improvements to its institutions to ensure accession to the European Union, has seen increased investment.

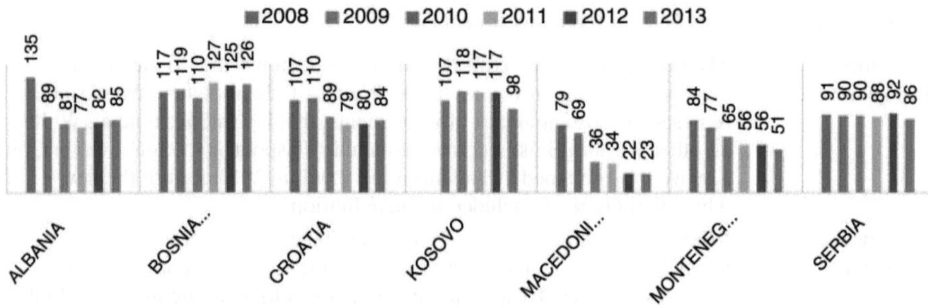

Fig. 7.1 Western Balkan rankings in the World Bank doing business report 2008–2013 (Source: World Bank Doing Business Report 2008–2013)

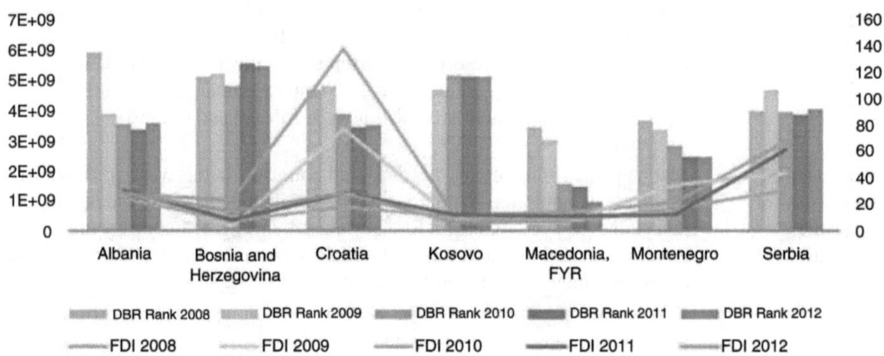

Fig. 7.2 FDI and DBR rank in the Western Balkans 2008–2012 (Source: World Bank doing Business Report (2013a) and Foreign Direct Investment in Western Balkans 2008–2013 (2013b))

The preferences of foreign investors differ, however, the existence of a favourable policy and legal framework are not enough to attract investors in one country. It is the proof of implementation of those policies and laws that remains crucial for investors.

On the other hand, looking at other indicators, such as Transparency International's Corruption Perception Index, we find that the region's rankings show little improvement, suggesting that efforts to fight corruption are either absent or ineffective. In the latest Transparency International Report on the Corruption Perception Index, Montenegro is ranked 66th with a 4.0 index, Macedonia is 69th with a 3.9 index, Serbia is ranked 86th with a 3.3 index, Bosnia and Herzegovina has an index of 3.2 and is ranked 91st, Albania has a 3.1 index and is ranked 95th, and Kosovo with a 2.9 index is ranked 112th—the worst in the region. These numbers indicate problematic rankings for the countries of the Western Balkans for perception of corruption.

The relation between the Corruption Perception Index and the flow of investments is expected to be the inverse, considering that the lower the perception of corruption, the more suitable the environment is for investing. As we can see, the

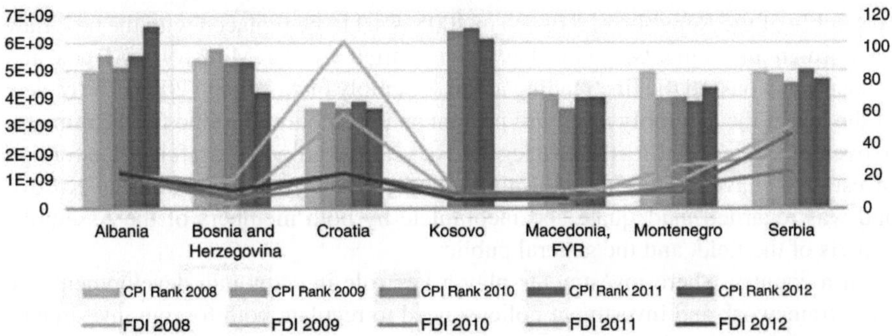

Fig. 7.3 FDI and CPI rank in the Western Balkans 2008–2012 (Source: Transparency International Corruption Perception Index and Foreign Direct Investment in Western Balkans 2008–2013)

Doing Business Rankings seem consistent with the Corruption Perception for the Western Balkan countries, although the two indexes are in no way directly interlinked to one another (Fig. 7.3).

5 Kosovo: An Overview

Investments, both domestic and foreign, play a highly important role in the economic development of Kosovo. In 2012, foreign direct investments (FDI) accounted for roughly 9 % of Kosovo's GDP compared with around 13 % in 2007.[1] Since 2000, there has been a visible decrease of FDI as a percentage of GDP, both due to decreasing FDI and to an increasing GDP in Kosovo. However, in 2010 and 2011 FDI increased from 2009 levels.[2] Based on data from the Central Bank of Kosovo, the trend of the sectors, which attract the FDI has changed over the past 5 years. There has been a significant increase in investments in the construction sector, particularly during 2010 and 2011, while investment in the finance sector has declined from around 35 % in 2008 to roughly 12 % in 2011.[3] Other sectors that dominate in attracting investments are manufacturing, real estate, telecommunications and transport. The data for 2012 is expected to show an increase of FDI in the energy sector, resulting from the privatization of the distribution and transmission network of the Kosovo Energy Corporation.[4] Investments in real estate and construction have grown steadily, largely reflecting investments by the Kosovo diaspora.

In Kosovo, apart from FDI, domestic investment plays a very important role in local economic development. The Law on Foreign Investments, adopted by the

[1] Government of Republic of Kosovo, Central Bank of Kosovo 2012, p. 81.

[2] Government of Republic of Kosovo, Central Bank of Kosovo, *Yearly Reports* 2001–2012.

[3] Government of Republic of Kosovo, Central Bank of Kosovo 2012, p. 65.

[4] Ibid., p. 82.

Assembly of the Republic of Kosovo in 2005 is set to be replaced with the new Law on Foreign Investments, which has been drafted by the Ministry of Trade and Industry and passed the first reading at the Assembly of Kosovo in 2013. The review of the law at the assembly level will present an important milestone for the ministry to overcome, since during the past legislative year the proposed draft laws on foreign investments have been returned to the ministry twice by the Assembly of Kosovo and was regarded inadequate and incomplete by both members of the Assembly, experts of the field, and the general public.

In a country where investments play a key role in economic development, the legal framework and investment policies need to regulate both foreign investments and domestic investments, while reflecting their importance and Kosovo's commitment to ensure a more suitable environment for these investments. As a step towards this, Kosovo has worked to improve the World Bank Doing Business indicators; however, many gaps—not considered by this report—still remain that affect the investment environment in Kosovo, and as a result contribute to lack of investments. Some of the most prominent tasks to encourage foreign investments include, but are not limited to, reducing the corruption level, improving infrastructure and ensuring a stable political state.

However, in developing economies, such as those of the Western Balkans, foreign direct investment remains both one of the most important goals of the government and one of the most common promises made during political campaigns. Considering the stagnating economic development, high unemployment rates, and low-to-average local production, countries in the Western Balkans rely heavily on FDI to improve the economic situation and generate employment. As such, policies facilitating investments have a hidden social dimension in that they play a role in easing social issues of unemployment and lack of growth.

5.1 Kosovo: An Analysis of the Policy-Making Process and Actors

Policy-making procedures in Kosovo are regulated by Government Regulation 13/2013 on Government Legal Services, which outlines the steps for drafting legislation with the government's initiative. This regulation was drafted in May 2013, and enacted on June 30, 2013, the first time such a regulation was enacted by the Kosovo government.

The steps for drafting legislation are outlined below. Responsible policy actors for each step are also shown.

The most important part of the policy-making process is the legislative component, the steps of which are outlined below. This procedure entails cooperation between the executive and legislative branches, and the inclusion of external interest groups. Figure 7.4 lists the steps in chronological order along with actors responsible for the steps.

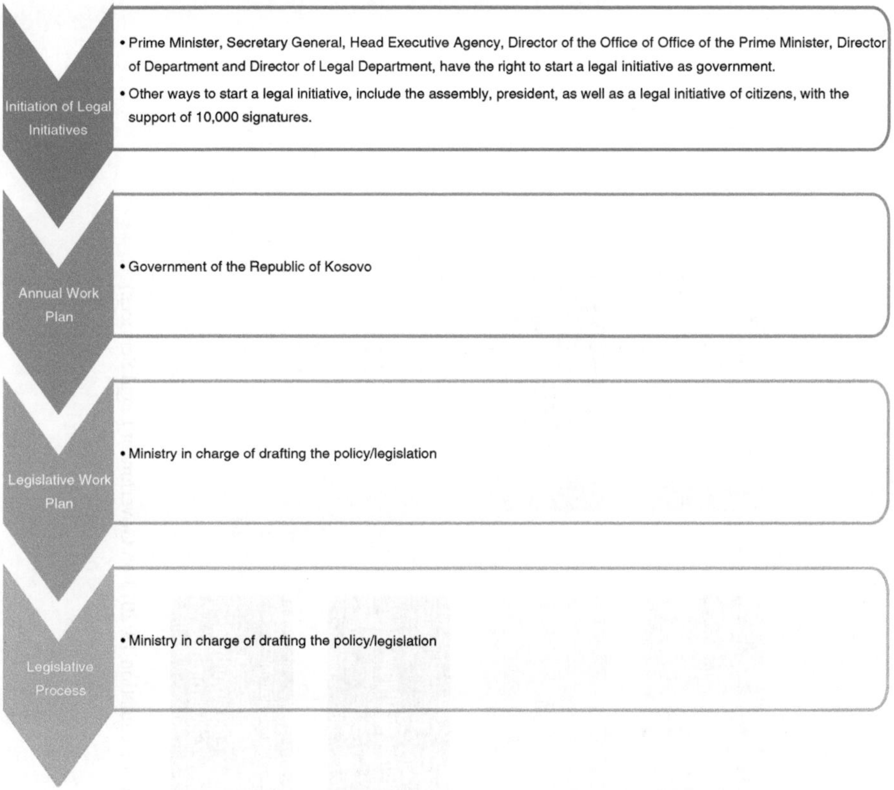

Fig. 7.4 Policy making steps and responsible actors in Kosovo (Source: Kosovo Government Regulation 13/2013 on Government Legal Services)

The ministry in charge of drafting the policy or legislation must draft the preliminary version of the draft law, and follow it up first by a preliminary and then a public consultation, The preliminary consultation takes place over a period of 15 days with relevant actors within the institutions as well as with other interest groups, such as members of the private sector and civil society. The public consultation is open for comments from the public. Through this process, civil society organizations (CSOs) as well as other relevant parties, which will be affected by draft legislation, are to be consulted both at the preliminary phase and at the public consultations phase. This enables the more active involvement of CSOs and the public at large in the policy-making cycle. Furthermore, this provides a unique opportunity for civil society to keep track of their recommendations on draft legislation, as line ministries for the draft laws must include explanations on consultation processes and subsequent recommendations in the Memorandum of Explanation for the draft law. After the first three steps are carried out by the ministry, the new draft including changes from the consultations is sent to the government for review and approval. The procedures are also sent to the government for review and approval. After approval by the government, the final draft of the law is completed by the ministry in charge and sent to the Assembly of Kosovo (Fig. 7.5).

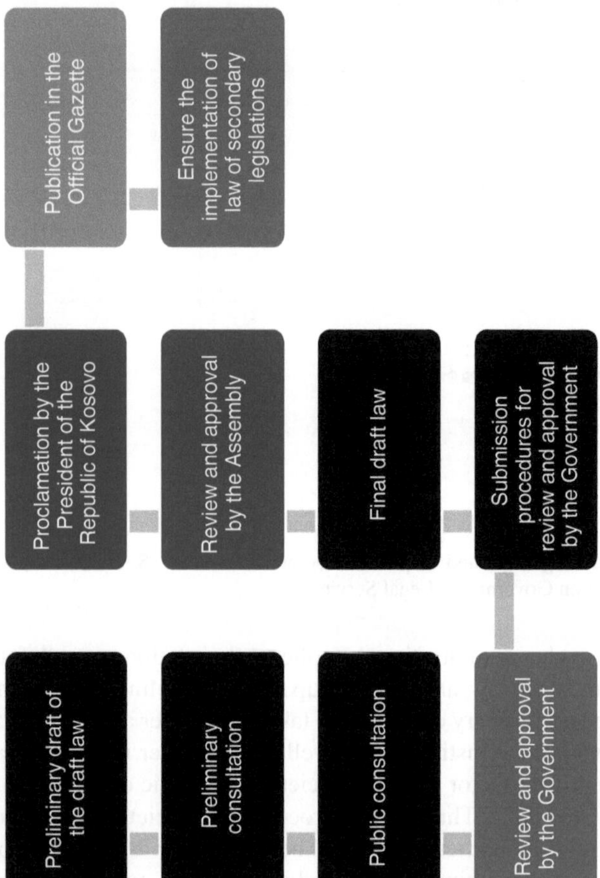

Fig. 7.5 Policy making process in Kosovo (Source: Kosovo Government Regulation 13/2013 on Government Legal Services)

The draft law is sent to the Assembly of Kosovo and is discussed by the members of parliament in the first hearing. If the draft law passes the first hearing, it is discussed by the functional committees within the assembly. The functional committees can propose amendments to the law during the working groups on the law. The working groups within the functional committees of the Assembly of Kosovo consist of representatives of the line ministry, members of the committee, civil society representatives, as well as representatives from other interest groups. After the proposed changes by the committee, they are sent first to the ministry and then to the government for approval. If these amendments are approved, they are sent to the Assembly of Kosovo for a vote; if it receives the necessary votes, it is sent to the president of Kosovo to be approved and signed into law. After this step, the law is published in the *Official Gazette* and implemented by the line ministry and the government of Kosovo.

The formulation of Kosovo's legislative framework and regulations allow the involvement of individuals from various areas in the policy-making process. However, these regulations are yet to be fully implemented, and the readiness of the government to cooperate with civil society seems to be the biggest obstacle to their implementation.

5.2 *Policy Actors in Kosovo*

5.2.1 Kosovo Government

As seen above, the policy- and law-making processes generally start at the government level. Ministries in charge of specific areas are also responsible for proposing and drafting laws and policies that regulate their particular area or its specifics. Moreover, ministries can also propose amendments to existing laws or propose new laws to replace old laws.

The executive branch of the Kosovo government, in addition to proposing legislation, is in charge of including other relevant actors in the consultation process, working closely with the legislative branch to include amendments to the proposed draft, as well as ensuring the implementation of the legislation once it is approved. If the proposed legislation does not pass the hearing at the assembly, the line ministry must submit a new draft of the law to the assembly, and go through the entire cycle of procedures again.

5.2.2 Assembly of Kosovo

The government sends draft laws to the Assembly of Kosovo for the first hearing of the draft law. If the law passes the first hearing, it is sent to functional committees that must hold a public hearing at the assembly level with all relevant actors. After the public hearing, work groups are formed by the members of the committee, representatives from the line ministry, as well as other interest groups such as representatives from the civil society and the private sector. However, the inclusion of external partners in work groups is not mandatory for the committees. The amendments made at the functional committee along with the proposed draft from the ministry are sent for approval to the standing committees.

The process continues in the second hearing at the assembly session, where the new draft of the law with the changes proposed by the committees is debated. After the debate, members of parliament vote on each article of the law, and finally on the law as a whole. If the law passes, it is sent to the president of the Republic of Kosovo to be signed into law.

5.2.3 Civil Society

Kosovo has a strong and diverse civil society, which, as external partners to the government, is active in policy making through public hearings and participation in working groups. However, cooperation between state institutions and civil society still leaves a lot to be desired. Civil society inclusion in policy-making processes is often undertaken as a mere formality (to satisfy requirements of the rules and regulations to consult all relevant parties); in rare cases, the inclusion of civil society reflects readiness for cooperation from both sides. The Assembly of Kosovo remains significantly more accessible to civil society, and cooperation between the two is more frequent; whereas the Kosovo government is still relatively closed to cooperation with civil society. At the government level, civil society continues to be consulted only when this is required by laws and regulation.

5.2.4 Private Sector

Kosovo is still developing advocacy and lobbying as part of the process of proposing and changing policies. As a result, the private sector is not yet adept at using all available channels to push its agendas and requests. Although there are a considerable number of chambers of commerce in Kosovo, there is little advocacy in policy making to represent the requests of business. Nevertheless, given that several members of parliament have experience and connections in the private sector, such issues are addressed by them. However, there is a need for more active involvement of the chambers of commerce as advocates for the private sector.

5.2.5 Actors in Investment Policies: Kosovo

In 2012, the Kosovo government, namely the Ministry of Trade and Industry proposed a new Law on Foreign Investments. As the most important legislation in regulating foreign investments, the new law aimed at improving the investment environment as well as transmitting the message that Kosovo was working towards a better environment for investors.

The main reasons behind the new law were to guarantee protection of investors; establish a framework for equal treatment of investors, foreign or local; and acknowledge investments from the diaspora as foreign investments. Furthermore, the law was drafted to establish the basis of a legal framework for investments, to be further expanded by laws and strategies.

Following the drafting procedures, the law was sent for review to the Assembly of Kosovo. This draft was considered inadequate in many aspects and was not passed by members of parliament, who required a more comprehensive draft to be sent within the designated time limit. The law did not receive the necessary votes to pass the second review by the assembly, and was returned to the Ministry of Trade and Industry. The issues marked as important by members of parliament had not been addressed in either of the proposed laws; thus the ministry was required to draft a new law.

The new draft law was drafted with extensive consultation and involvement of CSO representatives with expertise in economic policies and members of the chambers of commerce. The outlined procedures for drafting the law were followed in substantial detail. The drafting of the law was done in work groups comprising the Ministry of Trade and Industry, the Kosovo Investment Promotion Agency, legal experts, as well as the aforementioned third parties, business associations and CSO representatives. This cooperation between different institutions produced informed debate on the articles and regulations of the law, resulting in a law that passed the first hearing in the Assembly of Kosovo.

Inputs from all relevant actors were taken into consideration and included in the law to a reasonable extent. This law has shown the readiness of both the Kosovo government and other non-political actors to collaborate in drafting policies that work best for the country. The law is yet to be amended by the functional committee at the assembly, which will most likely include relevant institutions and organizations in the process.

5.3 *Policy Environment and Positioning of Policy Actors*

The major debate on the Law on Foreign Investments has taken place within the Assembly of Kosovo, where both ruling and opposition political parties have voiced their positions. While the parties that are in the Kosovo government have shown their support for the law proposed by the Ministry of Trade and Industry, opposition parties have largely deemed it inadequate and requested it be redrafted. The opposition called for an investment strategy, which would expand the investment policy framework and ensure implementation of the law. The debate on the third version of the law took place in September 2013 in a regular assembly session.[5]

The majority party, the Democratic Party of Kosovo (PDK), has voiced its support for the law while emphasizing the importance of this legislation in attracting

[5] Government of Republic of Kosovo (2013).

potential investors. The New Kosovo Coalition, a party in the government, has also supported the law, while emphasizing the importance of regulating foreign investments on a national level rather than through supranational treaties.

On the other hand, opposition parties highlighted the shortcomings of the law. As noted by the Foreign Investment Advisory Service (FIAS) report in 2007, corruption and absence of the rule of law remain the highest concerns and require policy improvement to attract potential investors to the Western Balkans (World Bank 2007). These two concerns also dominated debates over investment policies in Kosovo and were noted as the most urgently in need of reform, and most detrimental to investment if no measures are taken.

The main opposition party, the Democratic League of Kosovo (LDK) states that a primary concern is that the law envisions the merging of two different agencies, one responsible for investment promotion and the other for support to small and medium enterprises, as the majority of Kosovo's businesses fall within the small and medium enterprises definition. Furthermore, this merger undoes the Council of Foreign Investment within the Office of the Prime Minister due to its important role in analysing the business climate and aiding the government in designing policies, and thus it becomes an independent body outside of the Office of the Prime Minister. LDK also stated that the lack of a Strategy for Investment and an investment stimulation package are shortcomings in the overall investment policy framework. As a supplement to the proposed Strategy for Investment, LDK called for the implementation of the existing Anti-Corruption Strategy to tackle the most problematic issue in both Kosovo and the entire Western Balkans region. Moreover, government investment in education, as a means of creating an educated labour force, was also identified as an important strategy to attract investments.

The Vetëvendosje (Self-Determination) Movement has opposed the law entirely. The prevalent issues have been the importance given by the law to protecting investors but not Kosovo from bad investments. Political implications of non-discrimination of investors based on country of origin was another major issue. Given the political past and the current situation in the Western Balkans, such legislative provisions are cause for concern, according to Vetëvendosje. Furthermore, the importance of limiting sectors where foreign investment is allowed highlights a security concern; many Western Balkans countries have addressed that concern by prohibiting investment in certain sectors of the economy. The limitation of investment to only certain sectors also attracts foreign investment to those sectors, which have remained underdeveloped. The necessity of social responsibility as a component of investment was also suggested by this political party.

Another opposition party in the Assembly of Kosovo, the Alliance for the Future of Kosovo (AAK), also opposed the law as it was presented by the ministry. Besides stressing the importance of fighting corruption and organized crime, strengthening the rule of law and supporting a strategy for investment, AAK highlighted the need to support local investors as they remain the backbone of the economy.

The policy environment remains fragile due to a range of problems and institutional deficiencies. The widespread problem characterised by the close links between politics and economics in the Western Balkans is evident in the concerns voiced by Kosovo's policy actors. There is no clear separation of politics and the private sector, as is the case with most transitioning economies. This connection impedes unbiased policy making by the majority of policy actors, who are also involved in the state institutions and hold political offices. On the other hand, the overlap between trade unions and politics represents a similar problem.

Furthermore, corruption and the absence of the rule of law still remain major problems that must be addressed by institutions to ensure an environment that is desirable for doing business. The current political situation exacerbated by a troubled past also creates a barrier not only for each Western Balkan country, but for the region as a whole.

5.4 Implications of Investment Policy Changes

Apart from its importance in regulating foreign investment, this Law on Foreign Investments has been an important step towards showing the readiness of Kosovo institutions to reform its policies and create a stable environment for investment and doing business. Additionally, the cooperation between institutions and non-institutional actors shows positive signs in the improvement of the policy environment in Kosovo. The involvement of a wider spectrum of experts and stakeholders allows for better and more comprehensive policies, but more importantly, allows for policies that are more likely to be implemented.

However, positive developments will occur if along with existing policies, the new policies necessary to supplement the current legislative framework are implemented. As expressed by many policy actors, a strategy is required that considers all forms of investment, encompasses all existing legislation and provides an action plan for its successful implementation.

The final draft of the Law on Foreign Investments has eliminated some potentially negative effects for local investors, although much ambiguity still remains in the role of the state in investment and in providing a secure and stable environment for investment in all areas.

Based on existing legislation regulating the economy, many issues continue to be regulated through by-laws and secondary legislation. Investment policies, however, are a sensitive area and should be regulated largely through primary legislation. This remains a challenge for the future, especially in terms of the specifics of investments that derive from investment agreements.

6 Conclusions

While investments are determined by various factors, many factors are unchangeable such as the size of a national market or economy. Nevertheless, one of the most important factors, especially for the Western Balkans, remains institutional stability and the readiness of institutions for policy reform.

First, even though a lot of wide-ranging work has been done in the Western Balkans to ensure a better environment for investment, governance and institutional issues continue to determine the investment environment. Countries in the Western Balkans remain fragile democracies requiring support to build stable institutions.

Second, the Western Balkans suffer from "chronic corruption", which largely mars the attractiveness of these countries for investors. Although reports frequently assess the high level of corruption in these countries, little is actually done to combat corruption. One of the biggest priorities for the government should remain decreasing the level of corruption and improving the rule of law as cornerstones of a good investment environment.

Third, necessary policy reforms should be undertaken in a multidimensional manner by including a more comprehensive list of relevant actors. This will serve to design more comprehensive policies that encompass a wider spectrum of parties to ensure easier implementation of those policies. Cooperation between policy actors is key to both the design and implementation of policies.

Finally, policies must be implemented. While most Western Balkan countries have adopted sound policies, not all of these have been implemented; and those that are, are never fully implemented. Although this demonstrates institutions' readiness for sound policies, it also shows lack of effort in ensuring these policies in fact achieve their expected results. So far, the EU accession process has served as an effective incentive for the design of good policies; the EU must remain an incentive, but now for the actual implementation of those policies.

References

Botrić, V. (2010). Foreign direct investment in the Western Balkans: Privatization, institutional change, and banking sector dominance. *Economic Annals, LV*(187), 7–30.

Botrić, V., & Škuflić, L. (2005, June 3). *Main determinants of foreign direct investment in the South East European countries*. Paper prepared for the 2nd Euroframe conference on economic policy issues in the European Union, Trade, FDI and Relocation: Challenges for employment and growth in the European Union?, Vienna.

Carr, D. L., Markusen, J. R., & Maskus, K. E. (2001). Estimating the knowledge-capital model of the multinational enterprise. *American Economic Review, 91*(3), 693–708.

Demekas, D. G., Horváth, B., Ribakova, E., & Yi, W. (2005). *Foreign direct investment in Southeastern Europe: How (and how much) can policies help?* Washington, DC: International Monetary Fund.

Estrin, S., & Uvalic, M. (2013). *Foreign direct investment into transition economies: Are the Balkans different?* London: The London School of Economics and Political Science.

Government of Republic of Kosovo (2013). Kosovo Government Regulation 13/2013 on government legal services.

Government of Republic of Kosovo, Assembly of the Republic of Kosovo (2013). Transcript of the Assembly of the Republic of Kosovo Plenary Session held on September 19 and 26, and October 2.

Government of Republic of Kosovo, Central Bank of Kosovo (2001–2012). Yearly reports, 2013, Pristina

Government of Republic of Kosovo, Central Bank of Kosovo (2012). Yearly report, Pristina.

Haggard, S., & Webb, S. B. (1993). What do we know about the political economy of economic policy reform? *The World Bank Research Observer, 8*(2), 143–168.

Mateeva, M., & Tsekovb, I. (2012). *Do Central and Eastern European countries possess FDI advantages to more developed western countries?*, Paper prepared for the 2013 annual meeting of the Midwest Finance Association, March 13–16, 2013, Chicago.

OECD. (2010). *Investment reform index 2010: Monitoring policies and institutions for direct investment in South-East Europe*. Paris: OECD Publishing.

Rojec, M., & Penev, S. (2011). Attractiveness of Western Balkan countries for FDI. In *Serbia and the European Union: Economic lessons from the New Member States* (Vol. 1, 1st ed., Spring). Belgrade: Institute of Economics Sciences.

Rojec, M. (2005). *Balance of privatization policies related to foreign direct investment in the transition countries of Central and Eastern Europe*. Ljubljana: University of Ljubljana, Faculty of Social Sciences.

Transparency International. *Corruption perception index 2008–2013*, Berlin.

World Bank. (2007). *Attracting investment to South East Europe: Survey of FDI trends and investor perceptions* (FIAS the multi-donor investment climate advisory service). Washington, DC: The World Bank Group.

World Bank (2013a). *World Bank doing business report 2008–2013*. Washington, DC.

World Bank (2013b). *Foreign direct investment in Western Balkans 2008–2013*. Washington DC: World Bank Data.

Chapter 8
Montenegro: Enhancing Competitiveness and Accelerating European Union Integration – The Role of Higher Education

Danijela Jaćimović-Vojinović

1 Introduction

The speed and the success of the transition process in the Western Balkan countries, which started in the 1990s and faced numerous challenges including waves of destructive war, have relied heavily on the level of education of their citizens. The importance of education is huge for small countries and young democracies such as Montenegro which has a limited resource base to support a diverse and dynamic economy. Given Montenegro's commitment to European Union (EU) membership, its society and economy face far-reaching and deep changes in order to develop democratic politic institutions and a competitive economy that can withstand the pressures within the European single market. Education plays a defining role in achieving competitiveness and sustained economic growth, and also in ensuring the implementation of European values that underpin the EU membership.

The process of European economic integration has put pressure on prospective EU members to reevaluate the role of education as a resource for both economic and democratic development. The integration process foregrounds the establishment of new flexible labor market relations, which in turn, require flexible and dynamic education institutions and programs. For aspiring EU entrants, including Montenegro, this has crystallized into a need to implement significant education reforms to establish the necessary structures and organization to achieve the quality of education that reflects labor market changes and the demands of international competition.

The literature emphasizes the role of education for ensuring income growth. Cross-country regressions indicate that changes to education levels are positively associated with economic growth (Krueger and Lindahl 2000). Several empirical studies find strong positive links between education quality and national GDP

D. Jaćimović-Vojinović, Ph.D. (✉)
Faculty of Economics, University of Montenegro, Podgorica, Montenegro
e-mail: jacimda@hotmail.com

M. Thomas, V. Bojicic-Dzelilovic (eds.), *Public Policy Making in the Western Balkans*, DOI 10.1007/978-94-017-9346-9_8

growth rates (Hanushk and Kimko 2000), and evidence of the contribution of education quality to improved productivity in an economic environment open to foreign trade (Jamison et al. 2006; Topel 1999). These findings are confirmed in the research by Montenegrin economists that identifies human capital as the critical factor to improved growth rates and living standards in Montenegro (Montenegrin Academy of Science and Arts 2010a, b).

The role of highly educated individuals is equally important in the development of a society based on democracy. A large body of empirical work supports the view that higher education (HE) leads to more democratic politics (Barro 1999; Glaeser et al. 2004; Papaioannou and Siourounis 2005). Moreover, better quality HE environment is a good predictor of a transition from dictatorship to democracy, although not the reverse (Rander-Pehrson 1999). Finally, more educated democracies tend to be more stable than those with less well educated citizenry.

Following the above insights, harmonization of the European education system has been a prominent track in the integration process. Effective European-wide distribution of knowledge, and labor mobility to achieve increased EU competitiveness and greater prosperity of European citizens, prompted the package of educational reforms known as the Bologna Process. The Bologna Process aimed to establish a competitive European higher education (HE) area, and to attract students and instructors from outside the EU. The extensive education reforms to achieve a better educated and more competitive European citizenry are also intended to contribute to the realization of the Lisbon Strategy, a EU landmark document that sets the agenda for transition towards a knowledge economy in the EU. Achievement of the Lisbon objectives should set the EU on the path to becoming the most competitive and dynamic knowledge based economy in the world.

For the new EU member states, accession to the EU involves a complex process of adjustment to the "rules of the game" operating within the EU. The EU integration process has influenced and continues to influence the process of caching up with the knowledge economy agenda by new and aspiring EU members (Reinhile and Mrak 2009). In that regard, the Bologna Process is a powerful instrument for the essential reforms to the HE systems of all accession countries.

Since 2004, the Montenegrin HE system has experienced huge transformations in line with the Bologna Process as a major high education reform initiative (Lucin and Prijic-Samarzija 2011). In Montenegro, a newly established country following secession from Serbia in 2006, and with strong EU aspirations, the skills and experience acquired under the socialist system proved less marketable in the new economic environment. Expenditure on education was falling, with a significant negative effect on the quality of education outcomes (Campos and Dean 2003).[1] The need for HE reform to enhance growth and increase economic competitiveness was recognized early in the transition process, and has become the foundation to multiple transition reforms.

[1] A recent comprehensive review of education systems in the Western Balkan (Luca et al. 2007) concludes that the education systems developed under socialism focused on "memorized factual and procedural knowledge" to generate skills which were perhaps appropriate for a planned economy but not necessarily for the demands of a market-based economy.

Building on previous research, this chapter explores developments in Montenegro's education policy, looking at the relations and roles of key stakeholders that have shaped policy, and considering assessments of and reflections on major aspects of education policy. The first section critically assesses the socialist era education system in Montenegro, and its evolution in the course of economic and political transition. It focuses specifically on discussing the challenges of implementing the Bologna Process. Throughout, the emphasis is on capturing the main policy trends, identifying the key actors driving and shaping the policy reform process, and the development of a new policy framework. The discussion centers on deciphering how key policy actors negotiated their respective interests in pursuing (or not) education reforms, and the implication of this for reform outcomes. This chapter addresses the following main questions.

What is the role of HE for supporting and enhancing the process of economic and social development in Montenegro? Will Montenegro be able to compete in the knowledge economy and develop the skills required for the twenty-first century? How is the policy making process in HE being shaped? Who are the most important actors? What are the major obstacles facing HE reforms in Montenegro?

The analysis is at two levels. First, we provide an overview of the Bologna Principles, followed by an analysis of their implementation so far in Montenegro, based on an interrogation of the interactions among key stakeholders. This structure enables the application of different methodologies. To investigate the EU education framework as a baseline for new and aspiring EU member states, we analyze official documents and official European Commission (EC) and other relevant statistical data. The country-level analysis uses the main legislative and strategic documents defining the content of education policy. Analysis of the policy actors and their influence on policy outcomes is based on interviews with representatives from the Ministry of Education and Sport, the Ministry of Science, the Presidents of the Higher Education Council and the Science and Research Council, members of the quality-control bodies, students representatives, university deans, professors, and NGOs.

2 European Common Educational Policy: The Main Challenges

2.1 *Bologna Declaration and Bologna Process*

The basic HE framework for the EU was designed within the Bologna Process, through a series of meetings of ministers in charge of HE policy, conducted with the goal of establishing the European Higher Education Area (EHEA) by 2010. The signatory countries are 5 EU member states, 3 European Free Trade Association (EFTA) countries – Iceland, Norway and Switzerland, and 11 then EU candidate countries (Bulgaria, Czech Republic, Estonia, Hungary, Latvia, Lithuania, Malta, Poland, Romania, Slovakia, and Slovenia). This body has since been enlarged beyond EU borders to include a total of 47 countries.

In signing the Bologna Declaration, the ministers declared their intention to do the following:

- Adopt a system of easily readable and comparable degrees;
- Implement a system based on two main education cycles;
- Establish a system of credits (such as the European Credit Transfer System ECTS);
- Support the mobility of students, teachers, researchers, and administrative staff;
- Promote European cooperation in quality assurance;
- Promote European dimensions in HE (i.e. for curricula developments and inter-institutional cooperation).

The Bologna Process created a new sociopolitical area of HE that brought together the European states, supra and international organizations, civil society, and employers (Croshe 2009). The growing 'market share' of the EHEA in worldwide student mobility indicates that European HE has become more attractive since the Bologna Declaration came into effect (Campos and Dean 2003).

HE across the 47 EHEA countries looks substantially different from early 1999. Nevertheless, it is difficult to measure the achievements of this initiative because the realization of desired outcomes requires many years of post-implementation experience -especially labor market effects and the effects of all three cycles of study (undergraduate, postgraduate, and doctoral). Experience from the first 10 years of implementation of the Bologna Principle points to differential speed, and variation in the implementation modalities across the 47 country signatories to the Bologna Declaration. Since it is an intergovernmental declaration, the document is not binding in character, and requires no ratification; hence there is no political pressure to implement it (Garben 2010). During the first 10 years since it was signed, all countries have implemented most elements envisaged by the reform architecture, involving legislation and national-level regulation. States see the Bologna Process more as an instrument to resolve their national problems – to make their universities attractive for students from other continents – than as a way to harmonize their HE systems with those of their country counterparts (Charlier 2006).

From the beginning, the EU has played an important role in driving this process, and its role will continue to be crucial. Throughout the recent financial crisis, the EC reaffirmed its stance regarding the importance of HE, and the need for increased investment in this area in order to facilitate adaptation of its citizens to new economic, demographic, and social realities (European Commission 2010). To contribute to the goals of the Europe 2020 agenda, the European Commission adopted a new agenda for the modernization of Europe's HE systems in September 2011.

2.2 *Necessary Reforms Towards Europe 2020 and the Challenges Ahead*

The Europe 2020 strategy puts knowledge at the heart of the EU's efforts to achieve smart, sustainable, and inclusive growth. This is because HE and its links to research and innovation play a crucial role in individual and societal advancement, and in providing the highly skilled human capital and articulate citizens that Europe needs to create jobs, economic growth, and prosperity (European Commission 2011).

The main areas for reform identified in the new agenda are the following:

- To increase the number of HE graduates;
- To improve the quality and relevance of teaching and researcher training, to equip graduates with the knowledge and core transferable competencies they need to succeed in high-skill occupations;
- To provide more opportunities for students to gain additional skills through study or training abroad, and to encourage cross-border cooperation to boost HE performance;
- To strengthen the 'knowledge triangle', linking education, research, and business;
- To create effective governance and funding mechanisms to support the pursuit of excellence.

The suggested reforms are expected to produce several key outcomes by 2020, including a significant increase in the number of young people successfully completing HE; a reduction in school dropouts to below 1 %; and an increase in HE research.

The ultimate goal of the HE reforms to support the Europe 2020 agenda is to improve the quality of education and its relevance in a time of rapid and continuous change, through adjustments to curricula, introduction of practical experience in taught courses, staff and student exchanges, and flexible and innovative learning approaches and delivery methods. For the HE reform to be effective will require the involvement of employers and labor market institutions to contribute to the design and delivery of programs, and involvement in life-long learning programs. The provision of adequate funding is of overall importance to support the recruitment of high quality teaching and research staff, procurement of equipment, and improved working conditions. In 2010, the EU invested 1.3 % of GDP on average in education, compared with 2.7 % of GDP in the United States, and 1.5 % in Japan (European Commission 2011).

The initiative to make the EHEA more competitive and more transparent to international stakeholders is intended to increase Europe's appeal as a study destination. There is a growing number of third countries interested in the common educational policy and the instruments developed by the EU to support member states modernize their education systems (Official Journal of the EU 2010). By attracting the best students, academics, and researchers from outside the EU, and developing new forms of cross-border cooperation, international cooperation in HE could contribute significantly to improving the quality of HE (European Commission 2011).

The countries implementing the Bologna Process have faced different problems since 1999, from inefficiencies (high dropout and low participation rates), to limited systemic flexibility and slow quality upgrades. Ultimately, a country's achievements depend on its national agenda, the date of its joining the Process, the distribution of authority, its experience and policy making tradition, and not least, available funding. A balanced mix of supporting policy mechanisms (funding, regulation, communication, and information exchange) appears to be crucial for successful implementation of the Bologna reforms. Experience with their implementation so far shows that lack of resources and expertise to guide and influence the domestic policy process has been a significant handicap, particularly in countries where the Bologna Process is relatively new. The analysis in Sect. 3 describes Montenegrin experience in implementation of the Bologna Process against this background.

3 Implementation of the Bologna Process in Higher Education in Montenegro

3.1 Higher Education in Montenegro and the Main Reform Trends

The former socialist country of Montenegro started the process of transition and the shift to a market economy in the early 1990s. The broad scope of political and economic reforms put HE reform at the center of its reform efforts, and made it a priority to support the process of transformation towards building an efficient and competitive market economy. HE was recognized as one of the most important drivers of transition and its reform was strongly supported by government, the international community, and donors.

Montenegro is a small,[2] middle-income, and young country that gained independence in 2006. It was awarded EU candidate status at the end of 2010, and negotiations for EU membership began in 2012. Progress towards EU accession required Montenegro to improve its competitiveness significantly, and to that end, the efficiency and quality of HE alongside developing stronger links between research, innovation, and business are considered of paramount importance (World Bank 2011).

At the onset of HE reform which began in earnest with the signing of the Bologna Declaration in 2003, the state-owned University of Montenegro (UM) was the only HE institution. The Bologna Process has been the major reform initiative in the area of HE pursued over the last 10 years in Montenegro. Formal application started with the adoption of a new legal framework consisting of the Law on Higher Education (2003), and led to the adoption of a university and department book of rules (2004), and accompanying regulations for their implementation. This created a normative institutional HE framework in Montenegro.

The new Law on Higher Education stresses improvements to the efficiency of studies, and harmonization with the European HE system, in line with the principles of the Bologna Declaration and Lisbon Convention. Obligations assumed through membership of the Bologna Process and Lisbon Convention are aimed primarily at promoting a European HE system which as mentioned earlier, is the strategic goal underlying creation of the EHEA. A need for reform of the HE system in Montenegro

[2] Population is estimated at 623,000.

was evident long before adoption of the Bologna Declaration. In fact, HE was the weakest part of the former education system. Average years of study were usually 6–8 and even 9 for some programs, compared to the official time of 4 years as defined by the regulation. The UM had inadequate human resources, and there was chronic lack of investment in professional training of teaching staff. Learning practices and curricula were outdated and ill-fitted to the requirements of a market-based economy.

The changes introduced by the Law adopted in 2003 aimed at modernizing HE by putting in place a more open and flexible system. Implementation of this institutional framework in Montenegro has led to an increase in the numbers of HE institutions and students enrolled. There have been several directions of change. By promoting quality of public and private HE institutions, the new Law contributed to the expansion of private universities/faculties. In addition to the state UM which has 20 faculties, 3 research institutes, and 1 independent study program, located in 8 different towns throughout Montenegro, there are 2 private universities, Mediterranean University and the University of Donja Gorica, and 7 independent private faculties (Montenegrin Academy of Science and Arts 2010a). Private institutions represent between 20 and 25 % of the HE market in Montenegro.

The increase in the number of private HE institutions is important in so far as they tend to be more flexible and market oriented, offering programs that better fit labor market needs. Liberal policy implemented through education reform in Montenegro has been driven by expectations that private institutions will increase the competition and contribute to improving the quality of the education system. Reflecting these policy preferences, the latest changes in the Higher Education Law (2010) make it possible to exploit public sources for certain study programs offered by private HE institutions if they are deemed to be of strategic importance to government.

Private versus public HE is a much debated economic, education, and political topic in Montenegro, and it is increasingly evident that expectations about private HE institutions and their contribution to genuine change to the system have been overestimated. According to an interviewee, "the quality of the work of private HE is different, often poor; they lack qualified teaching staff, and provide narrow curricula, mostly oriented to low- cost social science programs, organized in small towns, with strong support by the local politicians" (Zgaga et al. 2013).

Another change resulting from implementation of the Bologna Process reforms is the significant increase in the number of students to approximately 25,000, of which some 20,000 students studied at the UM, and the remainder in other institutions. This increase in the number of students is due in part to the introduction of liberal legislation which is making it easier to set up private education institutions, and in part to lack of funding from public sources. Montenegro allocates 1.10 % of GDP to HE compared to 1.26 % in Slovenia and 0.72 % in Croatia, the regional peers with the highest and the lowest HE expenditures respectively.[3] To compensate for revenue shortfalls, a system of tuition fees has been introduced in Montenegro.

---

[3] Budget allocations for HE in the region are generally inadequate and tend to be spent inefficiently (World Bank 2012).

One of the primary goals of HE reform in Montenegro is to ensure greater employability of university graduates by addressing the mismatch in supply of and demand for skills – a long term problem in Montenegro (World Bank 2011). The Ministry of Education and Sport (MoES) does not have any systematic mechanism to collect, analyze, and disseminate information on Montenegrin graduates' employment outcomes. However, slow reform of the university curricula in a context of a fast transition in the labor market away from manufacturing and agriculture and toward the knowledge and service industries, has not been able to break the long term trend of high unemployment among graduates.[4]

There have been other setbacks in implementation of the Bologna Process. At the start of the reform, the UM as the only HE institution in Montenegro became engaged in the process almost overnight, and without adequate preparation. Over time, a variety of practices related to implementation of the Process developed, usually involving confusing interpretations of program duration, content, and learning outcomes. This was the result of introducing changes in a different institutional context, and equally importantly, of confronting different individual attitudes and preferences concerning reform of the HE system (Montenegrin Academy of Science and Arts 2010a). Overtime, the gaps between the formal adjustments and the required strategic changes have become more evident, and policy making has become increasingly problematic. Political pressure on the universities has increased, which is an unexpected outcome that goes against the Bologna Process ethos (Zgaga et al. 2013).

3.2 *Challenges to Implementing the Bologna Process in Montenegro*

In keeping with its commitment to the Bologna Process in relation to HE reform, Montenegro has two policy priorities -improving the quality of education, and decentralized governance of the HE sector. Enhancing the quality of HE requires further *curricula upgrading*, improved learning outcomes, and acquisition of knowledge that is adapted to the needs of the labor market to ensure greater employability of graduates. This in turn requires actions to improve the quality of academic staff, primarily through increased international mobility for teaching and non-teaching staff to encourage younger, less qualified staff to pursue masters and doctoral level studies oversees.[5] So far, levels of international mobility among

[4] To overcome the problem, the World Bank decided to finance research to collect relevant data and build the capacity of local institutions to monitor trends in graduate employment (World Bank 2011).

[5] Since the quality of human capital is crucial for improving quality of HE, the World Bank project 2011, component 2, provides € 2.1 million for this purpose. Also, teaching staff benefit from building closer links with the scientific diaspora who are interested in collaboration for teaching and research projects.

teaching staff are low for several reasons related to lack of awareness among staff of the importance of mobility, lack of institutional support to facilitate mobility, and so on.

Research and development (R&D) is a very important segment of HE which has implications for the quality of education outcomes (Havas 2009). Most indicators such as number of articles published in peer-reviewed journals per teacher show that Montenegro has a poorly developed R&D sector. Lack of funding, insufficient demand for scientific research from the business sector and especially small and medium enterprises, and the criteria for professional promotion which are much lower than in developed countries offer no incentives for pursuing a research career (Montenegrin Academy of Science and Arts 2010c).

The primary responsibility for education quality resides with the individual HE institution, and an international assessment is carried out annually at ministerial meetings monitoring implementation of the Bologna Declaration. Through several international projects (World University Service – WUS, Austria, and the EU Instrument for Pre-Accession Assistance -IPA), the UM has set up the Center for Quality Assurance and has adopted the Quality Assurance Strategy for the period 2011–2015. However, the quality assurance system remains largely framed around traditional understanding of learning outcomes, and burdened by a perception that quality assurance is an additional administrative burden on teachers' time. Indirect quality assessment of the relevant Bologna Principles is performed through a process of accreditation and reaccreditation by the Higher Education Council. Hitherto, the practice of accreditation and reaccreditation, to which all HE institutions are subject, mostly consists of application of procedures and standards related to the administration of the Bologna Process to the academic community. Introducing accreditation programs and setting criteria for them has been difficult for HE institutions in Montenegro.

Another policy priority in Montenegro is institutional integration and governance of universities. Procedures such as transfer of public funds, signing of official documents, internal quality assurance and communication with government and international institutions are defined at university level, and the faculties define curricula, enrollment, and employment policy. However, there are differences in and resistance to institutional integration mainly in the belief that it would lead to integration of financial resources. Consequently, the integration process has caused a lot of tensions in UM, mostly between the social science/humanities faculties and the technical sciences faculties, and also conflict – aggravated by the onset of the financial crisis in 2009 – between UM and the private universities.

The increase in the number of students as a result of implementation of the Bologna Process, mainly in social sciences and humanities faculties, has boosted their revenue and enabled an increase in investment in teaching resources and infrastructure (Laszlo 2008). This has increased the popularity of these fields of study among high school students and intensified the competition among private universities and faculties. Of course the latter are in favor of retaining financial autonomy and are reluctant to commit to institutional integration within HE. However, the recent financial crisis significantly constrained access to public funding and reinforced the arguments in favor of the process of integration which is being actively championed by the Ministry of Education. Nevertheless, there is resistance from the financially better off faculties. Antipathy to a model which means that faculties that generate the highest revenues cannot influence decision-making, goes against old habits and has led to increased conflicts and paralyzed change at the UM, which is the major player in HE in Montenegro. A further aggravating factor with direct implications for the reform process is the competition for students. This is an explicit policy of the UM, prompted by reduced public funding, and increases the ill feeling between the UM and private faculties.

3.3 The Regulatory Framework, Institutional Infrastructure and the HE Policy Making Process in Montenegro

Education reforms in Montenegro have been pursued as part of the overall reform process closely supervised and supported by the international community. The first rounds of reform were undertaken with World Bank support in the early 2000s through a project for pre-university education. Support from the EU followed in line with implementation of the EU accession process, through such schemes as TEMPUS support for HE, and IPA. Other international actors have participated including UNICEF, UNDP, USAID, Open Society Fund, Save the Children, and a number of development agencies and bilateral funders such as the UK DFID, Swedish SIDA, the Austrian WUS, and CARITAS. More recently in 2012, reflecting Montenegro's advancement along the European accession path, Montenegro temporarily closed Chaps. 24 and 25 (Education and Culture, and Science and Research). However, HE remains in need of further reform. In 2011 the World Bank launched a project in support of HE, and Research for Innovation and Competitiveness, which aims to increase competiveness by supporting strategic institutional reforms in HE, improve policy making, and foster research capacity building.

At the local level, the most important actor in the HE reform process is the *Government of Montenegro*. The intensification of relations between the Government of Montenegro and EU institutions and other international institutions (IMF, the World Bank) have largely defined the direction and pace of the changes required. Having signed the contracts with international financial institutions, and agreements with the European institutions, the Government of Montenegro has created the environment for a number of reforms.

Like most countries in the Western Balkans after a turbulent 1990s, Montenegro, has followed a specific development and reform path. This path is evident especially in the run up to becoming an independent state, Montenegro benefited from substantial international presence and funding, and engaged in a series of wide-ranging economic and political reforms. In 2003–2006, Montenegro was granted US $90 million of IDA loans, and in the period 2005–2007 received an additional US$ 42 million. This support was intended primarily for the development of policies and investments in key areas such as energy, health care reform, education, and pension systems. The pre-university education reform process was an initiative of the Government of Montenegro in 2001 supported by the World Bank, and was followed later by HE reform. There was a general consensus that high quality education was fundamental to improving Montenegro's economic development prospects, and that a comprehensive overhaul of the primary and secondary education was needed including curricula reform, new learning objectives, intensive teacher training, and preparation of new textbooks. The Montenegro Education Reform Project 2005–2008 supported by the World Bank aimed to strengthen the capacity of the school system to make continuous improvements, especially in the quality of classrooms, teaching materials, and learning outcomes. Additionally, the project supported the creation of the Examination Center for student assessment and the Bureau of Education Services (BES) for improving teachers' skills. The new Examination Center and the BES built the capacity and put in place the mechanisms for a system of monitoring and planning.[6]

The process of European integration, initiated by the signing of the Stabilization and Association Agreement (SAA) in 2010, and continued through the EU accession negotiations, has formally bound Montenegro to harmonize its legislation with the EU Acquis, and to regularise its attitudes and policies in all areas of cooperation. Thus, further changes and reforms have had to include HE. At the start of the reforms in the early 2000s, the government and the Ministry of Education were supportive of the reforms which initially involved only the UM; however, actual pressure on the UM to reform was quite weak because the reform process coincided with government's participation in activities to secure Montenegro's secession from Serbia. Under those circumstances, government was wary of antagonizing the academic lobby and potentially creating an enemy. The need to balance EU demands to pursue reforms with lack of enthusiasm for reforms from some sections of HE reluctant to change deeply entrenched practices and keen to protect vested interests, meant that there was little incentive to push the reform through. However, over time, and especially since the signing of the SAA, significant progress has been made in aligning the EU and Montenegrin institutional frameworks more closely, ultimately allowing Montenegro to open and close Chaps. 24 and 25 of negotiations with the EU. This means that in terms of procedures and administration of implementation of the Bologna Process, Montenegro has fulfilled its commitments. But strategic change, as the ultimate goal of reform, will still require further policy action as evident in the decision to have another World Bunk-funded program on education reform- the Higher education and research for innovation and competitiveness of Montenegro (HERIC) 2012–2017 is being implemented by the Ministry of Science in cooperation with the Ministry of Education and Sports, and funded by a World Bank loan of $16 million. The aim of the HERIC project is to strengthen the quality and relevance of HE and research in Montenegro by reforming the system of HE funding and quality assurance, and strengthening capacity for research and innovation.

[6] The scale and the results of the project were outstanding and the World Bank declared this project the best in the region in 2009.

Another important policy actor is the *Ministry of Education and Science*.[7] With the significant need for reform to the education process, and the need to manage a large public sector,[8] the Ministry has been led by a combination of university staff and the politicians. The reforms to education policy which started in 2001 with the efforts of the Ministry, were later supported by the World Bank which helped to establish a team of professionals, experts, and enthusiasts active in the field of education. Therefore, with the change of government in late 2002, it was a logical choice to appoint to the minister's position someone who was closely involved in the World Bank-supported project. From 2002 to 2008 the Minister was a university professor. This created a rift between the pro-reform and anti-reform forces within the education sector. However, the authority and enthusiasm of the Minister, and the political support he received from government for the proposed reforms, resulted in the introduction of many changes to the education sector.

However, some among the Ministry officials did not understand the reform process, and saw it as threatening their positions. This problem was partly overcome by recruiting young people, although it proved difficult to break the opposition from senior officers with significant political influence. A group of experts established and trained to participate actively in the World Bank project, was also often used as expert advisors to the Ministry during this period, in preference to the ministry's own staff.

A change in government led to the appointment of a new minister in 2008–2010, who like his predecessor was a university professor. Although familiar with the work of universities and the EHEA project, he lacked knowledge about primary and secondary education and public administration practice. This period was marked by frequent industrial action by teachers and students, who found it difficult to adjust to the changes being introduced. The expert team composed of young and skilled people which had supported the previous minister, left the ministry for better paid jobs outside the public sector. The new minister was forced to rely on ministry officers, who deliberately or unintentionally obstructed reform. At the same time, the application of the new curricula which increased teachers' and principals' workloads, and the announcement of external assessments, led to strikes, work absences and resignations from some school principals and directors of other education institutions. Maintaining normal operation of the education system was the imperative during that period.

In these circumstances, pressure on HE institutions to pursue the reforms entailed in the Bologna Process was minimal. Implementation of the new Law on Higher Education in 2003, was left to the universities. The UM began sporadic and arbitrary implementation of the legislation, choosing what and when it suited them from the reform package. A tradition of university autonomy was often evoked as justification to push back on pressure from the ministry to implement certain reforms.

[7] In 2010 the Ministry of Education and Science was reorganized into two separate ministries, the Ministry for Education and Sports, and the Ministry for Science.

[8] The education sector accounts for about 30 % of the budget of Montenegro and for some 30 % of total public sector employment.

Government for its part was reluctant to confront the university establishment. Ultimately, this situation resulted in another change of minister in 2010. The appointment of a new minister was closely linked to the problems in the pre-university education sector, which were supposed to be addressed as part of the package of reforms agreed with the EU. There was so much controversy that it took six months for the new minister to be appointed. The new minister was a political figure, trusted by the prime minister, and with significant experience in public administration.

The new minister lacked the experience of working in the education sector, and particularly in the field of HE. The main task for the new management was to establish normal operations in the education system, and to perform the tasks required by the imminent opening of negotiations with the EU. The minister relied on ministry staff, who this time adopted a more moderate anti-reform attitude because of the minister's strong political backing. Expedience and efficiency in performing the assigned tasks characterize this leadership.

In 2010, the Ministry of Education and Science was reorganized into the Ministry of Education and Sports, and the Ministry of Science. The Ministry of Science was tasked with coordinating research- related activities, and a professor from a private university was appointed a minister. The Ministry of Science performance was linked to the limited resources channeled into the research and poorly developed innovation system in Montenegro. Several internationally sponsored programs specifically targeted this ministry, such as the World Bank support for a Center of Excellence, grants for equipment, mobility of researchers, etc. The Ministry of Education and Sport has retained jurisdiction over HE policy, so that within the Ministry there is a HE sector with the Deputy Minister responsible for HE.

However, management of the education sector was difficult for ministers with academic and political experience alike. The complexity of the system, constant resistance to change at all levels, and the increasing pressure of the financial crisis, made for very slow change. Thus, the ministry generally complied with the requirements imposed by the EU negotiation process, mostly balancing different interests rather than acting as a strategic force for change.

The third important actor in the process of HE policy making is the universities as the principal service providers. In Montenegro there are currently three universities, one public and two private. UM is the largest one in terms of the scope of programs offered, and staff and student numbers. In order to understand the role of the UM in the policy making process, it is important to keep in mind its rigid understanding of university autonomy which often served to protect tenured academics, but also the politics behind the existing arrangements. In the political context of Montenegro, since the early 2000s, the leadership at UM was controlled by the minority coalition partner the Social Democratic Party (SDP), while the position of the Minister of Education was filled by the ruling party, the Democratic Party of Socialists (DPS). In the HE sector the SDP dominated with numerous positions filled by its members, including the Deputy Minister in charge of HE, the chancellor and the faculty deans. In the context of power-sharing and pressure to maintain the coalition during a very sensitive political period,[9] the DPS did not get closely involved in the activities around the university.

The traditional concept of university autonomy, including significant political autonomy, allowed UM to escape pressure from the Ministry of Education to reform. The result has been survival of historical practices and minimal changes to the curricula. The changes that were implemented were mostly cosmetic, leading to high enrollment rates, high pass rates, and increased revenues from tuition fees. Thus, despite progress in setting up the institutional framework corresponding to the Bologna process, reforms to the education system have been rather modest.

There are still programs in place which for decades have not seen any enrollment, or have had fewer than ten students but they continue to employ large staff (teaching and non-teaching) who in many ways have acted to maintain the status quo in the university system. The recent push towards financial integration in the university leading to a situation where more profitable institutions de facto subsidize less profitable ones while not enjoying input to decision making, has raised tensions within UM, and promoted further arguments about future education reform. Reduced budget allocations certainly put pressure on the university to step up the reform process, which would close some programs, change the profiles of others, and create a viable state-backed university structure. As a consequence of these developments, there has been a shift in the coalition partners' position towards the status of the UM in that the tacit division between the SDP and the DPS is being challenged.

There are some more specific attitudes emerging within the ranks of the DPS for a political takeover of UM through the appointment of the DPS members to the management structure of universities and faculties. These changes are certainly related to the pressure from the EU, and the policy of conditionality under the new loan agreement with the World Bank exclusively designed to support HE, to address many outstanding issues in education sector reform, including that of university funding.

Private universities in Montenegro are a relatively recent phenomenon formed mainly by significant political support, and suffering from lack of funds, premises, and administrative and academic capacity. Despite all the problems faced by UM, students and their parents share the view that it provides the highest quality HE and enrolls the best secondary school students. The, enrollment of mostly average secondary school students significantly affects the output of private universities. The financial crisis has also affected these universities, and has opened new legal opportunities related to accessing public funding for some specific programs, making the private universities more prominent policy actors.

The 2003 Act also created the *Council for Higher Education* as the foremost authority in the area of HE, entrusted with ensuring the quality of HE. The Council conducts analyses of HE, prepares expert proposals to government, and is endowed with special authority to (1) provide opinion on draft strategy for the development

[9] The academic community had a very important and influential role in supporting the project of Montenegrin independence.

of HE, (2) deliberate on standards for the issue, modification, and revocation of licenses, (3) provide advice on the criteria for selection of academic titles, (4) deliberate over standards for HE funding, (5) establish criteria for evaluating academic programs with regard to their compliance with professional requirements and international comparability, (6) conduct periodic quality control of licensed institutions and issue certificates of accreditation or re-accreditation, (7) perform other duties prescribed by this law and the founding act of the Council. The Council is responsible for achieving quality in HE and assisting institutions to improve and maintain the quality of their services. In addition, the Council for Higher Education is the accrediting body, and is responsible for implementation of the quality assurance system which is based on continuous monitoring, control, and reporting.

Despite the Council's extraordinary powers, it has neither achieved full autonomy or its stipulated role, nor has it developed organizational capacity to accomplish its tasks. For finance, the Council remains dependent on the government, and for administrative, physical, and organizational issues dependent on the Ministry (Montenegrin Academy of Science and Arts 2010a). The Council failed to constitute permanent bodies and thus to enrich the institutional framework, exercise control, or initiate significant regulatory action (Montenegrin Academy of Science and Arts 2010a). Its role effectively has been reduced to a formal accreditation body, which is at odds with its legal mandate to improve the quality of HE.[10]

One of the key concepts of the Bologna Process is to make HE more student oriented, so that *students* become partners in the education process, which represents a significant change in the context of HE in Montenegro. Student participation in relevant managing bodies currently stands at 15 % with the goal of increasing it to 25 %. However, despite formal representation, the actual influence of the student body in the decision making process is limited. There is no tradition of active engagement of students, and no effective system to disseminate the experience of working in education-related decision making bodies among the general student population.

The NGO sector is another potentially important policy actor. This role is quite new and underdeveloped in Montenegro. There is a clear lack of civic awareness related to activities in this area and only a very small part of civic sector is engaged in the work of HE institutions, e.g. the Center for Civic Education and the Center for Monitoring (CEMI). The NGOs so far have dealt mainly with issues of corruption in the field of HE. According to studies conducted by NGOs, 30 % of the population believes that the state university is corrupt, and the percentage is significantly higher (44 %) for private universities[11] (Center for Civic Education 2011, 2012).

The Chamber of Commerce and the Employment Agency do not play a formal role in creating HE output. This is a significant weakness in the overall policy making framework because the impact of the business community is critical for aligning

---

[10] Because of the importance of the Council, Component 1 of the World Bank loan is dedicated specifically to promotion of its work.

[11] Corrupt practices are evident in the allocation of places to student dormitories and admissions to university.

curricula with the needs of the labor market (Chamber of Commerce 2012). In summary, the Bologna Process has introduced institutional reforms in the Montenegro HE system in terms of putting in place the basic architecture of relevant institutions but in most cases this has not been fully developed and the influence of these institutions does not reflect formal provision. The institutional autonomy and coordinated activity of policy actors is limited since most continue to receive financial resources directly from the ministry. The Ministry of Education and Sports is the umbrella institution responsible for HE policy and the Higher Education Department, with the result that decision-making remains quite centralized.

4 Conclusions

Socio-economic changes in the young democracy of Montenegro have necessitated reform to the education system, especially the HE sector, in order to support and accelerate the process of transition and fulfill the European integration objective. Highly educated young individuals are the most important factor for building a modern, democratic society able to implement and develop European values of democracy, rule of law, and respect for minorities. The Bologna Process is the basic framework for the transformation and reform of HE on the European continent (Zgaga 2010), aimed at building more competitive and knowledge based economies, and it has been pursued by Montenegro as the major path to reforming this country's education system.

Implementation of the Bologna Process in Montenegro has resulted in significant reforms with varying effects on all the actors involved in this process. The changes introduced include Europe-wide recognition of university degrees, qualification frameworks, quality assurance, and accreditation systems. Overall, the principles of the Bologna Process have been implemented in Montenegro in a technical, normative, and organizational sense.[12] The specific changes to HE in Montenegro introduced as a result of the implementation of the Bologna Process include significant reduction in study duration, better organization of the education process, and the possibility to obtain an internationally recognized diploma. However, much remains to be done. For example, with regards to the role of private education institutions which were meant to fill the gaps in the state sponsored system and contribute to developing competitive skills.

In practice, the introduction of three-cycle training has been difficult, and the greatest obstacle to reform has been the structure of previously established universities, primarily the intransigence of UM in relation to undertaking the necessary reforms. Although the emergence of private institutions opened an opportunity to increase the competition and thus improve the quality of education, the regulator

[12]This is indicated by evaluations obtained at the Ministerial Conferences which measure the implementation of the Bologna Process among the signatory countries, where Montenegro has achieved the highest rating of 3.88 at the last Ministerial Conference held in Bucharest in 2012.

has lacked incentives to ensure creation of conducive environment (Montenegrin Academy of Science and Arts 2010a).

Having in mind relatively short period of implementation of the reforms in HE, it is hard to estimate real impacts and contribution to the development of a desirable level of skills for highly competitive markets of twenty-first century as one of the key drivers of HE reforms. On current reading of the progress in the HE reforms, it is fair to say that expectation of Bologna Process and its role in contributing to the development of skills in support of the knowledge economy in Montenegro has been exaggerated.

The implementation of reforms needs reliable expert and administrative teams, which were originally lacking among decision makers (Huge and Tauch 2001). Incentives and directions provided by the international community have affected the behavior of domestic interest groups, which ultimately has determined the scope and outcomes of reforms. The most important actor was the Ministry of Education and Science, and subsequently, the Ministry of Education and Sport, and the Ministry of Science. Reform in HE has been accompanied by governance reform, i.e. moving from a state-governance model to one of state supervision. Unfortunately, some elements of the new model were introduced but not fully developed and clarified (Montenegrin Academy of Science and Arts 2010a). Supervision of the HE system is still over politicized and centralized (Orosz 2008), with the Ministry of Education and Sport the most important and the most powerful institution in the HE policy making process. The reform path characterizes the tension among ministries' pro- reform approach, and resistance from the UM to fully accept reforms (Montenegrin Academy of Science and Arts 2010a).[13] After almost a decade of HE reforms, the institutional infrastructure of HE, and cooperation among different actors involved in the policy making process are still underdeveloped.

The next phase of reforms should focus on more substantial transformation which will mostly rely on decentralization of HE which should strengthen the policy actors. A history of central planning has proved inauspicious ground for developing a culture of active participation of all stakeholders – Councils (Higher Education and Science), Chamber of Commerce, labor market, students and NGOs – in the process of decision makings.

The changes is likely to be gradual, and the next phase of the Bologna process should focus on building capacity among stakeholders to allow better performance of their respective roles. In the next 10 years of Bologna Process implementation support will be needed from the EU and international partners to further develop the culture and practice of decentralization, and exchanges within the Western Balkans region and with international community in order to increase the quality of HE in Montenegro.

Acknowledgements I want to express especial appreciation to Mr. Predrag Miranovic, PhD, Rector of the University of Montenegro, Ms. Mubera Kurpejovic, Deputy Minister at the Department for Higher Education at the Ministry of Education and Sport, Ms. Biljana Misovic

[13] Reforms based on Bologna Process requirements.

Independent Counselor at the Department for Higher Education, Mr. Mitar Misovic, PhD, Director of Quality Assurance Center at the University of Montenegro, for valuable comments and guidance for this chapter. I also want to thank Mr. Igor Radusinovic, PhD (Council for Science), Mr. Mladen Perazic, PhD (Chamber of Commerce), Mr. Ilija Kaludjerovic, Student representative at the Faculty of Economics. In addition I want to express special gratitude to Ms. Danijela Grba Vukajlovic (World Bank office in Montenegro), Ms. Mladenka Tesic (the EU Delegation in Montenegro), Ms. Daliborka Uljarevic (Center for Civic Education), and Mr. Zlatko Vujovic (Center for Monitoring) for their help and cooperation.

References

Barro, R. (1999). Determinants of democracy. *Journal of Political Economy, 107*(1), 158–183.

Centar for Civic Education, & CEMI. (2011). Fight against corruption in higher education. Podgorica: CEMI. http://www.cemi.org.me/me/Borba-protiv-korupcije/487-Borba-protiv-korupcije-u-obrazovanju-u-Crnoj-Gori.html

Centar for Civic Education, & CEMI. (2012). *How much for exam? Knowledge in (not) for grant.* Podgorica: CEMI. http://www.behance.net/gallery/Poto-ispit/3285332

Chamber of Commerce. (2012). *High education in Montenegro*. Podgorica: Chamber of Commerce. www.pkcg.org

Campos, N. F., & Dean, J. (2003). After, before and during: Returns to education in Hungary (1986–1998). *Economic Systems, 27*, 377–390.

Charlier, J.-É. (2006). Qui veut encore harmoniserl'enseignementsupérieureuropéen'? *Reflets et perspectives de la vie économique, 45*(2), 23–30.

Croché, S. (2009). Bologna network: A new sociopolitical area in higher education. *Globalisation, Societies and Education, 7*(4), 489–503.

European Commission. (2010). *Focus on higher education in Europe 2010: New report on the impact of the Bologna process*, MEMO/10/68. Brussels: European Commission. http://europa.eu/rapid/pressReleasesAction

European Commission. (2011). *Supporting growth and jobs – An agenda for the modernization of Europe's higher education systems*. Brussels: European Commission.

Garben, S. (2010). The Bologna process: From a European law perspective. *European Law Journal, 16*(2), 186–210.

Glaeser, E., Florencio, R., & Shleifer, A. (2004). Do institutions cause growth? *Journal of Economic Growth, 9*, 271–303.

Hanushk, E. A., & Kimko, D. D. (2000). Schooling, labor-force quality, and the growth of nations. *American Economic Review, 90*(5), 1184–1208.

Huge, G., & Tauch, C. (2001). *Towards the European higher education area: Survey of main reforms from Bologna to Prague. Summary and conclusions*. www.eua.be/fileadmin/user_upload/files/EUA1_documents/OFFDOC_BP_trend_II.1068715483262.pdf.

Havas, A. (2009). Universities and the emerging new players: Building futures for higher education. *Technology Analysis & Strategic Management, 21*(3), 425–443.

Jamison, E.A., Jamison, D.T., & Hanushek, A.E. (2006). The effects of education quality on income growth and mortality decline. *NBER Working Paper, 12652*, 1–28.

Krueger, B.A., & Lindahl, M. (2000). Education for growth: Why and from whom? *NBER Working Paper, 7591*, 1–26

Laszlo, B. (2008). The impact of the Bologna process on higher education in Slovakia. *European Education, 20*(2), 46–65.

Luca, F., Paternostro, S., & Tiongson, E. R. (2007). Returns to education in the economic transition: A systematic assessment using comparable data. *World Bank Policy Research Working Paper, 4225*, 1–45.

Lucin, P., & Prijic-Samarzija, S. (2011). The Bologna process as a reform initiative in higher education in Croatia. *European Education, 43*(3), 24–42.

Montenegrin Academy of Science and Arts. (2010a). *Montenegro in the New Millennium. Education*. CANU: Podgorica.

Montenegrin Academy of Science and Arts. (2010b). *Montenegro in the new millennium. Macroeconomics*. Podgorica: CANU.

Montenegrin Academy of Science and Arts. (2010c). *Montenegro in the new millennium-science and technique*. Podgorica: CANU.

Official Journal of the European Union. (2010). *Council conclusions of 11 May 2010 on the internationalization of higher education*. Brussels: Official Journal of the European Union 2010/C 135/04. http://eur-lex.europa.eu/LexUriServ/OJ:C:2010:135:0012:0014:EN:PDF

Orosz, A. (2008). The Bologna process in Croatia. *European Education, 40*(2), 66–84.

Papaioannou, E., & Siourounis, G. (2005). Economic and social factors driving the third wave of democratization. *Mimeo*, London Business School.

Rander-Pehrson, J. (1999). *Germany and the revolution of 1848–1849*. New York: Peter Lang.

Reinhile, V., & Mrak, M. (2009). *The knowledge economy and catching-up member states of the Europen Union*. Report prepared for the Commissioner's Potocnik's expert group knowledge for growth. http://ec.europa.eu/invest-in-research/pdf/download_en/kfg_report_no5.pdf.

Topel, R. (1999). Labor markets and economic growth. In O. Ashenfelter & D. Card (Eds.), *Handbook of labor economics*. Amsterdam/New York/Oxford: Elsevier Science North-Holland.

World Bank. (2011). Project appraisal document on a proposed loan in the amount of Eur 12 million (us$15.98 million equivalent) to Montenegro for the higher education and research for innovation and competitiveness project. http://www-wds.worldbank.org/external/default/fficial0use0only090.txt

World Bank. (2012). Skills, not just diplomas managing education for results in Eastern Europe and Central Asia. http://siteresources.worldbank.org/ECAEXT/Resources/101411_FullReport.pdf

Zgaga, P. (2010). *Bologna: Achievements, challenges and perspectives 1999–2011*. Brussels: European University Association.

Zgaga, P., Klemencic, M., Komljenovic, J., Miklavic, K., et al. (2013). *Higher education in the Western Balkans: Reforms, developments, trends*. Ljubljana: Faculty of Education.

Chapter 9
Managing the Financial Crisis: Credit Crunch and Response in Serbia

Srdjan Marinković

1 Introduction

In the autumn of 2008, Serbia experienced combined banking and currency turbulence as the impact of the global financial crisis unfolded. The impact on the Serbian economy can be traced and synthesized through a series of inter-related events. First, the international banks started withdrawing funds from their local Serbian subsidiaries, causing a decrease in international reserves from March to September in 2008. This triggered depositors' anxiety, which, coupled with indecisiveness on the part of the authorities, immediately resulted in a run on the banks as Serbian depositors rushed to withdraw their funds particularly from the foreign-owned banks, which were perceived as the most fragile. For Serbia, this phase of crisis produced devastating results: foreign currency savings in the banking system were reduced by 20 % and some 977 million Euros in foreign currency deposits were withdrawn during the last quarter of 2008. Despite the Central Bank's massive intervention on the foreign exchange market, the Serbian dinar lost 20 % of its nominal value against the euro between October 10, 2008 and the end of January 2009. The authorities finally admitted that Serbia's available international reserves could not provide sufficient coverage, and, after drawing down precautionary credit line provided by the International Monetary Fund (IMF) sought additional support through a new Stand-by Arrangement.

This short episode is far more important than it appears at first glance since it was the first wave of a larger impending crisis. The credit contraction that immediately followed this incident was mostly a consequence of the bank run. The sudden stop in credit activities is the first issue that deserves consideration. That, together with an increase in deposit rates, loan rates and interest rate spread threatened to create a

S. Marinković, Ph.D. (✉)
Faculty of Economics, University of Niš, Niš, Serbia
e-mail: srdjan.marinkovic@gmail.com

M. Thomas, V. Bojicic-Dzelilovic (eds.), *Public Policy Making in the Western Balkans*, DOI 10.1007/978-94-017-9346-9_9

hostile credit environment. Preemptive action staved off worsening of credit conditions into a sharp credit crunch in the next year. The coalition consisting of the main stakeholders (foreign banks, National Bank of Serbia, IMF) was built up to alleviate the unfolding credit crunch. This firefighting measure postponed the issue, but not indefinitely.

In the Republic of Serbia, the late 2008 slowing down of credit activity came after years of continuously rising bank credit to the private sector. The credit boom raised the debt and made cost of funds increasingly dependent on the future exchange rate and on borrowing conditions in the global economy. The entire local economic system gradually increased its sensitivity to currency risk, which made the solvency-type of disturbance a plausible scenario for the future.

Was this a case of bad luck or bad policy? There are many economic variables (so-called fundamentals) that could possibly drive credit market conditions. In emerging markets none of the variables is purely market driven. They are strongly managed by policy makers, so that economic failure is most plausibly explained by citing the policy failure argument rather than by blaming market forces. This chapter examines the policy choices and the process through which the choices were made, with a close look at the role of specific policy actors. The chapter primarily investigates the case of Serbia, but also makes broader reflections on the Western Balkan.

1.1 Defining Credit Crunch

Despite its unquestioned practical importance in economic theory, *credit crunch* is not a uniquely defined concept. Udell (2009, 1) defines 'a credit crunch as a significant contraction in the supply of credit reflected in a tightening of credit conditions'. Similarly, Bernanke and Lown (2001, 207) definc it as 'a significant leftward shift in the supply curve for bank loans, holding constant both the *safe real interest rate* and the *quality of potential borrowers*' (italics added). Although, the latter definition might appear clear and elegant in theory, empirically, it is not easy to apply. First, both elements that must stay constant are expected to change as credit conditions worsen. Further, conditions of credit supply and demand are mutually dependent, and it is extremely hard to distinguish which comes first: does supply accommodate to changes in demand or vice versa.

It is difficult to determine if the credit crunch represents an exclusively supply-side phenomenon or a mixture of developments involving both the supply and the demand side of the credit market. The issue is important from the policy stance, since, if the contraction of outstanding credit is caused by weak credit demand, it is probably only another reflection of the economy's slowdown. If not, the causality is exactly the opposite and merits scrutiny.

Moreover, the credit crunch can be taken as an *independent* cause of economic slowdown if the credit contraction is not followed by simultaneous contraction in banks' financial resources. In that case, the credit cuts are the consequence of bank asset reallocation or other determinants that spur substitution out of claims (on the private sector) that are now perceived riskier.

If the contraction of funds available to creditors for lending (loanable funds) precedes credit cuts, fewer funds available to (private) business borrowers and households could be the consequence of shrinkage in available resources. If loanable funds are reduced to the same extent as financial resources (that is, without an additional amplifying effect from a portfolio shift towards safe assets), credit crunch is a channel that transmits already present crisis signals. Thus, it does not cause but only propagates economic crisis. In the search for culprits, analysis must address the forces that drive the most important bank resources. For a credit market (and banking industry), which depends on external funds, these are foreign capital and deposits.

2 Policy Description and Analysis

2.1 *Boom-Bust Pattern in the Dynamics of Credit Aggregates: Empirical Evidence*

An empirical study of any credit crunch episode must look at the changes in the amount of credit outstanding to find trend reversals. In the Republic of Serbia, slowing down of credit activity came after several years of continuously rising bank credit to the private sector. The trend was one of region-wide development, and the countries in the region differed mostly in their turning points (see Cottarelli et al. 2005). The data in that study do not cover the most recent period. In Table 9.1 I filled that gap. It is apparent that in the case of Serbia the trend continued. The growth rate of bank credit to private sector for the period 2003–2008 was on average 28.87 %.

The rapid credit growth in the region was extensively studied (Kraft and Jankov 2005; Cottarelli et al. 2005; Boissay et al. 2005; Égert et al. 2006; Kiss et al. 2006; Djankov et al. 2007; Zdzienicka 2009). Most earlier papers found that rising credit-to-GDP can be explained as convergence towards equilibrium. The findings of Boissay et al. (2005) challenge the aforementioned view in that experienced credit growth could not be explained solely on the basis of fast economic expansion, declining interest rates or catching-up in incomes. Additionally, the findings suggest that the choice of exchange rate regime can be usefully implemented as a determinant of credit growth. With strong reliance on foreign resources, as a common feature,

Table 9.1 Bank credit to private sector in Serbia (2003–2008)

	2003	2004	2005	2006	2007	2008
GDP real growth rate	2.5	9.3	5.4	3.6	5.4	3.8
GDP (EUR) growth rate	7.9	9.8	6.8	15.0	22.0	14.8
BCPS (EUR) growth rate	19.1	26.9	41.6	26.9	39.8	20.7
BCPS/GDP change	10.4	15.5	32.6	10.4	14.5	5.2

Source: National Bank of Serbia 2013, 'Statistical Bulletin', December (author's recalculations)

countries in the region were able to boost foreign credit inflow, opting for a more rigid exchange rate regime. The suggestion is in line with the findings of more recent studies of credit growth determinants in the region. For peer countries, Mladenović and Palić (2009) found credit growth significantly influenced by economic activity, real interest rate, and nominal and real exchange rate. Exclusively for Serbia, somewhat surprisingly, it can be attributed to the nominal exchange rate volatility, and to a much lesser extent to the real lending rate. However, a statistical inference based on time series analysis, which does not factor in a switch in regime, leads to spurious results. In the entire period the Republic of Serbia faced several types of regime change: the capital account was liberalised de jure (2006), while the switch in exchange rate policy happened several times. In the next sections I will address this issue.

In Serbia, the initial rise was fueled by a surge in deposits in early 2002. It was also the main force for maintaining the upward trend until the last quarter of 2008, when the banking crisis struck.

The evolution of bank liabilities was homogeneous throughout the period preceding the crisis (Appendix Table 9.2). In all the years, the increase in bank credit to private sector (BCPS) reflected increased bank intermediation. Deposits rose, as did outstanding credit. Interestingly, in all but one period (first quarter 2008) it was followed by increase in bank claims on the National Bank of Serbia (NBS).

The expansion of BCPS was not constrained by the availability of domestic funds. The rise in the BCPS ratio was also supported by increased net borrowing from abroad. Thus, foreign capital inflow played an equally important role in funding the lending boom. Serbia opened its doors to foreign banks in 2002; the channel opened widely in 2004 when foreign bank acquisitions expanded. Bank borrowing was very strong from early 2004 to 2006; then fell dramatically because a cheaper alternative was found: direct cross-border borrowings by local corporate businesses. In fact, early credit activity from local bank units was later substituted for credit support from parent bank companies, with or without explicit guarantees from their local bank units (Appendix Table 9.3). Direct cross-border borrowings by enterprises slowed down at the end of 2008, and there was a similar contraction in foreign trade credit. Simultaneously, the local banking industry faced a decrease of its foreign debt (EUR 132 million). After a reversal in December, foreign credit again turned into outflow in January 2009.

Although borrowing abroad and rise in deposits can be treated as two alternative sources for raising credit, those two flows are closely linked. It would be wrong to attach too much weight to deposit rise to explain credit growth. Because of the so-called deposit-credit multiplications, even a small initial rise in available funds (for example, from abroad) can eventually produce a much bigger increase in both credit and deposit levels. Thus, the real question is how much of the deposit rise is actually induced by increased foreign borrowings.

To explore details, annual data for the last 2 years have been divided into quarters (see Appendix Table 9.2). In the last quarter of 2008, the Republic of Serbia faced for the first time a reversal in growth of bank credit to the private sector (−5.0 %). By using methodology similar to that of Cottarelli et al. (2005), I calculated that net foreign liabilities contributed to the decline by 0.3 %.[1] Solely on the basis of deposit contraction, the rate of decline would be 13.3 %; however, it was completely offset by an outwards portfolio shift of bank claims on the NBS (14.1 %). The main components of the banks' claims on NBS (reserve requirements and repo stock) moved in the opposite direction. There was a meltdown of repo stock, the most effectively alleviated credit contraction (16.9 %), contrary to mandatory reserves, which were increasing at the time. Thanks to NBS' response of change in currency composition of mandatory reserves, liquidity-squeezed banks had mandatory reserves of foreign currency at their disposal. Effectively, excess dinar liquidity was converted into deficient foreign liquidity, which suffered the strongest pressure both due to foreign capital outflow and depositors' rush. This is why banks' dinar and foreign currency reserves at the NBS moved in the opposite direction. The measure helped the banking industry to back up full convertibility and 'redeemability' of customers' deposits, while at the same time mitigated the pressure on the exchange rate. A common assessment is that the local currency would have reported a more rapid drop in value against the reserve currency if this measure had not been enacted.

The regularity was similar to the first quarter of the following year. Thus, one can conclude that the deposit contraction induced by the bank run is almost solely responsible for the credit contraction that followed in the next two quarters. Asset portfolio readjustments (towards safe assets) as well as foreign capital movement did not provoke additional credit contraction.

2.2 *Was There Something Fundamentally Wrong?*

It is obvious that the swing in foreign credit flow contributed to the boom-bust credit cycle. How much, if any, does excessive local return explain foreign credit inflow? Local currency–denominated (nominal) return on the credit portfolio in Serbia was huge in comparison to other countries in the region. However, it plays a secondary role in explaining the extent of foreign inflow and consequently the lending boom. The prime role should be attributed to exchange rate dynamics. Namely, that high return was merely a consequence of continuously appreciated local currency. Figure 9.1 shows the excessive real appreciation of local currency.

The real exchange rate RSD/EUR is derived from a nominal exchange rate index, adjusted for relative consumer prices in Serbia and the Eurozone. First it is expressed as a base index (June 2005 = 100); then, since not all real appreciation reflects disequilibrium phenomena, I focus on deviations of the real exchange rate from

[1] The construction of the table needed some recalculations. Negative values indicate negative influence of the specific element on the rise of BCPS. In the case of 'bank credit to the public sector' or 'claims on NBS', as it is a bank asset item, negative figures mean positive contribution to the growth of BCPS. Other items, which are (generically or in net amount) sources of bank funds; positive values indicate rise in specific source and consequently its positive contribution to financing growth of BCPS.

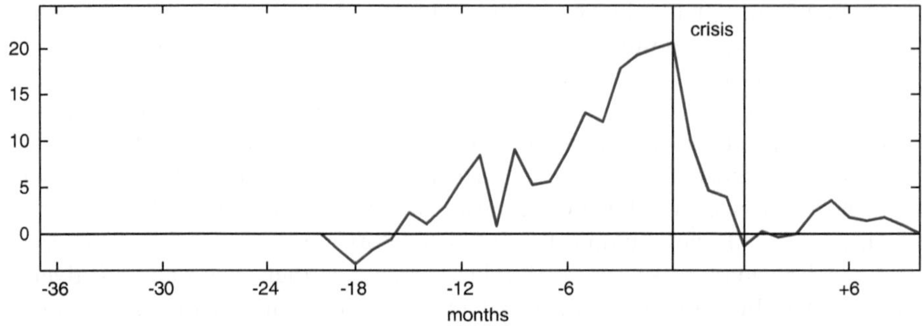

Fig. 9.1 Real exchange rate: deviations from the Trend (Source: NBS, Statistical Bulletin, Table 20: Exchange Rates, column 12 (for nominal exchange rate); NBS, Table 26: Consumer Prices, Cost of Living and Producer Prices, column 8 (for domestic consumer price index); *Eurostat* for percentage change m/m-1 HICP (Harmonised Indices of Consumer Prices) in euro area 10–13 (changing composition))

trend. The trend was specified as a linear 3-year time series—a slope coefficient is calculated for the period January 2007–November 2009, and the relevant monthly data are interpolated. The presented data are calculated as a percentage deviation of actual real exchange rate data from the data expressing the trend. According to this methodology, on the eve of the crisis, the local currency was at least 20 % above the purchasing power parity that presumably has been held seven quarters ago.

It is noteworthy that economic theory (Balassa 1964; Taylor and Taylor 2004; Lothian and Taylor 2008) supports the view that some extent of real exchange rate appreciation accompanies a fast-growing economy, which builds its competitiveness. However, it is never straightforward on how to read the data on real appreciation, as to aligning or misaligning in each specific occasion. However, economic theory still holds strong consensus that in the last decade currency appreciated more heavily in Serbia than in any other country in the region (IMF 2009, 9). Local authorities and some professional economists earlier on (for example, Stamenković et al. 2004) neglected threats from real appreciation, and responded that moving towards purchasing power parity would produce no real sustainable positive effect on the trade deficit, highlighting the necessity for structural reforms. As time went on, the gap widened and warnings from academia grew louder (Arsić et al. 2005; Madžar 2006). Despite this, some officials continued to argue that exchange rate depreciation would not boost export competitiveness (Dragutinović 2008). There is also some empirical evidence that partially supports the view of the weak response of exports (as well as imports) to real exchange rate (Tasić and Zdravković 2008). The study blames prodigal public expenditure for weak export performance. This is probably true, since the exchange rate is just one input in a complex formula of export competitiveness. However, it is clear that an overvalued rate could have a damaging effect on export. Furthermore, although some studies tend to capture long-term effects, the question is whether one decade is long enough to produce adverse effects from undermined incentives for businesses to enter export-oriented industries. This adverse effect would probably result after a longer time lag.

2.2.1 Feeding the Bubble

It is unclear whether foreign banks were attracted by a high return on the credit market or by being able to speculate on a risk-free NBS repo market. There is also the feeling that the way NBS sterilised growth in money stock and credit aggregates created a kind of speculative bubble. A preliminary analysis is that both motivations played a role in drawing foreign banks. Every year from 2003 to 2008, growth of bank credit to the private sector was reduced because increased available funds were partially diverted towards the claims on NBS. A peak was reached in 2006, when, on account of the rapid rise in banks' claims on NBS, bank credit to the private sector exhibited a 61.5 % smaller growth rate (Table 9.2, line 2.1). Given the economic meaning of the presented numbers, this suggests that the growth rate of BCPS would have tripled if the banks' position on NBS had not changed. In other words, in 2006 more than two-thirds of the increase of banks' financial resources was directed into the claims on NBS, leaving only one-third for the private sector. This change very nearly corresponds to the change in repo stock and other claims, predominantly mandatory reserves.

As a standard central bank monetary policy instrument, the NBS used repo operations to control the money supply and inflation. Although this was the second most intensively used monetary instrument, the rationale for using it must be considered in connection with a very stringent reserve requirement policy. Repos were introduced to complement and relax the pressure of the reserve requirements which some considered repressive. How excessive was the yield on NBS' short-term securities? The yield was just slightly above the consumer price inflation rate and several times lower than the rate banks regularly earned on consumer loans. Nevertheless, the real exchange rate appreciation is what made the yield on NBS' securities rather high, when converting it into its euro equivalent, as well as all domestic financial return. Finally, one should bear in mind that NBS bills are the only usable assets to serve as secondary liquidity reserve. From this brief narrative, it is clear that the increased capital inflows can be attributed to a considerable extent to high real return garnered by foreign creditors.

Therefore, a critical policy flaw was the way in which NBS sterilised money stock. Repo operations are surely beneficial in restructuring the size of assets on a bank balance sheet. The instrument is designed to induce a (voluntary) shift from the credit portfolio to risk-free claims on NBS, or to absorb the excess dinar liquidity of banks. It works well, at least theoretically. However, the risk of using this instrument for money sterilisation lies in the very design of the instrument. To be effective it must avoid misalignment. The gap in fundamentals (the interest rate differential) must be closed to stimulate the portfolio shift without any further stimulus for banks to raise additional external funds. However, if the differential remains persistently wide in favour of local assets, an increase of the repo rate would further sharpen it. The ultimate success of such a monetary policy instrument rests critically on the assumption that the liability side of the bank balance sheet remains intact. However, it never does. Interest rate differential stimulates foreign credit inflow. As the level of credit inflow rises, the higher volume of operations is expected to serve the purpose of sterilisation, and the operations gradually slip from 'fine tuning' to a peculiar speculative bubble. According to official statistics (NBS), since their introduction in January 2005, repo operations have recorded a steady increase. The operations gained momentum during 2006, when the repo stock literally exploded (sevenfold increase from the beginning to the end of the year). The repo stock continued to rise in 2007 in spite of the stop in direct bank borrowing from abroad. It reached a record high (RSD 234 billion) at the end of the third quarter of 2008, immediately before the crisis erupted. At that time repo stock accounted for 12.7 % of the banking industry balance sheet (together with other claims on NBS, the amount reached 31.4 %).

The size of the operations and consequently the size of the repo stock were demand-driven. On its regular weekly auctions NBS offers an unlimited number of the bills with a so-called fixed rate (price). Interviewed NBS officials stated that the excess demand for bills is attributable to politically driven expansionary fiscal policy, which boosted the money supply. As anecdotal evidence they emphasise the struggle between the IMF and government officials about the strong penchant for pension spending or irresponsible spending of public money on special occasions (for instance when a party left the government). There are also pure economic foundations for monetary expansion, for example, capital inflow from privatisations or foreign credits. The question is whether there was a better alternative to repo sterilisation. Casual empiricism indicates that there was not. For example, a prudent measure introduced in June 2006 to stop further expansion of consumer loans (and trade deficit), which linked outstanding credit for this purpose to twice the amount of bank equity, completely failed. The banks immediately drove additional equity from their parent groups, and boosted currency appreciation and consequently trade deficit.[2] The final result was exactly the opposite of what was intended. Sometimes, the cure and the poison are the same, but the quantity is what matters. It seems that the economy has taken too much cure. If the official (repo) rate has not been excessively high relative to the yield available on the credit portfolio, what makes it so attractive to banks?

2.2.2 Uncovered Interest Disparity

Another way for an overvalued currency to adversely affect the economy can be explained from a financial perspective. The authorities, by controlling the exchange rate (by rule or discretion) to slow ongoing domestic inflation, could potentially create a distortion in the capital market as well as the aforementioned trade implications. Namely, 'as long as the "peg" holds and domestic inflation continues, the effective rate of return, seen by domestic investors, falls below the real return garnered by foreign creditors. Thus, without exchange controls the differential encourages excess inflow of capital' (McKinnon 2000, 159). Thus, real appreciation

[2] The effect of banks' capitalisation is reported in the position *Other net liabilities* (Table 9.2, line 5) jointly with loan loss reserves, investment in fixed assets and some other positions.

potentially distorts a parity condition, probably the one that is most important for countries with liberalised capital accounts.

Uncovered interest parity (UIP) is a nonarbitrage-supported equilibrium condition that links the yield on two comparable assets denominated in different currencies. According to theory, the currency that earns the higher rate of return should depreciate until the end of the holding period. Unfortunately, empirical evidence largely contradicts the theory. UIP is frequently regarded as a good test of market efficiency (unbiased forecast) if all input variables are determined solely by market forces. However, in emerging markets none of the variables satisfies the 'free-market' condition. These are strongly managed by policy makers, so that the failure of UIP points more to policy failure than to market failure.

Prima facie, it may appear that strong local currency disfavours those who exchange foreign assets for local (Serbian dinar) assets—that is, foreign investors and creditors. However, this way of thinking is misleading. The effect of strong local currency is exactly the opposite. What really matters for foreign investors are the terms on which they enter the market relative to the terms available when they exit the market. If, in the meantime, the exchange rate remains the same, they would receive excess return that equals the interest rate differential.

In international finance literature, this excess return is often attributed to exchange rate risk or uncertainty over the future course of the exchange rate. However, if there is a strong commitment on the part of local authorities to support local currency (de jure or de facto), uncertainty vanishes and the excess return becomes 'easy catch'. If the exchange rate stays overvalued over a prolonged period, by extrapolation from the past, it heightens expectations over the future course of the exchange rate policy. Despite common assessment that such a policy cannot last forever, it is still plausible that it can last for some time. Instead of forecasting pure market forces, the market participants forecast a break or serious pressure that will force the authorities to leave the former policy course. If anticipated, the break will produce the opposite business strategy that will precipitate the crash. Everyone will join the queue for the most favourable terms to convert local to foreign assets. In financial terminology, one would say that before the crisis, foreign creditors took a short foreign and long domestic position, or they bet on a strong Serbian dinar.

Figure 9.2 presents what the 'short foreign, long domestic' position earns on interest rate differential net of exchange rate changes, posting the arbitrage on money markets. We see that in all times preceding and following the crisis, the (speculative) arbitrage gain was positive, while during crisis times, it was reversed.

Who else bet on the same side? For different reasons, but sharing the same assumption about the future, bank borrowers as well as many businesses took the same position. Bank borrowers were willing to take debt denominated (or indexed) in foreign currency since it was seen as a cost-effective alternative to taking dinar liabilities. Interestingly, overvalued local currency failed to stimulate savers to take the long position in local currency. Besides financing matters, business units show a strong propensity to place themselves in import-related activities and the nontradable sector, so that the decade was lost without any success in restructuring the economy towards a more balanced foreign trade.

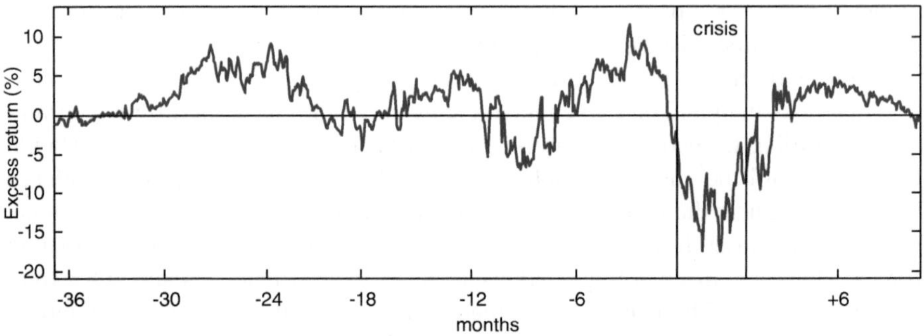

Fig. 9.2 Deviations from uncovered interest parity (Source: Deviations from UIP (excess return) are expressed as nominal interest rate differential subject to changes in exchange rate. Domestic interest rate is Belgrade Overnight Index Average (BEONIA), while for the foreign interest rates EONIA (European Overnight Index Average). It is calculated assuming position rollover and monthly trading (forecasting) window)

If UIP continuously holds, no participant will be awarded excess return. The policy (or mistake) of tolerating UIP deviations was not unique to Serbia. It was a South East Europe (SEE)-wide prescription, but not without exceptions. Slovenia, for instance, escaped this trap simply by implementing the UIP as an explicit rule in managing the exchange rate. The exchange rate was continuously managed to wipe out any extra stimulus for foreign (speculative) capital to enter the country. It may seem an unnecessarily isolating or protective measure with adverse consequence on credit growth, but ultimately it has proved the only beneficial policy.

Ultimately, all this contributed to excessive dollarisation, which made it extremely difficult to implement an effective crisis resolution package. From the central bank's perspective, a run on the currency and a run on banks in a highly dollarised economy have similarly dangerous implications. International reserves had to withstand all the pressure, being the only buffer to bank runs and reversal of foreign capital flow. In the case of Serbia the rationally (externally) driven rush of foreign portfolio investors, creditors and depositors coincided with and enforced each other. Three months after the eruption of the crisis, the banking system solved a full-blown liquidity crisis with fewer resources available.

Taken together, trade (deficit) and financial consequences (excessive credit growth and consequently credit crunch as well as financial dollarisation) mirror the ultimate scale of the issue of overvalued currency. The credit boom raised the debt and made cost of funds increasingly dependent on the future exchange rate and borrowing conditions in the global economy. Although banks were hedged against direct balance sheet exposure to currency risk (thanks to the prudential regulative), the overall economic system gradually increased its sensitivity to currency risk—making the solvency-type of disturbance a plausible scenario for the future.

3 Description of the Policy Process and Analysis

The analysis presented in the previous section indicates that there were some inconsistent or even conflicting policy choices, which contributed to the economy's vulnerability. This assessment is based solely on published hard data. The following analysis is based on soft data collected through interviews of a group of officials formerly in high executive positions in the government and the National Bank of Serbia. The author was able to challenge their positions and to delve into details of the peculiar process of policy making.

Two points will be addressed here. First, why have such misalignments (overvalued local currency) been tolerated for so long? Second, why has the authorities' response to crisis been weak and unconvincing? The foundations of the crisis were laid down years before it escalated, and its roots probably lie in the way public choices are made, e.g. in terms of exchange rate policy. The measures that are expected to realign fundamentals may face strong opposition. However, prompt crisis resolution measures rarely face strong opposition since they are urgently needed. Avoiding disaster is socially beneficial, so that a weak response is attributable to an inefficient policy-making process. Let us first discuss whether and, if so, why the authorities were not ready to take measures against the currency overvaluation.

3.1 Reluctance to Devalue or Fear of Floating

Let us first look at the policy of exchange rate. A pure float is an artifact of economics textbooks. In the real world, everywhere we see the influence of both pure market forces and official interventions, so that any departure from the equilibrium has to be assigned to some mixture of market and policy failure. First, I would like to review the recent history of the exchange rate regime and policy. From the very beginning of the reform Serbia started de facto pegging of its currency. Since the year 2003, the policy switched to the one most responsive to market forces. Former NBS governor (Jelašić 2010) describes this phase as the policy of real exchange rate stability. Since local inflation never fully converged with the inflation in countries of reference currency, it was actually the policy of slow but steady nominal depreciation. Some economists (Josifidis et al. 2009), are prone to mark this phase as a crawling peg regime, considering the way monetary authorities see the target level of exchange rate and pursue towards the target. The last phase of the exchange rate policy started in August 2006 (NBS 2006). At that time NBS shifted from de facto exchange rate targeting to the pure inflation-targeting monetary strategy. Exchange rate was no longer the variable of prime concern and had to be managed to prevent excess daily fluctuations (with no transparent threshold). According to the agreement signed with the government and the ensuing new memorandum (NBS 2008a, b), NBS was to avoid accumulating pressure from either side of the exchange market (buying or selling) in 'long-term' sequences. This meant that NBS was not expected to act against market forces. The entire period of the inflation-targeting framework can be explained if broken into the next subperiods. The first subperiod precedes the crisis; the second contains the last quarter of 2008 and the first 2 months of the next year, which was the time of the most acute currency and banking turmoil. As expected, those are the periods of highest exchange rate volatility. The first subperiod is also the period in which the local currency further appreciated (approximately 10 %). The crisis itself was accompanied with tremendous pressure from the buying side of the exchange market, which despite frequent and massive NBS interventions ended up with rapid depreciation of local currency (approximately 25 %). For the rest of the year, nominal exchange rate remained stable with no need for further intervention. The year 2010 brings back the practice of occasional interventions as already seen in the period of the anchoring exchange rate.

The following facts about exchange rate policy should be highlighted. First, many economists would probably agree that the most dangerous gap (real local currency appreciation) appears in the first 2 years of the reform. According to some assessments (Marinković 2006), the real value of the Serbian dinar (based on purchasing power parity) in March 2002 was four times that of October 2000. The gap might not be that huge if we benchmark the end-of-period value to some other prereform standings, but it would still look remarkable. Second, the next period that precedes the introduction of inflation targeting is the period of slow but steady nominal depreciation, but it is far from being assessed as the period of stable real exchange rate. In real terms, the Serbian dinar still continues to appreciate against the euro, although at a slower pace than before. Taking into account regular massive foreign exchange interventions,[3] I would conclude that the authorities recognised the issue, but still pursued it in a way to support the value of the currency.

The next period brings more flexibility to exchange rate policy, but with a huge gap inherited from the past. Moreover, the introduction of a more relaxed (independent) floating regime unfortunately coincides with de jure capital liberalisation. In this period NBS ceased to intervene heavily in the foreign exchange market. The massive direct interventions came out not only less frequently but also from both selling and buying side of the market. Nevertheless, for the first time, the abundance of foreign capital generated nominal appreciation of the local currency, together with an increase in exchange rate volatility. The nominal exchange rate trend shifted from appreciating to depreciating in long-term sequences. However, from the beginning to the outbreak of the crisis, in nominal terms the Serbian dinar appreciated about 10 %, and thanks to 'inflation inertia' even further in real terms.

There seems to be a kind of asymmetry in the way that authorities sought to correct market forces. If the market drove currency down, the authorities would take a contra-trend position (heavy selling of reserve currency), if the market drove currency up, they were not keen to act. Calvo and Reinhart (2002) coined the well-known phrase 'fear of floating', to describe the behaviour of the authorities.

[3] Starting from beginning of 2004, in the following ten quarters NBS was almost regularly present on the exchange market. In this period NBS net interventions from the selling side of the market reached 84.5 % of total interbank turnover. This means that almost half of total reserve currency supply was provided by the intervenient.

They found that countries that claim they allow their exchange rate to float in fact generally do not. Interestingly, the most relevant economic arguments (Josifidis et al. 2011) against pure floating (mostly depreciation) in transition countries are dollarisation of liabilities and an adverse pass-through effect of exchange rate on prices. Both arguments correspond to some structural weaknesses of the economy. A high and pervasive level of financial dollarisation (notably for long-term contracts) may indicate that key market participants do not see any real chance of local currency staying stable in the long run, so they are reluctant to lend in local currency. The adverse pass-through effect is as strong as the trade deficit. If imported goods dominate local goods in the structure of consumption, the pass-through from depreciation to inflation will be stronger. The adverse pass-through effect may be further enforced because of imperfect (asymmetric) price elasticity, let alone the trade deficit. Namely, prices tend to stay rigid when the costs decrease (for example, the prices of imported goods when exchange rate appreciates), while they increase when costs go up. Explaining this regularity calls for competition policy arguments (trading monopolies, import lobbies).

By exerting pressure on the exchange rate to support its value, authorities traded off long-run beneficial structural reforms for a short-run inflation target. However, the missing link in that line of thinking, which supports strong currency, is a reverse effect that comes from an overvalued exchange rate on the above-mentioned structural weaknesses: liability dollarisation, trade deficit, and consequently, the level of economy's dependence on swings in international credit conditions. The longer a country follows this trade-off policy game, the more damaging it will be to desert it, when this becomes unavoidable. Additionally after a certain point, misalignment is extremely hard to correct. Adverse consequences are far bigger, and reformers have to confront stronger and more unified societal opposition.

3.2 Key Stakeholders and Policy Actors

Therefore, the next step in the analysis is to look at the key stakeholders and policy actors. Who benefited from the several years of deviations? Overvalued exchange rates benefit net importers, borrowers who readily seek debt in cheap foreign currencies, foreign banks, and even the government itself. In a small open economy with a trade deficit, budget revenues predominantly come from imports (tariffs, value-added tax) and import-related economic activity (transport, retail trade) so that cutting back imports is costly even for the government budget.

In retrospect, one can conclude that almost no one benefited from currency depreciation under this particular episode of Serbian economic reforms. Who might be blamed for 'seating all the passengers on the same side of the boat'? Societal opposition against currency depreciation was at least partly inherited with the economic structure (primarily weak export-oriented production and high level of dependence on foreign financial resources). However, this resistance was reinforced by the authorities' unpreparedness for addressing the misalignment and the fragility of the economic structure.

There are also purely political drivers of the currency misalignment. The reform governments frequently used euro-denominated wages to communicate with voters. It is the overvalued exchange rate that must be credited with Serbia's respectable standing relative to its peers in per capita GDP and wage levels. It is interesting that at all times Serbia has imported a seasonal low-skilled labour force (for agricultural jobs) even from some neighboring EU countries. Therefore, the opposition seems strong, and voices for the status quo overpower pro-reform ones.

The electoral cycle argument is cited to explain the lag in implementing certain beneficial policies. Nordhaus (1975), by employing a formal analysis, found the policies involving inter-temporal choice to be biased against future generations. The policy started with relative austerity in the early years of the present term and ended with profligacy immediately before elections, generating a political business cycle. Many policies yield gradual payoffs, but the costs of reform are borne up front. For reelection purposes, the incumbent government would not allow such a policy to come to the table when elections approach. However, the electoral cycle argument is of little importance for the policy of real appreciation, since it survived several electoral cycles. But it can explain the change in severity of challenges the monetary and exchange rate policy faced over time. Many specific fiscal outbreaks happened during cabinet changes, right before the elections, and in other such politically sensitive times.

The complexity of the exchange rate policy for a small and open transitional country is attributed to the fact that it is simultaneously a mighty instrument used to reach different economic and social goals (inflation, balance of payment, credit growth), and it is also an extremely important independent social goal since it influences the public perception of economic stability. For instance, Crosby (1996) illustrated the difficulties of policy change given Honduran officials' reluctance to devaluate highly overvalued currency, simply because it is considered taboo. Similarly, Dornbusch, referring to the peso crisis, made this point forcefully: 'Exchange rate-based stabilisation helps bring under way stabilisation .... In the second phase, increasing real appreciation becomes apparent, it is increasingly recognised, but it is inconvenient to do something. ..... Finally, in the third phase, it is too late to do something. Real appreciation has come to a point where a major devaluation is necessary. But the politics will not allow that. Some more time is spent in denial and then—sometime—enough bad news pile up cause the crash' (quoted in Edwards 2000, 150). This frequently cited passage explains that policy makers are apt to stick to choices that yield short-run benefits even when the reality calls for prompt reversal. It also shows that economic stability is a complex social outcome, which may be presented in many different and sometimes conflicting ways. In moving towards one goal, the authorities may be actually laying the ground for catastrophic results for other stability goals. Later in the chapter I will return to question of why authorities often show the propensity to prioritise certain stability goals, to the exclusion of others.

An analysis framed only by societal groups or coalitions based on their specific interests may be inadequate. Since it implicitly assumes that any coalition or actor can perfectly anticipate specific consequences, and thus rationally articulate its political agenda. Valuable insights into the causes of a late policy reaction can be gleaned from the political economy of reform. Pioneered in Fernandez and Rodrik (1991), the approach introduced a novel idea that any reform produces uncertainty about the future position of stakeholders, which itself undermines the success of reform. Several features challenge the view on a rational and perfectly foresighted policy actor. First, 'individuals, households and firms occupy several positions in the economic structure simultaneously, with interest that often do not coincide' (Haggard and Webb 1993, 144). For instance, net exporters favour a weak dinar since they report higher revenue from export after it is translated into the local currency, but at the same time they may reject a weak dinar if their business operations are predominantly financed with foreign currency loans. A similar dilemma might arise for households that favour a weak local currency when looking at foreign currency savings, but exactly the opposite when looking at dinar wages, especially when salaries are not indexed in a foreign currency. Sometimes, stakeholders are not ready to support reforms simply because they are not able to assess the outcomes and impacts of the reforms on their particular interests or positions. Such uncertainties can lead to biases in favour of the status quo, since even groups that end up benefiting from the reform may oppose it if they fear it may make them worse off.

3.3 *Late Response to Immediate Threats*

The same remedy would be more effective if applied at the early stage of an incoming crisis. However, economic crises are infrequent and ever-evolving phenomena. They are never identical to the ones before. Often, even afterwards and with rigorous econometric techniques, it is not easy to identify which form the crisis takes, much less predict the probability or severity of an impending crisis. With events like these, even professional economists could fail. Therefore, in turbulent times ardent debate flourishes: too many are voluble, but few are ready to act.

Faced with an impending crisis, authorities' first reaction is forbearance. When the international crisis hit, the Serbian government stated that it would stop at Serbia's national borders, since the banking disturbance was not be a problem for peripheral economies. Some government officials even thought that in such an atmosphere, Serbia would gain a competitive advantage over some other countries. This is probably why the first actions of policy makers came too late. When action is necessary, policy makers wait, gambling on being 'hit or missed'; the reaction could also partly be due to myopia. Additionally if a worse scenario can be avoided by short-term preemptive actions, and since the public is unaware of the risks of going that route, it is complicated for policy makers to justify the more costly alternative.

More generally, policy legitimating is probably the most challenging issue. It may cause additional propensity to delay. 'In calculating pros and cons of any policy change, reformers sometimes have to wait until the pros accumulate at the level that opposition weakens enough to make the transition between preexisting policy regimes and new ones feasible. In turbulent times, like economic crisis, distributional effects still may be strong, but it is more likely that the right policy package will generate a socially beneficial outcome [efficiency-enhancing decision]. Status quo ceases to be an attractive option, and tolerance for remedial measures rises' (Haggard and Webb 1993, 153). However, despite public support, opting for the overall beneficial policy can be late for different reasons.

I now turn to a specific policy mistake. Special attention must be given to the unnecessary delay in desperately needed reform of the national deposit insurance system, which was expected to address depositors' anxiety—the most acute issue during the last quarter of 2008. The draft of the law on deposit insurance announced rapid increase in the coverage ceiling (from EUR 3,000–50,000 per depositor at each bank) and redefinition of insured deposits, as well as prompt resolution measures, but it passed in the parliament several months later (on December 22, 2008). Interviews with senior government officials and insiders reveal that the primary concern for policy makers was uncertainty over banking system solvency. The NBS warned the government about the inherent risk that the reform of deposit insurance could bring, but the responsibility for the action delay rests solely with the government. The more generous insurance scheme, which was proposed, could bring huge costs to the public funds if it failed to stop depositor anxiety. An extension of the public guarantee for private (mostly foreign-owned) banks was also a 'hot' political theme, but surely not one that might be addressed urgently. This highlights the fragility of the political coalition; namely, that the government structure also played a role.

If a government assembles a nonhomogeneous coalition, difficult but crucial reforms become even less likely. The weakness of coalition governments in controlling budget deficits or launching fiscal adjustments is well documented (Alesina et al. 1998). An interesting analytical framework for studying political reaction to crisis is 'veto-player hypothesis'. Political theory defines a veto player as an individual or collective actor whose agreement is necessary to change status quo policy. In an empirical study of several recent banking crises, Angkinand and Willett (2008) found rather strong support of the hypothesis that both too few and too many veto players leads to weak responses, and consequently to higher cost from banking crises.

What about the Serbian political structure, and how responsible is that structure for the late response? Serbia has a parliamentary system with a weak coalition government. All parties in the coalition are effective veto players since their votes are necessary to sustain a majority in parliament. However, in real political life, the parliament plays a secondary role since its members were elected according to the so-called 'open list'. Thus, the real power belongs to the government, which assembles party leaders or highly ranked party technocrats. Moreover, each political party often take control over a group of government departments responsible for the similar public goal—a way to control frictions inside the coalition. It transforms multiparty government into 'multi one-party' government. However, this 'free hands' approach weakens the possibility of much-needed consensus. Sometimes the government must coordinate its action with other policy makers. When pressing resolution measures must come to the table, the National Bank of Serbia becomes the main partner. Unfortunately, it so happens that heads of Ministry of Finance and

NBS are almost always from different parties. It is also worth noting that the position of the president is much stronger in Serbia than it is generally in parliamentary political systems. It seems obvious that in such a political milieu a coherent policy is not easy to reach. However, once a consensus about common policy is reached, any attempt to change it will be a political battle. Hence, policy is rigid, unresponsive and inefficient in dealing with serious challenges.

However, what the authorities persistently refused to do has ultimately been done by the market itself. The rush on banks and international reserves wiped out many landmarks of reform success (strong foreign liquidity, sustainable credit growth and banking sector soundness) but aligned fundamentals (purchasing power parity, interest rate parity).

3.4 The Role of External Actors

As underlined in Crosby (1996, 1404), 'the stimulus for policy change has more often than not come from the outside as intractable economic crises have forced governments to seek external assistance'. In this section, we discuss the role of two important external players. The first is the IMF, which monitors the reform process; and the second is a community of foreign banks, whose position is deeply affected by the above-mentioned policy. Although, sometimes in policy circles these two stakeholders are seen as coordinating their actions, academic support for this view is quite rare. As an exception, writing on the latest Argentina crisis, Marshall (2008) stressed the importance of the power struggle taking place at the time between the Argentina government and foreign banks, enforced by IMF.

Let me first discuss what I call the *evolution* of the IMF position on exchange rate policy. The IMF warned Serbia (as it did other countries in SEE) of stability threats from overvalued currency, currency substitution and trade deficit. All these dangers are related to exchange rate policy. Thus, IMF prescriptions seem to be shifting focus from sustaining competitiveness (avoiding excess real appreciation) to combating inflation (neglecting the appreciation). According to Vice Governor Dragutinović (2008, 21), the official IMF mission (the mission statement from November 6, 2007) argued for abandoning price-competitiveness (exchange rate) measures, noting that attempts to use depreciation to offset loss of competitiveness—which is rooted in wage increase, sluggish structural reforms and relaxed fiscal policy—would damage monetary policy credibility and have no effect on sustainable export recovery. Despite the very beneficial change of emphasis on the role of the government, the IMF's neglect of the role of exchange rate policy is what one must discuss. Note that when the attitude was changing, the new stakeholder—the foreign banking community—stood out as the major player on the local credit market. The policy gave impetus to capital import from abroad by 'allowing easy catch' to the foreign banking community, as discussed above.

What is closely linked with the changed IMF position on the exchange rate policy, is the IMF assessment of the role of foreign banks when banking system stability is at the forefront of policy discussions. It follows from IMF official reports that, at the very beginning, the organisation underestimated the problems that could have arisen with foreign banks. It is stated (IMF 2006, 13), 'as long as they earn high profits, the foreign banks in Serbia probably have access to new capital from their headquarters given that they account for a small share of the loan book of their international banking group. Their inherent strength and *strong reputations* [italics added] make a systemic loss of deposit confidence unlikely'. Immediately after that, the report warns that large depreciation could lead to a credit crunch with adverse implications for the economy at large. What was unforeseen at that moment was the external nature of the incoming shock. This is why the report stressed local shocks (increase of default rates) as the main stability threat.

Again, the reality forced IMF to revise the overly optimistic assessment of the role of foreign banks. The later IMF report for Croatia expresses less optimism over the role of foreign banks in sustaining financial stability. The reasons for the revised assessment are probably the new elements brought into the framework by the incoming crisis. IMF (2008, 14) assessed, 'the reliance on foreign funding has in turn increased vulnerability to contagion risks, with the exposure highly concentrated ….. Problems in a parent bank could be transmitted to local banks, given the high concentration of exposures to only a few countries. While reputational risks may render it unlikely that parent banks would not support their subsidiaries, the level and degree of their support would depend on general market conditions and cannot be assumed'. Wellons (1985) underlines that transnational banks tend to look at the foreign markets from the home country policy perspective. The author has given many reasons why a transnational organisation may see benefits to strongly weighing the interest of the home country, and behave as it has nationality.

Foreign banks have played an ambiguous role in transmitting global shock into the local market. From the very beginning they played a role in propagating the crisis, but lately their influence has been exactly the opposite. The foreign financial groups created an intraorganisational surrogate for interbank credit market, and stood up for their local subsidiaries, mitigating the credit crunch. However, the later behaviour had some measure of external stimulus. Specifically, the Vienna Agreement deserves special attention. This agreement was signed in early 2009 by representatives of parent banking groups and the NBS, but was initiated and operationalized under the auspices of the IMF. Although the agreement was made to provide the same extent of foreign bank credit exposure to the local credit market (initially assessed at EUR 10.8 billion) for the next year, it was rolled over for another year. In return, NBS offered some concessions to foreign banks—that is, full access to Serbian dinar and euro-denominated liquidity arrangements. It was then that the currency swap auction facility was introduced, but the facility was actually never used in full capacity. Although the Republic of Serbia had no real leverage in bargaining with international creditors, it is no surprise that all players were fully committed to the agreement. At the time, the credibility of all players had been seriously undermined so that they had to move fast towards a mutually beneficial outcome; no one had leeway to bargain.

3.5 *Stability Versus Growth Dilemma: Driven by Economic Policy or Politics*

Any reform process always implies a trade-off between immediate and long-term goals. Most frequently, stability appears to be an immediate goal, especially for countries that emerged from long periods of undermined stability. Societal collective memory in this case favours stability goals. There is also theoretical support that voters' reaction is coloured by the recent past (they are retrospective and prone to myopia), and those features favor the supremacy of stability over a growth stimulation–oriented policy. Nevertheless, when the aggregate level of consumption is rather low, growth stimulation is also a prominent goal, especially in communication with voters. Thus, main political actors must often follow an agenda with largely mutually exclusive goals.

3.5.1 Stability: Public View

Economic stability is an outcome of public policy continuously reassessed by the voters. In the remainder of the paper, I will try to shed some light over the issue of the right choice of a stability proxy. In opting for different economic stability proxies, public policy makers are not completely free. They are constrained by society's propensity to look at some proxies as better explanations of the same outcome.

From a purely economic standpoint, there is no difference between visible and nonvisible economic stability proxies. However, when considering account policy legitimacy, it becomes a relevant issue. For example, although exchange rate dynamics and inflation rate have common determinants, and often go hand in hand in the long run, they are crucially different in terms of visibility. Inflation rate can be polished by official statistics and takes time to become obvious. The data on exchange rates are published daily and can be carefully monitored by anyone. This is probably why exchange rate plays a greater role in shaping the public view about financial stability than do inflation reports. Senior officials from the National Bank of Serbia have occasionally advocated for neglecting exchange rates—sustaining long-term stable exchange rate has never been its goal—but have not persuaded market participants to shift their attention.

There are also stability indicators that are visible only to professional economists. Worsening of such indicators generates no immediate cost to anybody, but they can have a snowball effect, which can be triggered anytime. This is the case with numerous external fragility indicators—foreign debt, distress bank solvency, and budget and trade deficits. If academics remain silent, such stability indicators can be ignored by politicians for prolonged periods of time.

In this case it would seem that policy makers prioritised stability goals in the policy agenda, but they differentiated between goals according to visibility. Too much weight was assigned to the most visible ones (usable in communications with voters), neglecting the threats from slow but steady undermining of systemic financial stability. Glorifying the sound financial position of an economic system is of no use in political campaigns, which must be written in plain language, while it may, at the same time, bring immediate political costs. It is clear that hard-to-reach standards for long-term financial sustainability will be absent from a politically driven policy agenda.

Inherited similarities in economic structure and long-term goals have generated similar development trajectories throughout the South East European (SEE) countries and particularly in the countries that were formerly part of Yugoslavia. There are also apparent similarities in economic policy that need further evaluation beyond the scope of this chapter. However, given the global role of the International Monetary Fund (IMF) it is evident that key elements of economic policy in these countries have been developed and applied under the auspices of a common adviser. This is evident in both the policy prescriptions that were in place before the crisis (good command over inflation and exchange rate, capital account liberalization) and remedies applied in response to the crisis (e.g. unrestricted approach of banks to foreign liquidity, i.e. international reserves). In parallel, the European Union (EU) has played a significant role in SEE policy choices and policy making. In general terms, the EU accession window forced the supremacy of stabilisation goals over economic growth and influenced the region's policy orientation. Specifically in terms of the response to the crisis, it was right EU officials that suggested increase of deposit insurance coverage.

Moreover, even when economic policy prescriptions have not been imposed, the similarity may be because the countries follow each other's example. There is also a very intuitive behavioral explanation for that similarity. Keynes (1931, 156) put it forcefully, 'A "sound" banker, alas! is not one who foresees danger and avoids it, but one who, when he is ruined, is ruined in a conventional and orthodox way along with his fellows, so that no one can really blame him'. This story tells us that in choosing strategic solutions, decision makers (corporations and governments) can be guided by a 'safety in numbers' philosophy. Speaking of the current financial crisis, when it was spread out internationally, the precise assignment of responsibility among different policy actors became less feasible. The authorities in Serbia even responded that the solution to the crisis depended more on crisis-resolution measures are to be taken in major industrial countries than on the local response.

3.6 Ultimate Winners and Losers

The crisis itself prioritises crucial policy adjustments at the top of the agenda. Ultimately, what appears as the socially efficient decision in the short run, if sustained for too long, becomes the most damaging one. The latest credit crunch has neutralized all benefits accruing from reforms. Growth perspectives are undermined. Even the biggest winners from the precrisis period are worse off. The biggest corporations, which dominated the trade sector, have been rationed from the foreign capital market. Euro-denominated wages have dropped to the lowest level inside the SEE region. Businesses face a rise of cost of finance as well as credit cuts. Alternatives to bank finance have not developed thanks to abundant foreign credit. The SME sector was discriminated against twice: at the main sale and purchase markets by trade monopolies as well as at the financial markets.

3.7 Policy Alternatives: Agenda for the Future

It becomes clear that overvalued currency, in terms of purchasing power parity and interest rate parity, could undermine economic stability. Nevertheless, can currency valued according to fundamentals do better? Šošić and Kraft (2006) showed that in the case of Croatia, market participants responded in an asymmetrical way to real exchange rate misalignments. Undervalued local currency has induced a portfolio shift towards the strongest foreign currency, while overvalued local currency has failed to provoke a reversal. Underlined asymmetric response is nothing more than a consequence of slow confidence recovery. It is easy to undermine public confidence in stability but takes longer to reestablish it. The case of Serbia is clearly a case in point. The level of dollarisation has proved resistant to the battery of measures undertaken during the last decade.

The recently proposed policy agenda (NBS 2011) brings no novel approach to solve the issue. It is still based on three pillars: first, it advocates responsible fiscal and monetary policy to support macroeconomic financial stability and growth. The second pillar contains measures to promote the Serbian dinar as the right choice for long-term investments. Primarily, it is suggested that the government issue long-term debt in local currency. However, previously those attempts failed completely. To succeed, the tasks of the first pillar must be fully achieved. The same precondition holds in the case of the third pillar, which assumes the mutual effort of NBS and the banks to establish a private market of financial instruments for currency risk management. Private market protection against currency risk is prohibitively costly against the backdrop of monetary instability. The first pillar, if implemented fully, makes the other two pillars superfluous. Moreover, it cannot be enforced at the same time as the other two pillars because the ultimate effect of those measures critically depends on the first one.

Authorities also do not refuse to use a wider set of prudential measures in favour of local currency. It is a clear sign that they fear free competition. Preferable tax treatment of dinar-denominated saving instruments, discriminating policy of mandatory reserves, and policy of risk assessments affect the preference set. Those measures imply additional costs to those who are using (or indexed in) foreign currency. The ultimate effect is subject to the level of extra (regulation-imposed) levy, and has already proved limited.

Therefore, sustainable and responsible fiscal and monetary policy is the only way out of financial fragility. Note that globally even the most advanced economies undermined their prospects for stability and growth with prodigal government spending. This brings the austerity package to the forefront of academic and policy discussions as an urgent recourse to healthy finance.

4 Conclusions

This chapter examines the policy of commitment to an unreachable goal. In the case of Serbia, its protracted nominal stabilisation of the exchange rate, ignoring balance of payment fragility as well as threats from the credit bubble, has not been effective and largely anticipated by market participants as an unsustainable economic policy mix. Interest rate differentials stimulated credit inflows from abroad and fuelled the credit boom. The persistent difference between real yields available locally and abroad made the economy fragile and susceptible to external developments. Besides being frequently criticised for the adverse impact on competitiveness of exports, the policy is also responsible for making the economy dangerously exposed to currency risk.

Was there a capricious delinking of the local currency from its fundamentals? In the author's view, the official interventions drove exchange rates away from the fundamental determinants. Although the NBS as the Central Bank is required to fulfill its legal mandate on monetary policy which includes controlling currency volatility during this policy episode it worked to support rather than to restrain a strong national currency. This challenges the view of the central bank as a policy actor that is above partisan politics, and immune to political pressures. It may also be that the central bank operated on a narrow focus, with short-term inflation targets as its primary concern, what generated time-inconsistent monetary policy. Here I come to the crux of the debate. With expansionary fiscal policy and lack of effective structural reforms, the monetary authority must navigate a narrow road between pitfalls on either side. From one angle, it is depreciation-driven inflation; from the other, it is appreciation-driven balance-of-payment fragility in which speculative foreign capital drives out sustainable export revenue.

Finally, collective memory has also played a role. Despite strong efforts by local authorities to persuade the market that local currency can stay stable, no one really believed this was reachable in the long run. History of hyperinflation and severe devaluation contribute to the public perception that a weak economy cannot withstand a strong currency. Even in the period of a rather stable exchange rate, exchange rate dynamics were coloured by frequent short-lasting speculative attacks.

As for the delayed response to pressing and immediate threats, some key points emerge from the discussion. First, crises are not easily foreseeable. Rather, complex mechanics and multicausality make it difficult for authorities to offer immediate solutions to crises. Second, if the crisis is predominantly imported, local authorities can easily deny responsibility; this weakens the political will to undertake urgent resolution. Finally, when a crisis happens, authorities' forbearance as well as weak political coalitions increase the propensity to delay urgently needed action.

The role of external players raises the question of whether, when accelerating reforms, caution is required when offering stimulus to any specific actor, especially to actors who may have other interests. An equally important lesson concerns the right sequence of reforms. Trading off the more difficult but in the long run socially beneficial reforms in favour of the easy solutions will probably lead the economy down the wrong track.

Appendix

Table 9.2 Sources of financing the growth of the BCPS (EUR) in Serbia

(2003–2009)

						2008				2009		
Variable	2003	2004	2005	2006	2007	Q1	Q2	Q3	Q4	Q1	Q2	Q3
Annual/quarterly BCPS (EUR) growth rate	19.1	26.9	41.6	26.9	39.8	4.9	9.6	10.5	−5.0	0.7	1.4	2.1
Financing the growth of the BCPS												
1. Claims on public sector	−0.5	−4.6	−0.8	0.1	1.2	−0.4	−0.0	0.2	−0.5	−0.5	−5.2	−1.7
2. Claims on NBS	−2.2	−5.4	−28.6	−61.5	−17.3	3.5	−1.7	−4.6	14.1	5.2	−1.6	−2.9
2.1 Repo stock	–	–	−4.9	−28.7	−10.9	−0.3	1.3	−4.6	16.9	−0.6	−2.4	−3.7
3. Bank deposits	13.3	14.0	30.5	43.8	45.8	0.5	4.8	6.4	−13.3	−2.6	5.2	2.8
4. Net foreign liabilities	2.2	24.2	30.3	30.3	−10.9	−2.3	0.1	3.4	0.3	0.6	1.3	2.4
4.1 Foreign assets	−0.0	1.7	1.0	1.3	−9.5	3.3	0.5	−0.6	−2.1	3.1	0.4	−3.6
4.2 Foreign liabilities	2.2	22.5	29.3	29.0	−1.4	−5.6	−0.4	4.0	2.4	−2.5	0.9	6.0
5. Other net liabilities	6.3	−1.3	10.2	14.2	21.0	3.6	6.4	5.1	−5.6	−2.0	1.7	1.5

Source: NBS (2013) Statistical Bulletin, December (author's recalculations)

Table 9.3 Change of foreign debt levels for banks and enterprises

(2004–2009.Q3)												
						Q1			Q2			
	2004	2005	2006	2007	2008	Jan	Feb	Mar	Apr	May	Jun	Q3
Bank foreign debt absolute change	410	1,053	1,688	93	–59	–635	–21	174	–344	135	82	782
Enterprise foreign debt absolute change	327	1,054	1,428	3,100	3,814	56	51	–121	–30	–391	118	–309

References

Alesina, A., Perotti, R., & Tavares, J. (1998). The political economy of fiscal adjustments. *Brookings Papers on Economic Activity, 1*(Spring), 197–248.

Angkinand, A., & Willett, T. (2008). Political influences on the costs of banking crises in emerging market economies: Testing the U-shaped veto player hypothesis. *Macroeconomics and Finance in Emerging Market Economies, 1*(2), 279–297.

Arsić, M., Mladenović, Z., Nojković, A., & Petrović, P. (2005). *Makroekonomsko modeliranje privrede Srbije*. Belgrade: CES MECON.

Balassa, B. (1964). The purchasing-power-parity doctrine: A reappraisal. *Journal of Political Economy, 72*(6), 584–596.

Bernanke, B., & Lown, C. (2001). The credit crunch. *Brookings Papers on Economic Activity, 2*, 205–247.

Boissay, F., Calvo-Gonzales, O. B., & Koćluk, T. (2005). *Is lending in central and eastern Europe developing too fast?.*. Wien-Alsergrund: Oesterreichische Nationalbank.

Calvo, A. G., & Reinhart, C. R. (2002). Fear of floating. *Quarterly Journal of Economics, 117*(2), 379–408.

Cottarelli, C., Dell'Ariccia, G., & Vladkova-Hollar, I. (2005). Early birds, late risers, and sleeping beauties: Bank credit growth to the private sector in central and eastern Europe and in the Balkans. *Journal of Banking and Finance, 29*(1), 83–104.

Crosby, B. (1996). Policy implementation: The organizational challenge. *World Development, 24*(9), 1403–1415.

Djankov, S., McLiesh, C., & Shleifer, A. (2007). Private credit in 129 countries. *Journal of Financial Economics, 84*(2), 299–329.

Dragutinović, D. (2008). *Moć i nemoć monetarne politike u uspostavljanju ravnoteže između platnobilansnih ciljeva i ciljeva inflacije*. Belgrade: Narodna banka Srbije. Radni papiri, mart.

Edwards, S. (2000). Exchange rate overvaluation and currency crises: Lessons from Latin America and East Asia. In J. Bisignano & W. Hunter (Eds.), *Global financial crises: Lessons from recent events* (pp. 159–176). Boston: Kluwer Academic.

Égert B., Backé,P., & Zumer, T. (2006). *Credit growth in Central and Eastern Europe: New (Over) shooting stars?* (Working paper series 687 (October)). Frankfurt: European Central Bank.

Fernandez, R., & Rodrik, D. (1991). Resistance to reform: Status quo bias in the presence of individual-specific uncertainty. *American Economic Review, 81*(5), 1146–1155.

Haggard, S., & Webb, S. (1993). What do we know about the political economy of economic policy reform? *The World Bank Research Observer, 8*(2), 143–168.

International Monetary Fund (IMF). (2006). *Serbia and Montenegro: Serbia—financial system stability assessment, including reports on the observance of standards and codes on the follow-*

ing topics: Monetary and financial policy transparency, banking supervision, and payment system. Washington, DC: IMF. Country report 06/96, March.

International Monetary Fund (IMF). (2008). *Republic of Croatia: Financial system stability assessment—update*. Washington, DC: IMF. Country report 08/160, May.

International Monetary Fund (IMF). (2009). *Croatia: 2009 Article IV consultation—staff report', country report 09/185*. Washington, DC: IMF.

Jelašić, R. (2010). *Ključne determinante kretanja cena u Srbiji: empirijski pregled devet godina tranzicije*. Belgrade: Narodna banka Srbije.

Josifidis, K., Allegret, J. P., & Beker Pucar, E. (2009). Monetary and exchange rate regimes changes: The cases of Poland, Czech Republic, Slovakia and Republic of Serbia. *Panoeconomicus, 56*(2), 199–226.

Josifidis, K., Allegret, J. P., & Beker Pucar, E. (2011). Inflation targeting and exchange rate regime in Serbia and selected transition economies. *Eastern European Economics, 49*(4), 88–105.

Keynes, J. M. (1931).The consequences to the banks of the collapse in money values. In *Essays in persuasion, the collected writings* (Vol. 9). London: The Royal Economic Society.

Kiss, G., Nagy, M., Vonnák, B. (2006). *Credit growth in Central and Eastern Europe: Trend, cycle or boom?* (Magyar Nemzeti Bank Working Paper 2006/10). Budapest: Hungarian National Bank.

Kraft, E., & Jankov, L. (2005). Does speed kill? Lending booms and their consequences in Croatia. *Journal of Banking and Finance, 29*(1), 105–121.

Lothian, J., & Taylor, M. (2008). Real exchange rates over the past two centuries: How important is the Harrod-Balassa-Samuelson effect? *Economic Journal, 118*(532), 1742–1763.

Madžar, L. (2006). Marshall-Lernerovi uslovi i njihove ekonomskopolitićke implikacije. *Ekonomski anali, 51*(170), 90–124.

Marinković, S. (2006). A fallacy of the choice of an exchange rate regime: Some south-eastern Europe insights. *South East European Journal of Economics and Business, 1*(1), 28–42.

Marshall, W. (2008). Foreign banks and political sovereignty: The case of Argentina. *Review of Political Economy, 20*(3), 349–366.

McKinnon, R. (2000). Limiting moral hazard and reducing risk in international capital flows: The choice of an exchange rate regime. In J. Bisignano & W. Hunter (Eds.), *Global financial crises: Lessons from recent events* (pp. 159–176). Boston: Kluwer Academic.

Mladenović, Z., & Palić, M. (2009). Credit growth in upswing and credit contraction in recessions in CEECs: Econometric evidence from time-series and panel data analyses. In A. Prašćević, B. Cerović, & M. Jakšić (Eds.), *Economic policy and global recession* (Vol. 1, pp. 37–48). Belgrade: Faculty of Economics, University of Belgrade.

Narodna Banka Srbije (NBS). (2006, September). *Memorandum Narodne banke Srbije o principima novog okvira monetarne politike: Na putu ka ostvarenju ciljeva niske inflacije*. Belgrade: NBS.

Narodna Banka Srbije (NBS). (2008a). *Sporazum o ciljanju (targetiranju) inflacije*. Belgrade: NBS.

Narodna Banka Srbije (NBS). (2008b). *Memorandum Narodne banke Srbije o ciljanju (targetiranju) inflacije kao monetarnoj strategiji*. Belgrade: NBS.

Narodna Banka Srbije(NBS). (2011). *Izveštaj o dinarizaciji finansijskog sistema Srbije*. Belgrade: NBS.

Nordhaus, W. (1975). The political business cycle. *Review of Economic Studies, 42*(2), 169–190.

Šošić, V., & Kraf, E. (2006). Floating with a large life-jacket: Monetary and exchange rate policies in Croatia under dollarization. *Contemporary Economic Policy, 24*(4), 492–506.

Stamenković, S., Kovaćević, M., Savin, D., Nikolić, I., & Vuković, V. (2004). Privredni razvoj—kuda ide dalje? *Ekonomski anali, 44*(160), 39–73.

Tasić, N., & Zdravković, M. (2008). Osetljivost srpskog izvoza i uvoza na promene deviznog kursa u dugom roku, *Radni papiri, 16* (September). Belgrade: Narodna Banka Srbije.

Taylor, M. A., & Taylor, M. P. (2004). The purchasing power parity debate. *Journal of Economic Perspectives, 18*(4), 135–158.

Udell, G. (2009, March, 1–3). How will a credit crunch affect small business finance? *Federal Reserve Bank of San Francisco Economic Letter, 9*. San Francisco: Federal Reserve Bank of San Francisco.

Wellons, P. (1985). International debt: The behavior of banks in a politicized environment. *International Organization, 39*(3), 441–471.

Zdzienicka, A. (2009). *Vulnerabilities in Central and Eastern Europe: Credit growth* (Working papers 09–12, May). Lyon: GATE Groupe d'Analyse et de Théorie Économique Écully.

Part III
Policy Making and Governance: National and Sub-national Policies

Chapter 10
Local Governance and Regional Development in Albania

Mimoza Manxhari

1 Introduction

After half a century of centralized economic and political systems, Albania moved to a market-based economy and subsequent decentralized governance through a series of central and local level public reforms. Elda Gjergji noted that, "Albania, like other post-communist East Central European countries, has been undergoing a multiple transition: a political transition from one party to many, an economic transition from command to market economy, and a social one, from rural society to an urban".[1]

These decentralized governance reforms were driven mostly by different donors, and in the context of the European accession agenda, rather than reflecting the political commitment of the local authorities based on a common understanding and strategic thinking. As such, the process has involved much "toing and froing", which inevitably has led to ambiguities, functional overlaps, and unclear roles and responsibilities among the different levels of government. Domestic sponsorship for the reforms was split between the Ministry of Interior (MOI) and the Ministry of Economy, Trade and Energy.[2] Furthermore, the implementation of the reforms did not include proper capacity building of the civil servants tasked with the job.

This chapter provides a general overview of the decentralization reforms, the state of local governance, and the efforts made towards promoting regional

[1] Euro Academia: http://euroacademia.eu/presentation/the-albanian-transition-to-democracy-as-a-path-to-european-integration/

[2] The METE led on the regional development agenda, roughly until 2009 and the Ministry of Interior led on decentralisation.

M. Manxhari, Ph.D. (✉)
Management Department, Faculty of Economics, University of Tirana, Tirana, Albania
e-mail: Mmanxhari@yahoo.com

M. Thomas, V. Bojicic-Dzelilovic (eds.), *Public Policy Making in the Western Balkans*, DOI 10.1007/978-94-017-9346-9_10

development in Albania[3] as a state that aspires to full EU membership. It analyzes the decentralization process in Albania through an in depth study of its local government units (LGUs), their institutional set up, their strategic and functional roles, and their human and financial resources allocations. The institutional analysis is complemented by a bottom up perspective on the decentralization process and its outcomes as seen and assessed by the local elected bodies.[4] This examination will highlight the gaps in Albania's decentralization policies and outcomes, and focuses especially on the provisions regarding the main functions of local government. It explores potential approaches and interventions that would improve policy making at the local and regional levels (Fig. 10.1).

The chapter is organized in two main parts. Part 1 analyzes decentralization policy in Albania, which, in some key aspects, is comparable to FYR Macedonia experience.[5] Part 2 reflects on regional development in the EU member states as a model to which Albanian decision makers purport to aspire. This EU example serves as a benchmark when discussing the findings of this analysis, and formulating some recommendations.[6]

The study data were collected in four regional councils (Qarks)[7] and complemented by desk research involving scrutiny of relevant national and international documents, content analysis of important publications, and public statements, and presentations by key policy actors. Particular reference is made to the lessons learned from the latest Austrian Development Cooperation/Swiss Development Cooperation (ADA/SDC) funded regional development program.[8]

[3] As evidenced in the Albanian 2012 Progress Report, the progress of the reforms concerned with regional development is very limited. The draft National Strategy for Development and Integration (NSDI) 2013–2020 includes a range of policies pertaining to regional development, but the overall institutional framework still lags far behind the EU standards.

[4] Interviews with four regional councils' (Qarks) leaders and representatives were conducted in order to understand better their perspective as well their involvement in the process.

[5] FYR Macedonia is a Balkan country at a similar level of development and similar position in the EU accession process making it an interesting case to observe if not follow.

[6] Note that it is not the only driver. Discussion with the leaders of four Qarks and with regional council staff provided insights into and hints about the Albanian mentality which further informed our own views.

[7] The 2nd tier of governance in Albania consists of 12 regional councils. The Qarks studied in this chapter were chosen based on several criteria. Tirana is the biggest and represents the economically richest region of Albania which is simultaneously the weakest in its commitment to pursuit of decentralization. Shkodra and Kukes are the economically poorest Qarks, and Lezha has had considerable involvement of different donors to assist its decentralization and regional development (UNDP, Austrian Development Cooperation/Swiss Development Cooperation -ADA/SDC).

[8] The Regional Development Program (RDP) has been in place since February 2011 and runs till December 2014. One of its main expected results is development of a regional development agenda for Albania.

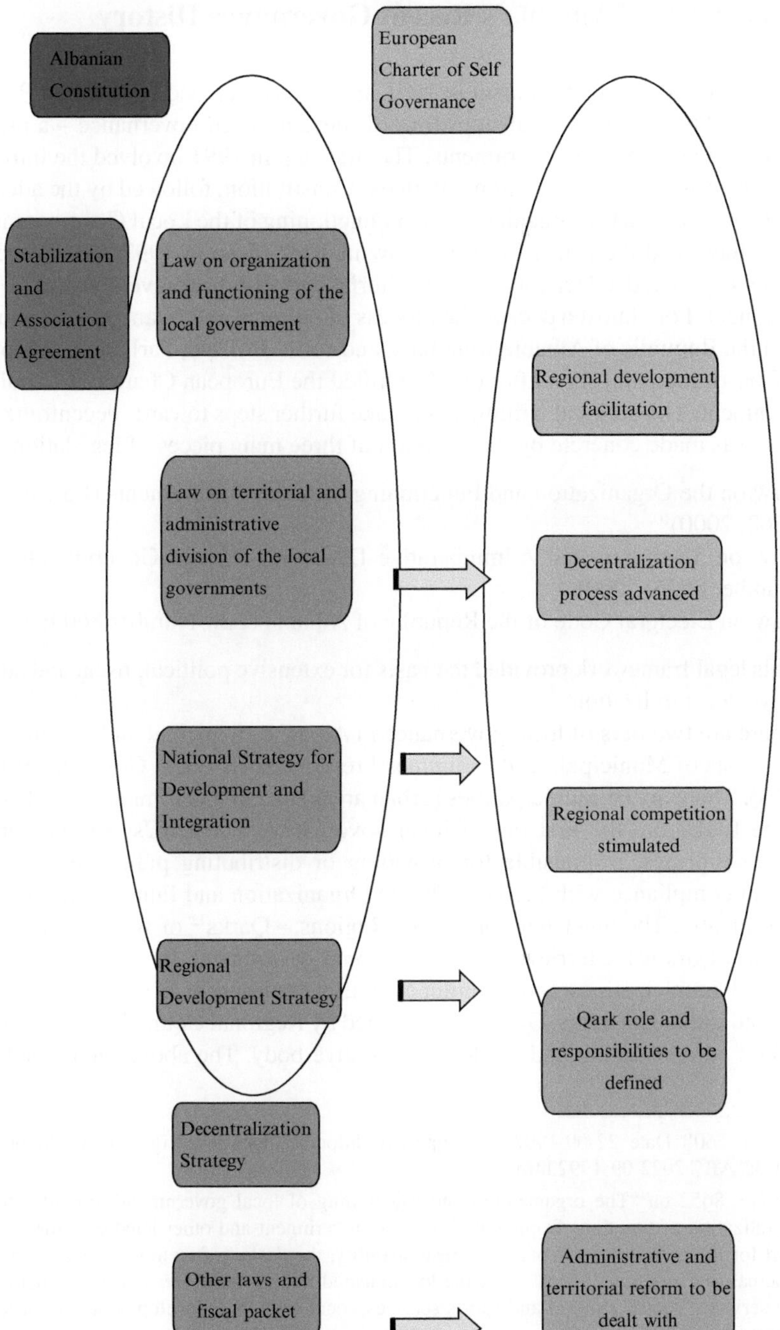

Fig. 10.1 Decentralization policy reform in Albania

2 Overview of Albania's Recent Governance History

Soon after the fall of communism in 1991, the government led by the then Party of Labour of Albania took initial steps towards decentralized governance – a process continued by successive governments. The first step in 1991 involved the introduction of the principle of local autonomy in the Constitution, followed by the adoption in 1992 of a Law on the Organization and Functioning of the Local Government, the Prefect Law[9] and the Local Elections Law in 1992. Also in 1992, the Council of Ministers approved a decision on the territorial and administrative division of local government. For almost a decade the process of political and financial decentralization in the Republic of Albania went back and forth. In 1998, Parliament adopted a new Constitution and soon after (1999) ratified the European Charter of Local Self Government. The political willingness to take further steps towards decentralization reform was made concrete by the adoption of three main pieces of legislation:

- Law on the Organization and Functioning of Local Governments (Law Number 8562; 2000)[10];
- Law on Territorial and Administrative Division of Local Governments (Law Number 8653; 2000);
- Law on Electoral Code of the Republic of Albania (Law Number 8609; 2000).

This legal framework provided the basis for extensive political, fiscal and administrative decentralization.

There are two tiers of local governance in Albania: municipal and regional. One tier consists of Municipalities/Communes[11] referred to as Local Government Units (LGUs). There are 65 municipalities (urban areas) and 308 communes (rural areas), and the LGUs are the first tier of local governance. The LGUs are autonomous public authorities, responsible for providing or distributing public services, and goods in compliance with the law (On the Organization and Functioning of Local Governments). The other tier consists of Regions – Qarks[12] of which there are 12 regions. A Qark is the territory of a sub-national government, which encompasses a cluster of municipalities and communes with a tradition of economic and social links, and mutual interests. Qarks are governed by Regional Councils, which include the Qark administration and the local legislative body. The above mentioned Law

[9] Law No. 7608 Date 22-09-1992 http://qpz.gov.al/doc.jsp?doc=docs/Ligj%20Nr%207608%20Dat%C3%AB%2022-09-1992.htm

[10] Law No. 8652 on "The organization and functioning of local government" provides for the decentralization of functions from central to local government and other legal documents allow support for the transfer of authority and responsibility, the design of methodologies, guidelines, and increased management capacity of the local elected bodies in the areas of infrastructure and public services, social, cultural and sports services, local economic development, and order and civil protection.

[11] Municipalities are entities covering a single urban area; communes are constellations of rural villages, mostly with small numbers of inhabitants ranging from 2,500 to 25,000.

[12] Qark is the Albanian acronym for the region.

8562, defines the role of the Regional Council as "developing and implementing regional policies and their harmonization with the national policies at the regional level, as well as any other exclusive function given by law" (Law 8562, Art. 13). Article 109 of the Constitution of the Republic of Albania provides for the formation of regional councils as local government bodies. Under these provisions, the regional council is elected by the representatives of the first local government tier; hence, there is no direct election by voters, which reduces the representativeness of the Qarks within the governance structure and is discussed later in the chapter.

At the level of mission, principles, and rights, the Law on the Organization and Functioning of Local Governments applies equally to the municipalities, the communes and the Qark. It assigns several exclusive functions to the municipalities and communes, but there is a lack of clarity about substantial functions and expenditures assigned to the Regional Council.

Our interest in this chapter is focused particularly on the Qarks because of the ambiguity related to regional level governance in Albania, which is not least a consequence of some major projects initiated to facilitate the decentralization process. Effective regional development requires close cooperation, and synergies between both levels of local governance, as well as joint planning and financing. Therefore, both elements need to be analyzed together.

3 Legal Framework and Instruments

In addition to the three main pieces of legislation referred to above, other laws were drafted and approved after 2000 and, together, constitute the legal decentralization and regional development framework in Albania. These laws, presented in Table 10.1, cover a range of specific issues such as taxation of small businesses, local taxation, social programs, and an amendment to the Constitution.

Following approval of the main legislative framework in 2000, Decentralization continued by adoption of the National Decentralization roadmap in 2007, which introduced a new set of reforms. The laws in Table 10.1, especially Nos. 8652, 8653 and 8654, lay down the principles for the functioning of LGUs. The principles of good democratic governance relevant to the present study include the principle of local economic development, governance at the closest level to the population, the principle of subsidiarity, and collaboration among LGUs.[13] More importantly, these laws endow LGUs with rights to property, governance, fiscal autonomy, and development. Law No. 8562 establishes the mission, rights, and principles of municipalities, communes and the Qark. However, while it assigns several individual (exclusive) functions to municipalities and communes, this Law does not allocate substantial functions or budgets to the Regional Council (Qark). This hampers the

[13] The 12 principles of good democratic governance at local level are defined in the EU Strategy for Innovation and Good Governance at Local Level available at: http://www.coe.int/t/dgap/localdemocracy/strategy_innovation/strategy_brochure_e.pdf

Table 10.1 Local governance legal framework

Law Number	Year	Title
8562	2000	Law on the organization and functioning of local governments
8653	2000	Law on territorial and administrative division of local governments
8609	2000	Law on Code of the Republic of Albania
8654	2000	Law on the organization and functioning of the municipality of Tirana
8743	2001	Law on real estate properties of the state
8744	2001	Law on the transfer of the real estate properties of the state to the local government units
8978	2002	Law on local small business tax (revised)
8979	2002	Law on some additions and amendments to Law no. 8438, date 28.12.1999, "On the income tax" with the respective amendments
8980	2002	Law on some amendments to the Law no. 8560, date 22.12.1999, "On the tax procedures in the Republic of Albania (revised)
8982	2002	Law on the system of local taxes (amended)
8991	2003	Amendments to Law no. 8405 on urban planning
9232	2004	Law on social programs on the inhabitant housing in urban areas
9632	2004	Law on social programs on the inhabitant housing in urban areas
9632	2006	Local tax system
9675	2007	Changes to the Law no. 8417, date 21.10.1998 Constitution of Republic of Albania
9719	2007	Changes and additions to the Law no. 9232, date 13.05.2004 for social programs on residential housing in urban areas
9745	2007	Changes and additions on the Law no. 9632, date 30.10.2006, local tax system
9743	2007	Changes and additions to the Law no. 8405, dated 17.09.1998 for urban planning, amended.
9869	2008	Law on the loan for local governance

(scattered) efforts to facilitate regional development. On the other hand, responsibility for shared functions – such as health, education and the environment – rests with the respective ministries in cooperation with municipalities and communes, not with the Regional Councils. Similarly, Law 8562 does not assign substantial spending powers to the Regional Council. Most (between 90 and 99 %) of Qark budgets[14] come from central government as part of an unconditional transfer. There is also a budget line within the membership quota for the LGUs comprising each Qark. However, according to the Qark leaders interviewed, this is not paid regularly by the LGUs. The third largest budget line is the conditional transfer for the delegated functions (e.g. the cadastre). Only a very small portion of the Qark budget comes from taxes and fees that are related to the services provided by the Qarks or the fines they impose. This clearly shows the Qarks' weakness and dependence on central

[14] As reported by the leader of Shkodra Qark, Mr. M. Cungu, the annual budget is approximately €640,000 99 % of which consists of is unconditional grant from central government.

government based on the limited range of functions and services that generate revenues allocated to the regional level.

In Albania, there are considerable disparities and ambiguities with regard to the implementation of the principle of local economy and governance. The term decentralization is understood as "the transfer of authority and responsibility for public functions from the central government to subordinate or quasi-independent government organizations and/or the private sector" (Litvack et al. 1998). Decentralization can help national government/ministries reach larger numbers of local areas with services; allow stronger political representation for diverse political, ethnic, religious, and cultural groups in decision-making, and lead to more creative, innovative and responsive programs by allowing local "experimentation". It can increase political stability and national unity by allowing citizens to better control public programs at the local level (Crucq and Hemminga 2007, p. 7). Of course, there are many ambiguities associated with implementing decentralization[15] which have not been carefully assessed in Albania given that the main incentive is closely linked to the country's aspirations to join the EU. Despite the merits of the general principle that LGUs are responsible for basic services, in Albania provision of services (e.g., drinking water, urban waste management, rural roads maintenance, primary health care services) suffers from a clear lack of capacity in some municipalities – and especially the communes – to offer an acceptable level of quality, and to do so efficiently. An example is the failure of all LGUs in Albania to deal with urban waste management as envisaged in the national strategy. Some municipalities and communes use almost 30 % of the unconditional transfer for this service while national level generation of revenue for this service remains very low. The main reasons for this capacity deficit are lack of human resources in these LGUs combined with limited economies of scale in the small LGUs.

In parallel with decentralization efforts aimed at the LGUs, policy makers have pushed ahead with a regional development agenda mostly because of the interest in supporting this level from various international development partner organizations such as USAID, UNDP, ADA, and SDC. The first efforts to promote regional development can be traced back to 1990 when a USAID financed program established Regional Development Agencies (RDAs), followed in 2000 by the UNDP program aimed at implementing the Millennium Development Goals in each Qark. In 2007, the Albanian Government drafted a Regional Development Cross-cutting Strategy 2007–2013 (CSRD) whose main aim was to strengthen regional development. The CSRD is important in so far as it was the first attempt at an Albanian concept of public policy for regional development. It did not define clear responsibilities or structures for the Qarks in relation to developing capacities to participate in EU Cohesion or Regional Development Policy; nor did it aspire to setting the directions to achieve this. Although the CSRD proposed a platform for regional development through the establishment of Regional Development Agencies in each Qark, there was insufficient clarification of the role of the Qark. The key shortcoming was a failure to integrate in one policy platform other important sectors and/or crosscut-

[15] Rosen 2002; Kalin 2003; Crucq and Hemminga 2007; Toto 2010.

ting policies/strategies, such as rural development, tourism, environmental protection, water management, education, social issues, transportation etc., to make regional development policy more effective.

Nevertheless, the CSRD was ambitious in its proposal for a regional development institutional framework, and it tried to establish several coordination mechanisms, but unfortunately this strategy was never implemented.[16] In 2009, a draft Law on Regional Development was prepared based on the CSRD strategy objectives and recommendations from various policy actors,[17] but was never passed by Parliament and remains on hold. Soon after the drafting of this Law, the UNDP and the EC initiated a program to support the Albanian Government to move forward more decisively with implementation of its regional development policy,[18] with the involvement also of other actors. In 2011, ADA/SDC proposed a program to promote regional development of the northern part of Albania, based on a bottom-up approach. Mr. P. Gjoni,[19] in the kick off meeting of the ADC/SDC financed Regional Development Program, the new bottom up approach implied by this initiative was intended to overcome the previous difficulties and shortcomings related to managing regional development by fragmented decentralized functions and structures. This 'lessons-learned' informed approach by the donor community acknowledged the necessity of pursuing a twin-track approach to addressing regional development issues given the generally weak commitment to regional development of local authorities. The policy development timeline and diversity of donors active in the sector clearly reflect this donor driven regional development policy reform in Albania. In contrast, at municipality level there was much stronger political will to push forward with decentralization along the path dictated by the European accession agenda.

4 The Importance of Qarks for Regional Development in Albania

Albania's authoritarian history and experience of a command economy meant that Albania's public services were largely centralized. It is the task mainly of various line ministries to formulate sectoral policies and to manage economic and social development issues related to public sectors such as transport, education, health, communication, the environment (especially waste management), and trade. These

[16] This is the fate of almost every single strategy in Albania; the policy strategies frequently lack financial bills to implement them.

[17] IDM and Co-Plan are two think-tanks that contributed to this agenda and identified various ambiguities and shortcomings in the existing strategy during several round tables organized by these NGOs.

[18] The program was named "Integrated Support for Decentralization – a Regional Development Program".

[19] Opening speech of the Regional Development Program kick off meeting in 2011.

ministries have an institutional presence in the capital Tirana and several decentralized offices for provision of services to citizens through regional or even district level institutions. Inspired by the National Strategy for Development and Integration (NSDI) 2007–2013[20] and in response to pressure from the international community, since 2007 Albania has worked on developing 38 sectoral strategies, of which 27 have been approved by the Council of Ministers, 7 are in the process of approval and 4 are still in a draft version.

Sectoral strategies and priorities are mostly implemented in parallel, with funds channeled from the national budget and donors in a top-down fashion, mainly through decentralized institutions controlled by the ministries, but also through local government. These sectoral policies have an impact at the regional and local levels, although their impact at regional level is difficult to assess due to the lack of instruments for their full and effective implementation. There are significant regional disparities in social and economic development, and education outcomes, in Albania. For example the Tirana region has the lowest regional poverty levels (8.7 % of the population were below poverty line in 2008) while poverty levels in the so called Mountain area of Albania were 26.6 % in the same year.[21] The extent of disparities in the level of regional development is illustrated by the number of registered enterprises; at the end of 2012, there were 41,742 active enterprises registered in the Tirana region, followed by Shkodra (6,377), Lezhe (2,883) and Kukes (914).[22] In addition, the decision of the Council of Ministers (No. 1037, dated 15.12.2010) to split Albania according to three Nuts II[23] levels, is being questioned following the results of the latest census. The population threshold for NUTS II according Regulation EC no.1059/2003 is 800,000–3,000,000 inhabitants and according to the 2011 census the population of Albania is 2,800,138 inhabitants.[24]

Overall, the efforts of the Albanian political class to initiate a constructive approach to regional development policy have been very fragmented. Although the limitations of the LGUs to deliver some key services such as health, education and environment, are evident, there have been no attempts made by government to address the problem by considering the regional level as a potential solution. This experience contrasts sharply with neighboring FYR Macedonia, where the local political authorities seem to be in more control of the regional development policy process. The reforms there have been driven by the local actors and been much less influenced by implementation of projects to meet the Stabilization and Association Agreement's milestones than in Albania. Although both countries embarked on developing regional development policy around the same time (1999–2000) and in

[20] National Strategy for Development and Integration, Albanian Government available at http://dsdc.gov.al/dsdc/National_Strategy_for_Development_and_Integration_7_2.php

[21] INSTAT Albanian poverty trend 2005–2008.

[22] INSTAT Business registration Survey 2012.

[23] Regulation (EC) no. 1059/2003 of the European parliament and of the council on the establishment of a common classification of territorial units for statistics (NUTS).

[24] Once Albania becomes an EU candidate country, the statistical regions' classification will have to be negotiated. which may require abrogation of the above-mentioned decision.

the context of the EU's accession agenda, the difference in the outcomes is clearly visible. FYR Macedonia has made much more tangible progress in the development of its eight regions; it has achieved greater fiscal decentralization and balanced regional development while Albania still struggles to clarify the role of the Qarks. Table 10.2 shows a wide discrepancy among Qarks in terms of the number of constitutive LGUs and the population size.

Administratively, each Qark is composed of one major municipality and one or more smaller municipalities, and several communes. Mayors and local councilors, who are elected through popular vote, head municipalities and communes. Regional councilors are chosen indirectly by the commune and municipal councils. Local officials are appointed by the mayors and approved by the local councils.

As already mentioned, progress towards decentralization during 2000–2012 in Albania mostly bypassed the Qarks. Their role is perceived more as a coordination office providing a range of functions and services (Law Nr. 8562), whose implementation has lagged or has even reversed in recent years.[25] The leaders of the four Qarks included in this study pointed to several areas of weakness and backsliding in regional development.

One of the key areas is developing and implementing regional policies and their coordination with national policies. Some Qarks, such as Shkodër and Kukës, have been more active in this regard. This is mainly because of the proactive approach of their leadership and support from the donor community. However, although strategic documents have been approved, the strategies have not been implemented due to lack of funding, human resources and instruments for their enforcement.

There is widespread underperformance in some basic service provision e.g. construction and maintenance of rural roads. Construction and maintenance of rural roads is an area of Qark responsibility whose implementation is lagging mainly due to lack of funding from central government. No central government funding was allocated for either maintenance or construction of new roads in 2000–2006. Since 2006, the Albanian Development Fund has provided substantial funding for the construction of new rural roads, but on condition that their status is upgraded to national roads, implying a change in responsibility for their maintenance. This policy shift is due to the central government's and respective donors'[26] dissatisfaction with the Qarks' performance. However, the Qark leaders interviewed claim that Qark performance is undermined by insufficient allocation of funds by central government.

Performing delegated functions by one or more LGUs situated within the Qark (based on mutual agreement) has not been widely implemented. The Qarks can be delegated to undertake urban planning by LGUs with insufficient human resources in the communes and smaller municipalities. However, over the years, LGUs have assumed this function, which had reduced the range of services the Qark offers. Urban planning is one area that is tightly controlled by the local political structures and serves for patronage purposes- hence resistance to shift it under Qark mandate.

---

[25] Interview with the president of Shkodër Qark, November 2012.

[26] Mostly the World Bank, European Bank for Reconstruction and Development, and the European Investment Bank.

Table 10.2 Albanian regions (Qarks)

Qarks	Berat	Diber	Durres	Elbasan	Fier	Gjiro-kaste	Korec	Kukes	Lezhe	Shkoder	Tirane	Vlore
No. of LGUs	25	35	16	50	42	32	37	27	21	33	29	26
Population ('000)	141	137	265	296	311	75	220	85	136	217	764	184

Source: Albanian Institute of Statistics

There is also an issue with maintaining the cadastre of agricultural land and protecting agricultural and forestland (as a function delegated by central government). This function so far has been performed by the Qarks, but according to the leader of Shkodër Qark,[27] enforcement of this function is difficult because the LGUs represented in the regional council are the steering body of the administration.

Thus, there is some evidence that the decentralization policy reform has slowed in recent years. For example, in 2006 the competitive grant fund for LGUs was set up. The financial resources for the fund were carved out from earlier LGUs budgets on the grounds that the LGUs neglected capital investment.[28] The decision making for fund allocation was thus moved to the central state level and the competitive grant allocation system was introduced. Unfortunately, this policy shift was implemented by central government without involvement of the LGU representatives in the decision making. At the beginning of the scheme, in 2006–2007, the Qarks played a crucial role in implementing the allocation scheme, which provided firm ground for pursuing a regional development agenda; centralization of the grant allocation process effectively put an end to this. With the amendment of the law on local taxes in 2009, the fiscal decentralization policy experienced a further setback. The background to or reasons for this initiative by the Democratic Party (DP) Socialist Movement for Integration (SMI) coalition government, were related to obligations stemming from the Albanian EU Stabilization and Association Agreement, but were not a response to requests from interested stakeholders and government did not consult the affected LGUs for their views. Thereafter, the LGUs' fiscal autonomy was reduced and the collection of the small business tax was partly centralized (USAID 2009, p. 27). This is reflected in the decreasing share of tax income from small business in the LGU budget with no corresponding compensation by way of unconditional transfers from central government. In this way, the ruling party opted for financial weakening of the big municipalities such as Tirana, Durres, Vlora, and Korca which at the time were under Socialist Party (SP) rule, a minority party in the Albanian Parliament.

Although the RDF has remained in place, it is administered by central government with no substantive role for the Qarks. One of the interviewed Qark leaders told us that the decision for control of the fund by central government both hindered the regional development agenda and comprised unfair and unequal treatment

[27] Interview with Mr. M. Cungu, November, 2012.

[28] As highlighted by the Institutional and Capacity Assessment to implement the Regional Development Program in Northern Albania, www.rdpnorthernalbania.org. The competitive grant scheme was replaced by the regional development fund in 2009 with the idea of boosting regionalization, but without clearly defined criteria. The purpose of the regional development fund is financing of capital investment in local roads, water and sewerage systems, health and education facilities, culture structures, local food markets, drainage and irrigation, and forestry. The system that administers this fund for regional development is quite complex and several bodies are involved in the allocation, distribution and implementation. The final approval of the projects to be funded through regional development fund, is made by the Committee for the Development of the Regions, whose work is facilitated by the General Technical Secretariat (DSDC – Department for Strategies and Donors Coordination), within the Prime Minister's Cabinet.

among LGUs, since those heading the ruling party were favored compared to those controlled by the opposition.

The Open Society Forum monitoring report on progress towards the Stabilization and Association Agreement (2010, p. 40) concludes that "the decentralization reform in Albania has almost entirely been brought to a standstill". Like the FYR Macedonia, Albania must respond very soon to both the decentralization and regional development reforms required by the EU integration process. Issues such as territorial reform, the role of the Qarks, structures required to access IPA (Instrument for Pre-accession Assistance from the EU) funds require immediate attention from policymakers. Failure to attend to these issues, and to do so soon, will result in Albania not being able to comply with EU cohesion policy rules and standards and being unable to access funds from IPA III, IV, and V.

Progress toward regional development legislation has been hampered, and the CSRD passed in 2007 was not fully implemented. In 2010, the UNDP and the EU initiated the Integrated Support for Decentralization (ISD) program to prepare a revised regional development policy framework for 2010–2020 in order to outline a long-term roadmap for Albania's EU accession process. The revised policy was approved by the program steering committee (including representatives from the MoI, Ministry of Economy, Trade and Energy, and the Department for Strategies and Donor Coordination), but it never reached the senior government level of the Council of Ministers which makes the final decisions. In addition, the project operated top down and excluded participation of local players such as the Qarks and the LGU representatives. The result is summarized in the EU Progress report 2012 (p. 52): "Considerable efforts are needed to establish the necessary institutional and administrative capacity at central and local levels and to develop a pipeline of mature and quality projects. Overall, preparations in the area of regional development are still at an early stage".

5 Decentralization: Achievements and Challenges

Decentralization in Albania has advanced since the early 1990s, but continues to face several challenges related to the establishment of local government units, their roles and financial resources, accountability, and the position of the Qarks. The territorial and administrative reform of 2000 abolished the former 36 districts and established a new structure of 12 regions or Qarks), 65 municipalities, and 309 communes. The boundaries to communes and municipalities remained in place; average population number are 22,500 in municipalities and 5,200 in communes, and include 48 % of local government units with less than 5,000 inhabitants.[29] The mayors and the heads of communes are directly elected by majority vote; the municipal/commune councils are elected according to a proportional voting system based on

[29] Albanian Regional Development: Opportunities and Challenges, UNDP Mission Report September 2005.

party lists. The regional institutions (Qark) do not have individual own democratic legitimacy in so far as they are indirectly elected. Local governments are organized in three national associations: the Albanian Association of Municipalities, the Albanian Association of Communes, and the Albanian Association of Qarks. The associations are performing an increasing role of bringing the views of municipalities/communes into the political debate, and increasingly are successful in influencing political decisions on decentralization issues at central government level. However, they complain about lack of capacity and limited interest among local governments in joining forces for political lobbying. To influence political decision-making in their favor, mayors and heads of communes still seem to prefer direct and personal links to central power holders.

In relation to the principle of subsidiarity, the organic law of 2000[30] and its recent amendments, define a range of exclusive, shared, and delegated functions to municipalities and communes. The main exclusive functions include: water supply and sewerage, construction and maintenance of local roads and public spaces, public lighting and urban transportation, public cemeteries, parks, sports activities, household waste collection, urban planning, cultural and historical heritage, social services and administration of nurseries and homes for the elderly. Joint responsibilities of the municipalities/communes include school and pre-university services, healthcare and social assistance, public order, and environmental management and protection. In reality, these responsibilities are treated as delegated functions, and in many cases there is no clear division of responsibilities between the decentralized services and the municipalities and communes, resulting in a strong trend toward seeing the municipalities and communes as another decentralized services delivery unit. The transfer of responsibilities is not complete in some areas, and the delivery of local public services is not operating as intended for a variety of reasons. In some cases, there is an absence of specific legislation (e.g. urban planning), delays in property transfer (e.g. roads, water supply, sewerage systems), and in others, lack of financial resources and/or professional capacity in the municipalities/communes. Municipalities/communes also complain about poor transparency and predictability of the transfer process: some competences were transferred at very short notice, with no proper preparation and information. Moreover the regional policy making scheme is unclear, as is how local government units (municipalities/communes) should implement policies drafted at the regional level.

In addition, many competencies that have been transferred to municipalities and communes require a regional approach in order to be cost efficient. A nation-wide or regional legal and policy framework, financial equality, or at least, inter-communal cooperation are needed to avoid each municipality acting in isolation and taking no account of the needs and interests beyond its boundaries. Although the organic law foresees the possibility of inter-communal cooperation, there is little real cooperation, and no real incentives for collaboration.

The municipal/communal budgets are covered by central government grants and local revenues. The unconditional grant covers about 50 % of the local budgets. It is

[30] Law 8652 (31.7.2000) on "Organization and Functioning of the Local Government".

calculated according to particular criteria, and a formula that is subject to annual negotiation. Conditional grants are used to finance "shared" municipality/commune functions, and competitive grants have been introduced to finance small local level capital investments e.g. for roads, water supply, education, and health. Since 2006, municipalities/communes have been allowed to collect property taxes on buildings and agriculture land, property transfer taxes, infrastructure impact taxes, small business taxes, simplified profits taxes, and vehicle taxes. In general, the potential of local revenue has not been exploited fully and tends to privilege municipalities and communes with a certain level of economic potential. At Qark level there is no possibility for raising local revenue. Qarks are entitled only to some conditional grants from central government for delegated functions. Thus, not all proposed regional policies have real opportunity to be implemented by the Qark or its members.

In view of the strong totalitarian version of communism in Albania compared to the rest of the Western Balkans, state institutions, legal procedures, and political processes have changed substantially. However, state power at central and local levels is often managed and administrated by a generation of (male) politicians and officials who were schooled in a deeply hierarchical, centralist, closed, and authoritative system. The politicians, administrations, and civil society are only very slowly learning new roles and attitudes. While it is generally assumed that local authorities are more accessible to citizens and local civil society groups than the central authorities, so far civil society seems to contribute little to shaping political decisions in Albania. Although there are some good examples of changing attitudes among authorities, and growing self-confidence, trust, and engagement among citizens, civil society still plays a very limited role as a counterbalance to state power. A culture of public debate and dialogue within and among the authorities has yet to be established, and most decisions are non-transparent and controlled – even at local level – by a still centralized and very personalized power system within the two main political parties. It appears difficult for citizens to hold local (and central) authorities accountable for illegal or inappropriate action. Although they are allowed to go to court to challenge individual decisions, this is not seen as a viable option by many citizens. There is also very limited public space for raising political issues, demanding accountability, or challenging political decisions at local or at central level. As in the case of other countries in the Balkan region, there are several NGOs working on development and human rights issues but they often lack a broad local constituency.

We referred to the fact that, according to the constitution, the regional councils and the heads of regional councils do not have direct political legitimacy. Since the Qark councils consist of representatives of municipalities and communes, they are often considered local government associations rather than an intermediate level of government. Although the Organic Law No. 8652 provides a basis for regional taxes and fees for public services, the regions lack fiscal autonomy. Qarks are primarily financed by transfers from central government (particularly to fund a relatively well developed administration) and municipalities/communes which are supposed by law to transfer an agreed percentage of their revenues to regional budgets, however, this does not always happen. Initially, the regions were established to optimize the provision of public services, to provide a platform for achieving common regional interests, and to ensure the alignment of local regional and national priorities and harmonize local and regional policies with national objectives.[31] The Organic Law No. 6852 vaguely outlines the roles and responsibilities of the regions (Qark), stipulating that the main functions of the council are the "development and implementation of regional policies and their harmonization with the national policies at the regional level". However, the Qarks have neither the administrative instruments nor the financial means or professional capacities to deal with this task. It seems that big municipalities are particularly unwilling to accept regional guidance or intermediation in their direct dialogue with the central authorities. Moreover, it is still the Prefect's responsibility to check the legality (but not the political appropriateness) of the decisions taken by the municipalities/communes. In spite of the Qark's responsibility for regional coordination and planning, there is no clear role in overseeing the action of municipalities/communes, or fostering much needed cooperation among local institutions.

Qarks also have the right to exercise executive competence in the delivery of public services: tasks can be delegated by the central government or by municipalities/communes. For example, Qarks contribute to managing rural roads and – most recently – to the police force. In 2005, central government transferred responsibility for the allocation of funds in the area of primary education and health care to the regional councils. A year later, these responsibilities were taken back and replaced by the competitive grant system, directly allocating investment funds to municipalities/communes in need. The transfer of responsibilities resulted in a widespread waste of funds and a number of unfinished school constructions. The transfer was done with little preparation or consultation, and took no account of the limitations of Qarks to favor regional interests over the local interests of their members, which contributed even more to the failure of this process.

The Qarks seem to be in a relatively uncomfortable intermediate position between central government, the line ministries, the Prefect, and the municipalities/communes. While many observers agree an absolute need for an intermediate level of decentralization, others say that the territorial dimension of Qarks is not adequate for Albania, suggesting either bigger slices in line with EU/NUTS II regions or smaller ones similar to the old district system. In addition, the Qarks are considered entities with relatively broad scope but limited tasks and capacities, limited political legitimacy, and dependent on municipalities and communes for funding. Figure 10.2 provides a graphic visualization of public institutions and processes at Qark level.

A new decentralization strategy[32] was elaborated by the MoI (2006), to address some of the challenges mentioned; however it was never approved by the Council of Ministers. Neither local government units nor the Qarks' were adequately involved in the design of the strategy. The same can be said for the Regional Development Crosscutting strategy prepared by the Ministry of Economy, Trade

---

[31] Albanian Regional Development: Opportunities and Challenges, UNDP Mission Report September 2005.

[32] http://www.moi.gov.al/drupal1/pdf/Strategjia_decentralizimital.pdf

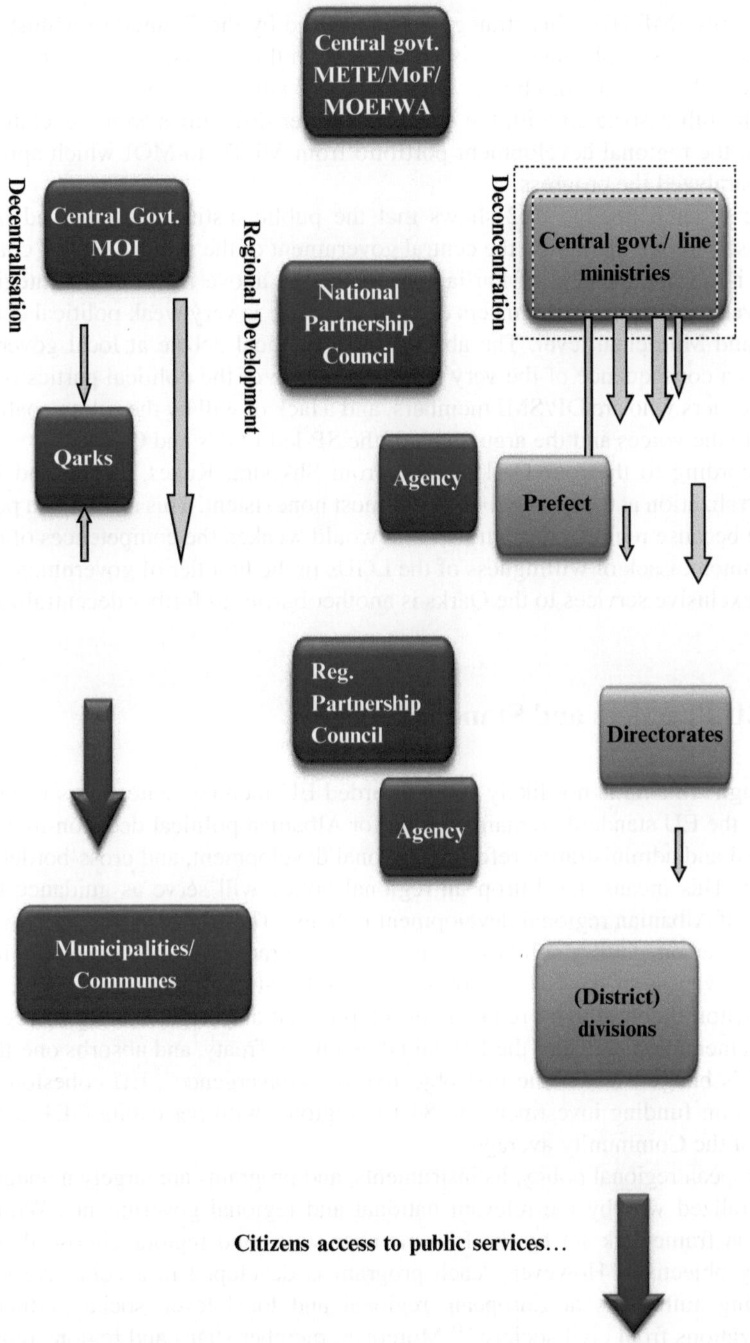

Fig. 10.2 Public institutions and processes at Qark level

and Energy (METE). This strategy was approved by the Council of Ministers and adopted, but its implementation is far away from the targets. The main reasons for this are lack of ownership by the Qark and LGU administrations, and absence of a financial bill associated with the strategy. Further difficulties were generated by a shift in the regional development portfolio from METE to MOI which appears to have paralyzed the progress.

The scheme in Fig. 10.2 shows that the public institutions involved in both processes are led mainly by the central government of the ruling DP/SMI coalition. There is no involvement of Parliament (since the above mentioned strategies are approved by Council of Ministers decree) and there is very weak political debate at Qark and Municipal level. The absence of a political debate at local government level is a consequence of the very strong influence of the political parties over the Qark leaders who are DP/SMI members, and a lack of will by the ruling coalition to listen to the voices and the arguments of the SP-led LGUs and Qarks.

According to the four Qark leaders from Shkodra, Kukes, Tirana and Lezha, decentralization at the regional level is almost nonexistent. This is mainly a political choice because regional decentralization would weaken the competences of central government. Lack of willingness of the LGUs in the first tier of government to delegate exclusive services to the Qarks is another barrier to further decentralization.

6 EU Practices and Standards

Although Albania is not likely to be afforded EU member state status in the near future, the EU standards remain a guide for Albanian political decision-making on political and administrative reforms, regional development, and cross-border cooperation. This means that European regional policy will serve as guidance for the design of Albanian regional development policies. The EU's regional policy 2007–2013 aimed at putting solidarity principle into practice, while strengthening the competitiveness of the EU economy as a whole. Strengthening economic, social, and territorial cohesion by reducing developmental disparities among its regions is a fundamental objective of the EU, laid down in its Treaty, and absorbs one-third of the EU's budget. Under the first objective of "convergence", EU cohesion policy focuses on funding investments in 84 EU regions, with per capita GDP less than 75 % of the Community average.

European regional policy, its instruments, and programs are largely managed in a decentralized way by the relevant national and regional governments. Within the common framework set by the EU, member states and regions choose their own priority objectives. However, "each program is developed in a collective process involving authorities at European, regional and local level, social partners and organizations from civil society."[33] Moreover, member states and regions must prepare "National Strategic Reference Frameworks" as well as national and regional

[33] EU regional policy principles http://ec.europa.eu/regional_policy/how/principles/index_en.cfm

operational programs. Strategic guidelines on cohesion policy have been developed to support effective planning at national level. According to these guidelines, programs should concentrate investment in high-growth areas, invest in drivers of growth and employment such as innovation and education, establish comprehensive medium term development strategies, contribute to trans-European infrastructure and environmental sustainability, mobilize additional resources, and develop partnerships among different levels of government and other actors.[34] These programs are negotiated and agreed with the Commission, but implementation is the responsibility of member states. There is a whole set of criteria these programs are required to comply such as for example respect for EU legislative practice, particularly on procurement, competition and environment; implementation of multi annual programs and strategic planning; building institutional framework and capacity of public administration to ensure programming, implementation, monitoring and evaluation of programs, and so on, EU regional policy is composed of a range financial and political instruments whose implementation facilitates reductions in economic and social disparities among different Community regions. Some framework instruments were designed in 1957, and cohesion policy was formalized in 1986. If Albania were to follow the same principles as EU policy, it would need to give more weight in its regional development agenda to the development of the poorest Qarks.[35] In the EU this is achieved by multi-year strategic programming of investments involving mostly local regional players. The current state of the Qarks and experience of decentralization policy in Albania more broadly, provides no foundation for such a process.

The Maastricht Treaty[36] formalized the cohesion fund and regional development committees, and affirmed the subsidiarity principle, leading to cohesion policy consolidation phase. With EU enlargement (2000–2006), the disparities in GDP deepened and the problems for new member states to cope with this policy intensified. As a result, major changes were made to the cohesion policy for the 2007–2013 phase including concentration of resources to poorer countries and regions in the EU, changes to priorities to stimulate growth, employment, and innovative technology. At the time of writing, Albania is far behind the EU priorities; its objectives for regional development remain at the level of defining the roles and responsibilities of the Qarks.

7 Conclusions

Regional development has added a new dimension to the Albanian institutional framework based on deconcentration and decentralization. To be effective, regional development must be a common objective, and its implementation should involve

[34] EU Regional Policy 2007–2013, Working for the regions, http://ec.europa.eu/regional_policy

[35] Qarks located in the northern part of Albania are considered the poorest and include Kukes and Shkodra. For this reason ADA/SDC decided to fund the regional development program for Shkodra and Lezha Qarks.

[36] The Maastricht Treaty came into force in 1993.

all ministries. The current rivalry observed among various ministries and institutions is hampering cooperative efforts. Furthermore, lower level government officials still prefer direct and personal links to power holders. A culture of public debate and dialogue within and among the authorities has yet to be established.

Regional development should be a comprehensive concept including economic, social, political, and institutional development. As referred to in the EU Lisbon Agenda, it is about making poor regions more attractive places to live and work in, to improve knowledge and innovation for growth, and to create more and better jobs. A new approach to the election and composition of regional councils should be discussed and approved. The composition and election of regional councils should be in compliance with the European Charter of Self-government. This would give more hands on implementation of policies and strategies to the regions and increase the chances of success of regional development policy. In addition, the driving forces of these processes in Albania should be local stakeholders. EU, UNDP and other development partners should and could support the process by providing know-how, examples of best practice from the region, and lessons learned rather than ready-made solutions. The Association of Qarks, Association of Municipalities, and Association of Communes as the main representations of these stakeholders' interests should be dominant in the process in order to provide ownership and implementable solutions.

One of the key challenges in many decentralized systems is transparency and accountability, and access to information. Practical experience from the regional/local level should be systematically used to nurture discussion at national level, with a view to better informed decentralization policy and regional development policy.

Quality and accessibility of public services (e.g. water, sewerage, household waste management, education, health) are key to making poor regions more attractive or maintaining their attraction for businesses, professionals, and families. The principles of subsidiarity need to be enforced and this can be done mainly through revision of Qark roles as well as greater inter-local cooperation. At the same time, local partnerships should be encouraged as an important factor in promoting regional development, particularly in view of the capacity constrains at the local government level.

References

Council of Europe. (2007). *EU strategy for innovation and good governance at local level*. Brussels: Council of Europe.

Crucq, P., & Hemminga, H. J. (2007). *Decentralization and economic growth per capita in Europe* (Groningen University Working Paper EC171). Groningen: Groningen University.

European Commission. (2012). *Albanian 2012 progress report*. Brussels: European Commission.

Government of Albania (2007). National strategy for development and integration: http://dsdc.gov.al/dsdc/National_Strategy_for_Development_and_Integration_7_2.php. Accessed 10 Oct 2012.

Government of Albania: Ministry of Interior. Albanian decentralization strategy. Available at: http://www.moi.gov.al/drupal1/pdf/Strategjia_decentralizimital.pdf. Accessed 10 Oct 2012.

INSTAT (2012). Business registration survey 2012. Tirana.
INSTAT (2013). Albania trends in poverty 2002–2005–2008. Tirana.
Litvack, J., Ahmad, J., & Bird, R. (1998). *Rethinking decentralization in developing countries*. Washington, DC: The World Bank.
Nikolov, K. (2003). UK inflation in the 1970s and 1980s: The role of output gap mismeasurement. *Journal of Economics and Business, 55*(4), 355–356. Elsevier.
Rosen, H. S. (2002). *Public finance*. New York: McGraw-Hill.
Schappi, E., et al. (2009). *Supporting regional development in Northern Albania*. Available at: www.entwicklung.at/uploads/media/Swiss-Austrian_Feasibility_Study_on_regional_development_final_version.doc. Accessed 20 Mar 2013.
Toto, R. (2008). *Rajonalizimi i Shqiperise perkundrejt Reformës Territoriale*. Tirana: Co-PLAN, Instituti per Zhvillimin e Habitatit.
Toto, R. (2010). *Trilogy of the region – policy followers or policy makers*. Tirana: Co-PLAN.
USAID. (2009). *Albanian regional development: Opportunities and challenges*. Mission report USAID 2009 (p. 27).
UNDP. (2005). Albanian regional development: opportunities and challenges. Tirana.
UNDP. (2008). Integrated support for decentralization project (ISD). Available at: http://www.undp.org.al/index.php. Accessed 20 Jan 2012.

Chapter 11
Strengthening Competitiveness in the Republic of Macedonia: A Regional Development Policy Perspective

Silvana Mojsovska

1 Competitiveness: Definition and the State of Affairs in the Republic of Macedonia

Competitiveness is increasingly being invoked as a critical factor for emerging and transition economies, particularly with regards to the discussions evolving around the level of development of national economies, rates of economic growth and prospects for further progress. Regardless of its frequent use at the macro-economic level, the concept of competitiveness is in fact poorly defined and strongly contested (European Commission Directorate 2003). Despite the fact that improving a nation's or a region's competitiveness is often stated as a central goal of economic policy, arguments abound as to what this precisely means, and whether it is even useful to talk of competitiveness at a macro-economic level at all (European Commission Directorate 2003). Strong criticism about the misconceived use of the term competitiveness at macro-level was put forward by Paul Krugman in the 1990s, asserting that the countries operate under different conditions than the companies, and therefore, no ground for reasonable comparison exists (Krugman 1994).

On the other hand, there are various proponents of the concept of macro competitiveness. This stream of thought has produced a degree of consensus on the meaning of competitiveness:

"Competitiveness may be defined as the degree to which, under open market conditions, a country can produce goods and services that meet the test of foreign competition while simultaneously maintaining and expanding domestic real income" (OECD 1992) and

S. Mojsovska, Ph.D. (✉)
Institute of Economics, University St. Cyril and Methodius, Skopje, Republic of Macedonia
e-mail: s.mojsovska@ek-inst.ukim.edu.mk

M. Thomas, V. Bojicic-Dzelilovic (eds.), *Public Policy Making in the Western Balkans*, DOI 10.1007/978-94-017-9346-9_11

"An economy is competitive if its population can enjoy high and rising standards of living and high employment on a sustainable basis. More precisely, the level of economic activity should not cause an unsustainable external balance of the economy nor should it compromise the welfare of future generations." (European Commission 2000–2002)

It could be argued that these definitions have their shortcomings, in so far as they mostly refer to the outcomes rather than the factors of competitiveness. Nevertheless, they provide basis for consideration of economic discrepancies among the nation states. The statistical data on the rates of economic growth, GDP per capita, unemployment and other macroeconomic indicators provide evidence of such differences, provoking endless scholarly discussions about the methods to boost country's ability to increase the well-being of its citizens and related policy making efforts. In this context, the competitiveness lays at the very center of these debates. We believe that, despite the lack of a widely accepted definition of the term, competitiveness could be perceived as a bridge or a route from economic underperformance to nation's welfare, and as such deserves attention in the studies concerned with the individual country's positioning in the international economic system. Indeed, the concern for how country fares in the global market has led to the development of different approaches for measuring competitiveness.

In the past three decades, several multi-country Reports dealing with competitiveness have been launched, including IMD World Competitiveness Yearbook, World Economic Forum Global Competitiveness Index (GCI) and European Competitiveness Report, each providing ranking of competitiveness of selected countries, according to the chosen indicators and methodology. Also, numerous studies devoted to competitiveness have been undertaken by OECD, World Bank and other international organizations. Regardless of the differences in the indicators used, the measurement of national competitiveness always includes indices on infrastructure, institutional set-up, human resources (demography, education and labour market), as well as factors related to the development of industry and services (through innovation and technology).

This chapter does not intend to go into the findings presented in those reports but is primarily concerned with the competitiveness profile of the Republic of Macedonia based on various indicators they use. In this context, the World Economic Forum Global Competitiveness Report (GCR) which provides a detailed overview of national competitiveness of a wide range of countries, ranks the Republic of Macedonia at 80th position (out of 144) in 2012–2013 with score of 4 (out of 7), as presented in Table 11.1. The score represents a minor improvement compared to 2008–2009, but also a slight decline compared to 2011–2012, suggesting a lack of significant and sustained positive changes.

As is evident in Table 11.1, the competitiveness index is based on 12 pillars on competitiveness (sub-indexes), grouped into three categories – "basic requirements", "efficiency enhancers" and "innovation and sophistication factors". The Republic of Macedonia had best ranking in the "basic requirements" (71st position out of 144), and the lowest in "innovation and sophistication factors" (110th position out of 144). The indicators of particular relevance for the competitiveness of the

Table 11.1 Macedonian global competitiveness indexes and sub-indexes 2008–2012

Year	2008–2009		2009–2010		2010–2011		2011–2012		2012–2013	
Indicator	Rank (out of 134)	Score (1–7)	Rank (out of 133)	Score (1–7)	Rank (out of 139)	Score (1–7)	Rank (out of 142)	Score (1–7)	Rank (out of 144)	Score (1–7)
Global competitiveness index	89	3.9	84	3.9	79	4.0	79	4.1	80	4.0
Basic requirements	68	4.4	73	4.3	70	4.4	69	4.6	71	4.5
1. Institutions	90	3.6	83	3.7	80	3.8	81	4.6	78	3.8
2. Infrastructure	89	2.9	90	3.0	91	3.5	86	3.7	81	3.6
3. Macroeconomic environment	31	5.5	49	4.8	47	4.9	37	5.3	47	5.0
4. Health and primary Education	55	5.7	60	5.5	69	5.7	80	5.5	77	5.6
Efficiency enhancers	92	3.6	85	3.8	83	3.8	87	3.8 .	84	3.8
5. Higher education and Training	73	3.8	70	3.9	72	4.0	80	4.0	81	4.0
6. Good Market Efficiency	98	3.9	76	4.1	57	4.2	63	4.3	68	4.3
7. Labour mark et Efficiency	113	3.9	86	4.2	71	4.4	72	4.3	94	4.1
8. Financial market Development	83	4.0	75	4.1	87	4.0	82	4.0	79	4.0
9. Technological readiness	83	3.0	52	3.9	64	3.6	67	3.7	71	3.8
10. Market size	104	2.7	103	2.9	106	2.8	107	2.8	104	2.8
Innovation and sophistication factors	105	3.2	93	3.2	97	3.2	104	3.1	110	3.1
11. Business sophistication	107	3.5	96	3.6	96	3.5	105	3.5	111	3.4
12. Innovation	99	2.9	92	2.9	97	2.9	105	2.8	110	2.8

Source: Global Competitiveness Report 2008–2009, 2009–2010, 2010–2011, 2011–2012, 2012–2013, World Economic Forum (www.weforum.org)

Macedonian industry, so called "the efficiency enhancing indicators", were also not particularly encouraging. Along with the sophistication and innovation which scored rather low – 3.4 and 2.8 (out of 7) in 2012–2013, respectively, the infrastructure, higher education and training, as well as technological readiness in the Republic of Macedonia are in need of substantial improvement.

Despite an unfavourable competitiveness ranking, as of mid-2013 the Republic of Macedonia has not yet developed an explicit policy approach or policy-making process aimed at increasing competitiveness of the national economy. The individual sector policies relevant for the competitiveness pillars are in place, such as those dealing with industry, technology and innovation, research and development (R&D), education and infrastructure. Apart from industrial policy created in 2009, which provides rather overall (not sector-oriented) strategic goals for improving competitiveness as well as certain actions for boosting micro-competitiveness at the company level, the other policies do not have distinctive focus on the competitiveness. Nonetheless, competitiveness has been included in the Government's programme 2011–2015, as a strategic priority under the title "Business climate and competitiveness".[1] As suggested by the title, the government activities projected in this sphere mainly focus on improvement of macroeconomic environment, rather than on delivering a comprehensive outlook on competitiveness. Such an approach was applied in the country in 2008–2012, with a result that a macroeconomic environment improved, providing the best ranking on Macedonia's sub-indexes (Table 11.1).

The reason was the implementation of regulatory reform, the so called "regulatory guillotine" aimed at establishing business-friendly climate.[2] Improvement in business environment is undoubtedly important for competitiveness, but, as evident from the indicators, it did not result in substantial rise in overall competitiveness. In this context, it is necessary that other policy areas are also treated by the policy-makers from the competitiveness perspective. For this to happen, serious changes in the policy-making settings are required to shift the policy making approach from sector-oriented to inter-disciplinary policy with the purpose of increasing competitiveness.

In terms of existing interdisciplinary policies in the Republic of Macedonia, more serious treatment of competitiveness has been applied within the framework of regional development policy. The main policy document in this area – Strategy for Regional Development comprises two main objectives[3]:

1. (Establishing) competitive planning regions characterized by dynamic and sustainable development and

[1] Programme of the Government of the Republic of Macedonia 2011–2015, http://vlada.mk/node/262?language=en-gb

[2] Since 2006, Macedonian government undertook a "Regulatory guillotine" – an intense reform aiming to eliminate many administrative barriers to the business. The government's efforts in this area were recognized in the World Bank Doing Business Report, which distinguished Macedonia as the 4th, 3rd and 3rd reformer in the world in 2008, 2010 and 2012 respectively (http://www.doingbusiness.org/reforms/top-reformers-2013).

[3] Strategy for regional development of the Republic of Macedonia, Official Gazette of the Republic of Macedonia 119/2009.

2. (Achieving) greater inter and intra-regional demographic, economic, social and spatial cohesion.

Implicit to the first objective, this policy deals with regional competitiveness. At the first glance, the two concepts of national and regional competitiveness are logically connected, but the nature of their linking in terms of the extent to which each aspect of competitiveness boosts the other has not been extensively explored in the literature. Given that regions are segments of the national economy, it could be presumed that increase in the competitiveness of the regions should have positive influence on the national competitiveness. On the other hand, if the policy-makers focus solely on the national competitiveness, this approach could (directly or indirectly) result in favouring certain regions against the others and provoke widening of inter-regional disparities in development. This is particularly important for countries with deep inter-regional disparities, such as the Republic of Macedonia, as eventual increase of national competitiveness might be at the expense of some regions lagging further behind.

The available statistical evidence at the regional level in the Republic of Macedonia does not allow measurement of regional competitiveness in the manner of the GCI. However, it provides a clear picture of the disparities among the eight regions in the country.

As presented in Table 11.2, Skopje region (around the capital) contributed to the creation of around 48.5 % of the country's gross value added (GVA) in 2007, followed by the Pelagonia region with a share of 11.2 %, while the least developed – the Northeast region- had a share of only 4.2 %. The situation did not changed significantly by 2010, as Skopje region participated with 43.7 % in the national GVA, while Northeast region had again the lowest share in the total GVA (4.4 %). Thus, the Skopje region had a predominant share of around 37.6 % and 32.5 % in the total industrial output in 2007 and 2010, respectively. Furthermore, most investment (including foreign investment) has been concentrated in the Skopje region (around 54 % of gross capital formation). Economic disparities among the regions are most evident with regards to the GDP per capita. As indicated in Table 11.2, Skopje region had three times higher GDP per capita compared to the lowest ranked Polog region (EUR 5,228.4 against EUR 1,719 in 2010). Nevertheless, despite having the highest GDP per capita, Skopje region also faces high unemployment as in other parts of the country and has serious problems related to poor transport infrastructure. The country is lagging far behind the EU member countries with GDP per capita at about 30 % of the EU average. This indicates that comparatively, the Skopje region is underdeveloped, while the situation is even worse in other regions.

The disparities among the regions reflect a mono-centric model of development in the Republic of Macedonia, with the capital (Skopje) being the most developed region. This suggests that the above mentioned GCI indicators effectively reflects the performance of the Skopje region, given that other regions are seriously lagging behind in terms of economic activity, gross capital formation, employment and other competitiveness factors. Implicitly, it could be assumed that the competitiveness of other regions, Skopje excluded, is below the level of national competitiveness

Table 11.2 Major development indicators of the planning regions in the Republic of Macedonia

Regions	Population	GDP per capita (in EUR)		Gross value added (in mil.EUR)		Share in gross value added in industrial sector		Share in gross capital formation (in %)		Unemployment rate (in %)		Local roads (in km)
	2010	2007	2010	2007	2010	2007	2010	2007	2010	2008	2012	2012
Macedonia	20,550,044	2,819.2	3,631.8	4,923.8	6,197.5	100.0	100.0	100.0	100.0	33.8	31.0	9,355
Vardar	153,858	2,921.1	3,712.6	384.5	454.0	13.5	11.2	6.2	6.1	43.6	35.9	989
East	179,770	2,065.5	3,362.2	318.8	530.7	8.8	143.9	7.5	9.6	20.0	18.5	1,180
Southwest	221,855	1,801.1	2,638.3	342.0	492.7	7.3	8.0	6.7	4.8	39.3	42.3	1,276
Southeast	172,858	2,591.0	4,198.9	381.2	542.2	6.2	6.4	6.0	6.9	11.7	13.8	957
Pelagonia	234,137	2,740.8	3,703.0	551.6	753.5	15.0	19.1	5.6	7.6	34.5	25.3	1,208
Polog	314,804	1,306.8	1,719.0	347.9	444.2	6.5	4.6	11.7	7.9	26.4	34.2	1,381
Northeast	175,045	1,405.4	2,366.7	209.1	271.6	5.1	3.3	2.3	2.6	58.0	52.8	1,026
Skopje	602,677	4,709.3	5,228.4	2,388.6	2,708.6	37.6	32.5	54.0	54.6	37.3	31.3	1,338

Source: Regions of the Republic of Macedonia (2009, 2012) State Statistical Office of the Republic of Macedonia

presented in the GCI. This points out at the complexity of the problem of low competitiveness in the Republic of Macedonia and suggests that it should not be treated solely as a national, but also as a regional phenomenon. Therefore, we argue that the logical implication for the Macedonian case would be to link the concepts of national and regional competitiveness in a unified policy framework in order to promote competitiveness. A lack of national competitiveness policy and the existence of regional development policy (which includes competitiveness among its objectives) provide a starting ground for the analysis of the possibility for employment of regional development policy as a tool for increasing national competitiveness in the Republic of Macedonia. The main queries about the viability of this proposition are related to the context and implementation of the regional development policy. These questions are discussed in the remainder of the paper.

2 Regional Development Policy in the Republic of Macedonia

The idea for the deployment of regional development policy in pursuing national competitiveness by reducing inter-regional disparities, has been vaguely explored in the literature (Batchler and Raines 2002). However, a distinctive policy approach partly related to this subject was introduced by OECD in 2007, with the idea of promoting regional clustering as an instrument for competitiveness building (OECD 2007). The main policy stream of this approach combines the postulates of regional policy, science and technology development as well as industrial and enterprise development policy. In this chapter, our focus is solely on the policy trends in the area of regional development.

Table 11.3 indicates the conceptual changes in regional development policy (new versus old approach) which have added a more complex substance to the policy. In turn, this reflects the changes in the global environment in the 1990s and the 2000s, mainly related to increase in the competition on the global market, due to the inclusion

Table 11.3 OECD approach to regional development policy

Policy stream	Old approach	New approach	Cluster programme focus
Regional policy	Redistribution from leading to lagging regions	Building competitive regions by bringing local actors and assets together	Target or often include lagging regions
			Focus on smaller firms as opposed to the larger firms, if not explicitly than de facto
			Broad approach to sector and innovation targets
			Emphasis on engagement of actors

Source: Competitive Regional Clusters: National Policy Approaches, OECD Observer (2007, p. 3)

of the post-communist countries in the world economic system, intense liberalisation of trade and capital flows, rapid technological changes, etc. The new approach promotes proactive behaviour and networking among the leading actors (regions, networks and groups of firms), in place of passive mechanism which dominated in the old policy approach (OECD 2007). The new policy approach encourages integrated policy making as a supplement to the sector oriented policy making. Regional development policy is by its very nature an integral policy (a policy that deals with different segments of development – economic, social, cultural, etc.) which could be proactive or passive, depending on the leading concept. The new OECD approach promotes active regional development policy, striving toward increased regional competitiveness. In this respect, we consider this policy making approach relevant as only proactive regional development policy could contribute to the development of competitive regions.

Regional development policy is a relatively new[4] policy in the Republic of Macedonia, introduced in 2007–2009, following the adoption of two major documents - the Law on Balanced Regional Development (2007)[5] and the Strategy for Regional Development (2009).[6] The Law stipulated creation of planning regions which territorially correspond to the statistical regions at EU NUTS 3 level.[7] Eight planning regions were established in the country: Vardar, East, Southwest, Southeast, Pelagonia, Polog, Northeast and Skopje (Fig. 11.1). The planning regions have no independent administrative power, as they have been created to serve only for development planning purposes.

The formulation of regional development policy has been attributed to the need to address wide disparities among the regions (Table 11.2), as well as to comply with the EU recommendations for the country to set up the institutional structure for supporting regional development (Commission of European Communities 2006). The EU Report on the Progress of the country in November 2006 stated that "a Law on Regional Development to align with the EU Structural and Cohesion Funds regulations is needed", as well as "an implementing agency for the regional and social components, which will be the precursor of the authority for implementing structural and cohesion funds, still needs to be established" (Commission of European Communities 2006). This has been emphasized in the Report, as the country obtained EU candidate status in December 2005, implying that it should start to prepare for the use of the structural and cohesion funds, upon eventual EU membership. Following this important step in the EU integration of the country (the

---

[4] This note refers to the period since the country's independence in 1991. Previously, Macedonia has been included into a regional policy of the Former Socialistic Federal Republic of Yugoslavia.

[5] Law on Balanced Regional Development, Official Gazette of the Republic of Macedonia 63/07.

[6] Strategy for regional development of the Republic of Macedonia, op.cit.

[7] Division on NUTS 3 regions serve for statistical purposes and measurement of the disparities within and among EU member states, as well as candidate countries. According to the demographic criteria for NUTS 3 region, it could cover territory with 150,000–800,000 inhabitants. Due to the territory and specifics of particular areas, eight NUTS 3 (statistical) regions have been established in Macedonia.

Fig. 11.1 Planning regions in Macedonia (Source: Regions of the Republic of Macedonia 2013, State Statistical Office of the Republic of Macedonia)

candidate status), the newly appointed Government in August 2006 led by the rightwing political party – VMRO-DMPNE[8] has shown strong enthusiasm for conducting EU related reforms, which resulted into prompt action towards the elaboration of the legal and strategic framework of the regional development policy. However, taking into consideration that according to the EU criteria, the Republic of Macedonia represents one region for using the EU Structural and Cohesion Funds, the regional development policy was formulated as a domestic policy addressing regional disparities.

2.1 Institutional Structure

According to the Law, the policy-making competences for regional development were divided among following institutions:[9]

[8] The political system in the Republic of Macedonia consists of two dominant Macedonian parties – SDSM (socialist) and VMRO-DPMNE (conservative) and two dominating Albanian parties – Democratic Union for Integration and PDP (Party for Democratic Prosperity). The Government elected in 2006 (still in office) is a coalition of VMRO-DPMNE and DUI.

[9] Law on Balanced Regional Development, op.cit.

- Parliament of the Republic of Macedonia that adopts the legal framework, as well as Strategy for Regional Development;
- Government of the Republic of Macedonia, which has a competence to propose legal and strategic framework for regional development policy to the Parliament, as well as executive power for the implementation of the policy;
- National Council for Regional Development, consisting of 18 high level representatives from different ministries and planning regions,[10] with a competence to harmonise regional development policy with macroeconomic and sectoral policies;
- Ministry of local self-government of the Republic of Macedonia with competence to participate in the formulation, and, particularly, in the implementation of regional development policy; and
- Council(s) for the development of the planning region (eight Councils in total – one for each planning region), consisting of the majors of the municipalities that compose the planning regions, which has a competence to create and implement development programme(s) of the respective region(s).

The Law also stipulated the establishment of the Bureau for Regional Development (on the national level) and Centres for Regional Development (eight in total – one for each region) to serve as operational units for the implementation of regional development policy. The Bureau for Regional Development operates under the umbrella of the Ministry of Local Self-Government, while the Centres for Regional Development are subordinated to the Councils for Regional Development of the planning regions. Also, municipalities were delegated with specific roles in the regional development planning process – to develop joint, regional projects that will contribute to the advancement of the regions.

The system of regional development policy is project-based, meaning that the state financially supports selected regional projects. The legal obligation of the Government is to allocate funding in the amount equal to 1 % of the GDP from the state budget, earmarked for regional development.[11] With regards to the distribution of these funds, the Law specifies eligibility of all regions to apply for the projects, but they are entitled to different share of available funds, depending on their level of development. In this respect, a share of the most lagging Northeast region was set at 16.6 % of the total funds, while the share of the most developed Skopje region was set at 6.4 % in 2009–2012.[12] The major criteria for the selection of projects include contribution of the project proposal to the development of at least two municipalities from the region, which ensures municipal cooperation. In addition, certain financial or in-kind contribution from the municipalities involved is encouraged, in order to ensure ownership and implementation of the project. Moreover, the criteria stipulate that the project must comply with strategic priorities set in the Strategy for

[10] Decision of the Government of the Republic of Macedonia for establishing the National Council for Regional Development, Official Gazette of the Republic of Macedonia 110/2007.

[11] Law on Balanced Regional Development, op.cit, Article 27.

[12] Other regions were entitled with the following shares: 14 % to the Eastern region; 13.5 % to Vardar, 13 % to Polog, 13 % to South-western region, 12.9 % to Pelagonia and 10.6 % to South-eastern region.

regional development of the Republic of Macedonia. The decision about the project financing is within the competence of the Government of the Republic of Macedonia, following a proposal from the National Council for regional development.

The organisational structure for formulation and implementation of regional development policy is rather complex, and requires strong coordination of the involved actors. Ministry of local self-government had the leading role in the process of the elaboration of the Law and Strategy for regional development (2007–2009), and has shown strong commitment to the realisation of both documents. In this respect, the personal engagement of the Minister for local self-government in the period August 2006–July 2007, Mr. Zoran Konjanovski, ought to be distinguished, as the regional development was set as top priority in the Ministry and necessary resources were provided for completion of the legal and strategic framework (primarily the needed expertise) for regional development. The Law was adopted in May 2007 and the team for elaboration of the Strategy has been formed in April 2007, which was recognised as a Progress in the EU Country Report for 2007 (Commission of European Communities 2006). However, due to the political agreement among the leading parties – in July 2007, the Ministry for local self-government passed from Macedonian VMRO-DMPNE to Albanian coalition partner DUI.[13] With change of the Minister, the elaboration of the Strategy was completed in 2009, but the general drive for further reforms in the Ministry seemed to have decreased. Following the adoption of the legal and strategic documents, the current role of the Ministry could be said to be rather passive and oriented toward the assignments deriving from the Law, while at the same time there is a lack of initiatives for further reforms in this sphere.

With regards to the implementation of the regional development policy, the coordination role has been lodged with the National Council for regional development, chaired by the Vice-President of the Government of the Republic of Macedonia in charge of economic affairs, which should ensure harmonisation of this policy with other policies, as well as its efficient implementation. The mandate of the National Council, as well as its structure, enables this body to give really strong impetus to the regional development. In this context, the National Council played important role in the process of elaboration of the Strategy for regional development, as it had to approve the Strategy as precondition for the document to be submitted to the Government and later, Parliament. At this phase, the National Council, along with the other actors in the process (Parliament, Government and Ministry of local self-government) has shown strong commitment to the completion of the strategic framework. However, when the actual implementation of the regional development policy started, the National Council mainly focused to the operational assignment stipulated in the Law – evaluation of the submitted project proposals for regional development. The decision about the project financing is within the competence of the Government of the Republic of Macedonia, following a proposal from the National Council for regional development. The allocation of the grants should be done on an annual base, and National Council should meet once a year for this

[13] As of 2013, DUI is still in charge of this Ministry.

purpose. In the period 2007–2013, the Council held only eight meetings, mostly devoted to the mentioned evaluation.

2.2 Strategic Framework

The Strategy for regional development (2009–2019), adopted by the Parliament of the Republic of Macedonia, serves as a main document in the domain of regional development policy. The Strategy provides insight into the major demographic, economic and social specifics of the regions, labour market and infrastructure, as well as natural and energy resources and cultural heritage. Moreover, the Strategy identifies as common problems for all the regions – poor infrastructure, high unemployment rates and unfavourable educational profile of the workforce, the concentration of industry and other economic activities mostly in Skopje and few other cities, population ageing process translating into social problems to sustainability of the pension and health care system, etc.

As noted in the Strategy, as well as confirmed in the UNDP study "Mechanisms for linking national, regional and local development planning processes in the Republic of Macedonia" (Mojsovska 2010), the methodology used for elaboration of the document incorporated participatory and consultation principle. In that context, efforts to ensure coordination on both levels – horizontal and vertical, were undertaken. The horizontal coordination among the mentioned policy-makers was done by Inter-ministerial body (National Council for Regional Development), and included participation of the representatives from the relevant institutions in the team elaborating the Strategy. Furthermore, a procedure of review of the draft document by the relevant state institutions before its adoption was applied to the Strategy. Vertical coordination has been ensured by the organization of regional workshops aimed at collecting inputs from the regional stakeholders, as well as having a public debate about the draft version of the Strategy prior to its adoption. Cross-cutting with other strategic documents is evident in the Strategy, and illustrated with references to the specific documents. According to the structure of the document, the vertical coordination should have been helpful for identification of the most demanding issues with regards to the development of the regions. As previously mentioned, increased competitiveness of the regions has been one of the main objectives of the Strategy. In this respect, the need for infrastructure improvement which is clearly the most demanding aspect at the current level of development has been elaborated from the perspective of each region. Furthermore, leading industries have been also identified for each region, along with the assessment of the potential for their further development and creation of competitive advantages. Also, special attention has been given to natural resources and energy potential of the planning regions as a foundation for the development planning process.

In addition to the Strategy, the Law stipulated elaboration of the development programmes of the regions, as main planning documents of the planning regions. According to the Law, the Programmes should identify goals, measures and instruments for development of the planning region, as well as funding, time frame and indicators for monitoring the implementation of the Programme.[14] While elements stipulated by the Strategy have been incorporated in the Programmes of all eight regions, it is interesting that a direct reference to the Strategy and other relevant documents has been generally absent. All Programmes include a note on increasing competitiveness, although not focusing on selected activities, but on a wide spectrum of economic activities (different industries, tourism, agriculture, services, etc.), which, to a certain extent makes those Programmes appear more as an aspirational agenda rather than a realistic foundation for policy.

The Strategy and the Programmes represent the basic framework for pursuing regional development policy in the Republic of Macedonia. In terms of competitiveness, as noted, the Strategy identifies the main areas for improvement in the regions, but the document does not include tailoring of the priorities to the projected budget for regional development. This task should be performed by the National Council for Regional Development, leaving in practice the success of the implementation of the Strategy to the capacity of the Council and other actors in the process as well as the available finance.

2.3 *Prospects and Constraints of Using Regional Development Policy to Boost National Competitiveness in the Republic of Macedonia*

The overview of the policy framework for regional development in the Republic of Macedonia indicates its complexity and involvement of numerous actors with specific roles in the policy formulation and implementation. If analysed from the perspective of the OECD new policy approach, it could be noted that the regional development policy of the Republic of Macedonia formally complies with the former's main postulate of: "building competitive regions by bringing local actors and assets together". This is evident in the inclusion of competitiveness among the main objectives of the Strategy, and the establishment of the mechanism for regional policy implementation based on joint projects undertaken by the municipalities from the region(s). Furthermore, regional development policy of the Republic of Macedonia primarily targets the lagging regions and puts an emphasis on engagement of the actors (either on policy or operational level) while at the same time allows for the identification of the sectors in need of improvement. In terms of the cluster programme focus on smaller firms, given that over 98 % of the Macedonian companies belong to the category of small and medium companies, regional development policy is bound to evolve around SMEs. Hence, one conclusion that can be drawn is that regional development policy in the Republic of Macedonia has been designed following the modern policy-approach which concentrates on the

[14] Law on Balanced Regional Development, op.cit, Article 14.

competitiveness, and puts an emphasis on the networking of relevant actors. However, the formal setting of the policy is such that it does not guarantee its successful implementation. The following section takes a closer look at the prospects for a shift to regional development policy becoming an anchor of and a framework for policy process geared towards increasing competitiveness of Macedonian economy, as well as the constraints therein.

The prospects of regional development policy in the Republic of Macedonia to contribute to increased national competitiveness are based on the following postulates:

- It represents an interdisciplinary policy that treats the most important determinants of competitiveness, disaggregated at a regional level;
- It relies on the detailed overview of the level of development of the regions, along with identification of the main problems and potential sources for further development;
- The policy-making process includes consultation and participation of the major stakeholders as a main precondition for making sure their interests are reflected in the actual policy;
- The policy strives towards application of polycentric development model in the country, by prioritising the most lagging regions to reduce regional disparities, but without excluding the more advanced regions.

As discussed above, the formal institutional set-up for regional development policy has been designed to promote improvement in regional competitiveness. The claim that regional development policy has the potential to contribute to national competitiveness is based on the fact that it addresses all the main determinants of national competitiveness. Furthermore, the National Council for Regional Development has legal obligation to harmonise the policy with other related policies. The point is that regional competitiveness largely depends on structural reforms that are conceived by and pursued at the national level – in the field of education, labour market, demography, health services, as well as macroeconomic environment, financial markets, etc. Implicitly, in the case when national competitiveness policy is absent, these reforms should be induced by the regional level development policy makers. This in turn would contribute to improvement in national competitiveness. Furthermore, the detailed overview of the regions' problems and potentials enables formulation of policy making actions involving prioritisation and rational use of available resources, which could alleviate negative consequences of a lack of focus on competitiveness in the existing sectoral policies in the Republic of Macedonia.

In developing the potential of regional development policy to serve as an anchor for (national) competitiveness, an important concern is the feasibility of such a policy. In this context, consultation and participation of the main stakeholders is of utmost importance in the process of policy formulation. Application of the participatory approach in the process of Regional Development Strategy elaboration has enabled to gather valuable information, which could form a solid base for planning of the activities contributing to the overall national competiveness. The relevance of participatory method extends to the development of the regional development model in the country. The polycentric model of regional development promoted by the Strategy is in line with the notion of competitiveness as relating to the well-being of all citizens, which provides an additional argument in support of considering the use of regional development policy in the context of national competitiveness.

However, the potential to go in that direction in the Republic of Macedonia is largely determined not by the formal institutional setting for regional development policy, but its actual implementation. There are several critical constrains that ought to be taken into consideration. Regional development system in the Republic of Macedonia is rather complex and requires high capacity and superb coordination of all actors in order to produce satisfactory results. In practice, such coordination is very difficult to achieve. This is because the recent introduction of regional development policy in the Republic of Macedonia has hit against relatively low capacity of the actors in the system, which has caused problems in policy implementation. Moreover, the policy-makers tend to neglect the issue of financing of regional development policy, regardless of its vital importance (Mojsovska 2011).

With regards to the first concern, the complexity of regional development policy system, along with the fact that it has been fairly recently introduced, makes threatens its effective implementation. The practise has shown that the driving force for formulation of the regional development policy was related to two factors – personal commitment of the head of the respective institution (such as Minister for local self-government or Vice-President for economic issues) and prioritisation of the policy with regards to the EU agenda. Since 2006, there have not been political changes in the ruling structures in the Republic of Macedonia, i.e. no changes have occurred with regards to the political discourse of the Government. As already mentioned, the change in the party affiliation in the leadership of the Ministry for local government, was associated with a perceptible slowdown in the development of regional policy.

Nevertheless, it is worth noting that the commitment of the initial structures within the Ministry at the start of the reforms was largely related to the pursuit of the EU agenda, as the EU requirements were specific with regards to the need for elaboration of the Law and Strategy for regional development. This agenda was also followed after the leadership change in the Ministry, up to the adoption of the Strategy. Since 2009/2010, the EU requirements within Chapter 22 on regional policy and coordination of the structural policy have mostly focused on the establishment of institutions for administration and management of the IPA Funds. In this respect, the regional development policy, as formulated, has been predominantly domestic policy, aiming to increase of the competitiveness of the region. This is rather an important aspect, but it could be concluded that overall, EU Agenda had a major impact on the dynamic of formulation of the policy. On the other hand, it must be emphasized that the process of the formulation of the legal and strategic framework has been simpler compared to the implementation in so far as it by its very nature makes it easier to solicit higher commitment by the actors involved.

With regards to the implementation of the policy, the National Council for Regional Development, that should have crucial role in the harmonisation of regional development policy with other policies, and, therefore, contribute to setting-up of better system for development planning and hence improvement in national competitiveness, managed to hold only eight meetings in 2007–2013.[15] The meetings were mostly focused on evaluation of the submitted project proposals for regional development, in line with the Council's legal obligation to deliver the preliminary list of selected projects to the Government for a final decision. Just on these two facts- the frequency and the contents of the Council's meetings, it is clear that no pro-active approach towards the harmonisation of the regional development policy with other polices or improvement of the quality of coordination with regards to the implementation of the policy exists at the moment.

It could be argued that the driving force for more substantial treatment of the regional development issues is missing. This role should be either performed by the Vice-President of the Government in charge for economic issues (chair of the National Council) or by the Ministry of Local Self-government. As the legal framework stipulates rather operational role in the implementation of the regional development policy to the latter, it could be argued that there is high risk of lack of the interest in the Ministry to perform assignments or undertake initiatives which are not implicitly stipulated in the Law. On the other hand, the cabinet of the Vice-President for economic issues and its limited number of staff have been delegated with many responsibilities from different economic areas.[16] This means that the process of regional development largely depends on the capacity and willingness of the National Council and other actors to act, given the "top-down" approach of the regional development policy. In our view, this could seriously endanger the process of implementation of the policy, implying more critical attitude of the policy-makers towards the capacity of individual institutions.

Furthermore, deficiencies in the cooperation among the actors involved in regional development policy have been registered at other levels, too. According to the UNDP study in 2010, the Centres for regional development that have major operational role in designing regional development project proposals and to ensure the implementation of the selected projects, have indicated that the cooperation with other actors exists, but is not fully satisfactory. The main problems indicated by the Centres include non-existing/non-adequate regional databases, lengthy procedures in an official communication, lack of regular communication with the national level institutions and an absence of adequate expert support from the relevant institutions (Mojsovska 2010). Since the publication of the study, the situation has somehow improved with regards to the availability of the regional data, as the State Statistical Office started to provide wider range of regional statistics. At the same time, the online availability of the official documents related to regional development is still rather limited, as none of the actors in the regional development policy publishes a complete set of legal frameworks on their respective web-sites. This is primarily related to the limited human resources that can be engaged to perform information dissemination tasks. In sum, deficiencies in the coordination of the system for regional development present a serious burden to achieve the projected policy outcomes.

---

[15] http://www.vicepremier-ekonomija.gov.mk/?q=taxonomy/term/4&page=1

[16] http://www.vicepremier-ekonomija.gov.mk/?q=frontpage&page=2

The second constraint for the implementation of regional development policy and the possibility for its deployment in increasing national competitiveness is related to the capacity and the level of awareness about the regional development system among its actors. As previously noted, regional development policy in the Republic of Macedonia was introduced in response to the problem of large disparities in regional development, and as an element of the Europeanization agenda. While the development of regional policy institutions and framework involved consultation and participation method, the novelty of the topic among the actors involved certainly imposed some constraints on the outcomes of this process. Furthermore, consultative process was pursued in the early phase of policy formulation, while used rarely during the policy implementation process. In the mentioned UNDP study (Mojsovska 2010), the Centres for regional development noted the need for more serious approach towards regional development by all actors involved in the process, including raising awareness about regional development concept, transfer of foreign practices about regional development and higher participation of business and non-governmental sector in the process of regional development planning and implementation.[17] Apparently, these activities should be part of a regular process of professional upgrading of the capacity for regional development, while ignorance about these problems might provoke vacuum in the implementation of the policy.

The most challenging constraint to the implementation of the regional development policy is related to finance. Although the Law on regional development stipulates allocation of 1 % of the GDP for this purpose, the practice indicates that much lower amount was designated for regional development. In absolute terms, the mandatory amount in 2012 should have been around EURO 76 million; the projected finance in the budget was around EURO 2.8 million, and actual allocation amounted to just EURO 1.3 million.[18] It could be argued that even if the legal stipulation were respected, there is a need for increased funding towards regional development. Another important aspect that, if addressed, would result in more efficient allocations for regional development concerns a disconnect between the financial allocations for development programmes/projects within the sectoral policies and those earmarked for regional development. This is a direct consequence of a lack of coordination in the policy-making process, which results in the compartmentalization of funding and a loss of sight of the synergies that can be created among various policies. In this context, National Council competence in the area of regional policy should be deployed in order to harmonise regional and sectoral policies. This would not only mitigate the threat of insufficient funding for regional development but also provide a realistic grounding for using regional development policy to strengthen national competitiveness.

---

[17] Ibid.

[18] Revised budget of the Republic of Macedonia 2012, Ministry of Finance (http://www.finance.gov.mk/files/REBALANS%20ZA%20OBJAVUVANJE.pdf)

3 Conclusions

The issue of competitiveness in the Republic of Macedonia has been very important, but not thoroughly treated by the policy-makers. There is lack of single competitiveness policy or policy-making process focusing on wide range of competitiveness' determinants. Instead, the policy-makers mostly concentrate on the improvement of the macroeconomic environment through legal reforms striving to create business friendly climate, while the sector policies in education, labour market, infrastructure and other fields do not have distinctive focus on competitiveness. Given the low performance of the country with regards to the Global Competitiveness Index measurement, there is a need for more serious approach towards the issue of competitiveness. Taking the concern to use available resources rationally, this paper has explored the possibility to use the existing regional development policy in the Republic of Macedonia as a policy anchor for boosting the national competitiveness.

The main findings of the research which has focused on the policy making side of the issue, indicate that the formal setting of the regional development system offers substantial potential with regards to our proposal. Regional competitiveness has been at the centre of attention of the policy-makers in this field, particularly evident in the Strategy for regional development, which offers an insight into the state of affairs of the major determinants of the competitiveness of the regions (human resources – education, labour force, economic basis, infrastructure, natural resources, social protection, etc.), as well as identification of the main problems and areas that need improvement. Furthermore, the regional development system the Republic of Macedonia has been designed to ensure harmonisation of this policy with other macroeconomic and sector policies by the National Council for regional development, providing a basis for coordination of the activities in different policies related to the competitiveness. Also, the system has assigned active roles to the actors on national, regional and local level, which should result in an improved synchronisation between the needs of the regions and policy measures, and therefore, provide positive impact on competitiveness. The policy focus on the lagging regions, the goal of which is to reduce inter-regional disparities and boosting competitiveness of the regions could also have impact on the national competitiveness, provided that it contributes to improved well-being of the citizens in the regions.

However, the formal setting of the regional development system cannot by itself guarantee for satisfactory outcomes. In this respect, the proper implementation of the policy is of utmost importance. The practice indicates several constraints which hinder functioning of the system. These particularly include the deficiencies in coordination of the policy-actors, along with a lack of active engagement in harmonising regional development policy with other policies and insufficient capacity of the policy-actors. Nevertheless, the most serious threat to the implementation of the regional development policy is related to finances. The policy-makers tend to take a neglectful approach to the financing of the regional development policy, despite the legal stipulation to allocate 1 % of GDP for regional development. In addition, there is no link between the financial allocations for regional development and other policies, which could contribute to the regional development or increase of competitiveness. In this respect, improvement in the operation of the system are vital for harvesting potential benefits from the regional development policy to improve national competitiveness of the Republic of Macedonia.

References

Batchler, J., & Raines, P. (2002). *A new paradigm of regional policy: Reviewing recent trends in Europe*. European Policies Research Centre, Glasgow: University of Strathclyde.

Commission of the European Communities. (2006). EU Progress Report on the Republic of Macedonia 2006, Brussels, 2006, 2007, 2008, 2009, 2010.

Competitive Regional Clusters: National Policy Approaches, OECD Observer, May 2007.

Decision of the Government of the Republic of Macedonia for establishing the National Council for Regional Development, Official Gazette of the Republic of Macedonia 110/2007.

European Commission. (2000–2002). European competitiveness report.

European Commission Directorate – Regional Policy (2003). A study on the factors of regional competitiveness.

Global Competitiveness Report. (2008–2009). World Economic Forum.

Global Competitiveness Report. (2009–2010). World Economic Forum.

Global Competitiveness Report. (2010–2011). World Economic Forum.

Global Competitiveness Report. (2011–2012). World Economic Forum.

Global Competitiveness Report. (2012–2013). World Economic Forum.

Krugman, P. (1994). Competitiveness: A dangerous obsession. *Foreign Affairs, 73*(2), 28–44.

Law on Balanced Regional Development. Official Gazette of the Republic of Macedonia 63/07.

Mojsovska, S. (2010). Mechanisms for linking national, regional and local development planning processes in the Republic of Macedonia. UNDP study.

Mojsovska, S. (2011). *Decentralization and regional development in the Republic of Macedonia: Policy and perspectives* (LSEE Research Paper. No 4). London: LSEE-Ifri Research Programme on South East Europe.

Organisation for Economic Cooperation and Development (OECD). Programme on Technology and the Economy (1992).

Programme of the Government of the Republic of Macedonia. (2011–2015).

Regions of the Republic of Macedonia. (2009). State Statistical Office, June 2009.

Regions of the Republic of Macedonia (2012). State Statistical Office, June 2012.

Regions of the Republic of Macedonia (2013). State Statistical Office, June 2013.

Revised budget of the Republic of Macedonia. (2012). Ministry of Finance, 2012.

Strategy for regional development of the Republic of Macedonia. Official Gazette of the Republic of Macedonia 119/2009.

Chapter 12
Conclusions

Margo Thomas and Vesna Bojicic-Dzelilovic

Developing and transition economies face a myriad of challenges in achieving and maintaining political stability and promoting economic growth to assure national security, the social and economic well-being of their citizens and sustainable environments for future generations. Countries compete for scarce resources, investment, and innovation amid political instabilities, economic and financial crises, and environmental uncertainties (Thomas 2010). The Western Balkans region provides a compelling prism for examining policy reform following the 2008 financial crisis in light of the region's historical, political and economic significance in the European Union neighborhood.

An important starting point is the recognition that this is a complex region comprised of countries that share a common, often inter-linked political, economic, and social history and yet are not homogeneous. The countries that emerged from the former Yugoslavia cover a spectrum in political and economic terms – from Bosnia and Herzegovina with deep scars from the conflict that has shaped the politics, administration and economics of the country to Serbia – the largest economy. Albania bears the distinction of not being part of Tito's Yugoslavia and yet having striking political and economic parallels. It is also worth noting the exclusion of Slovenia from this discussion. Slovenia "followed a different path" (Cviic and Sanfey 2010) and despite the fact that it is one of the countries that emerged from the former Yugoslavia serves as a testament of the richness and complexity of the tapestry of the Western Balkans.

M. Thomas, Ph.D. (✉)
International Finance Corporation, World Bank Group, Washington, DC, USA
e-mail: mthomas@ifc.org; thomaswgb@gmail.com

V. Bojicic-Dzelilovic, Ph.D.
Department of International Development, London School of Economics and Political Science, London, UK
e-mail: v.bojicic-dzelilovic@lse.ac.uk

M. Thomas, V. Bojicic-Dzelilovic (eds.), *Public Policy Making in the Western Balkans*, DOI 10.1007/978-94-017-9346-9_12

This book explores policy making in the transition economies of the Western Balkans, by examining the role of policy actors in driving the policy agenda as well as the design and implementation of policy reforms making the case for strengthening the policy making process and building capacity in government, academia, the private sector and civil society in order to improve the quality, ownership, credibility, and sustainability of the policies that are critical for economic growth and social development. The case studies in this book focus on social and economic policy making on the national and sub-national levels while exploring and analyzing the roles and contributions of various policy actors (including parliaments, government, private sector, NGOs, various special interests, IFIs, donors and the EU) in policy design, process, implementation and outcomes.

As noted earlier, the book is organised into three main sections starting with a broad view of the economic and social policy reforms taking a regional perspective while highlighting the political, social and economic complexities; drawing on case studies of reform episodes from Kosovo, Montenegro and Serbia to examine distinct aspects of national policy issues such as regulatory governance, financial policy, investment policy and trade liberalisation; and, finally looking at local development and regional competitiveness by drawing on case studies from Albania and the Republic of Macedonia.

Each chapter and case study attempted to addresses a core set of questions:

1. What is the policy issue being addressed? What are the political, economic, and social context and drivers of the reform?
2. Who were the stakeholders and policy actors involved in designing, implementing and evaluating the impact of the policy? What were their specific roles? What kind of collaboration, collusion, competition occurred during the policy design process?
3. Was there evidence of policy networks or coalitions and how did these networks or coalitions work to put the policy reform on the agenda and to implement the reform? How did these networks and coalitions influence the scope, timing, and pace of reforms? How was power distributed within the coalitions – who were the leaders and what were their spheres of influence and special interests? What was the scope of these networks and coalitions e.g., national/ sub-national levels, across borders – regional?

In reviewing the chapters, three main themes have emerged:

First, the case studies addressed the core set of questions in different ways and with varying scope. In fact, there is no single case study that addressed these three sets of questions completely.

On the surface, one can attribute this unevenness to: deficiencies in the methodology since there was no systematic, standardized collection of data from a well-defined population of respondents or (e.g., a survey); or poor training of the analysts; or the fact that the analysis is retrospective thereby posing particular challenges for the contributors.

On a deeper level, it is evident that part of the explanation can be attributed to the opacity of the policy process and the political economy of reform. Since these are economies in transition from some variant of communist and socialist traditions, the policy process in a democratic, market-driven sense is nascent at best and absent in substantive terms since the 'new approach' to policy making is often a façade or relegated to the formality of checklists as entrenched coalitions work to protect their interests (Thomas 2010; Staranova 2002).

Secondly, based on the evidence provided through the case studies, policy making remains solidly the realm of government and public actors (since the formal role of civil society and the private sector appears to be limited to varying levels of consultation initiated by the governments) (Penev 2009). In many respects the case studies highlight the weakness of the policy making processes in these countries and the obscurity afforded to key stakeholders, special interests, and coalitions. These factors often conspire to limit accountability, transparency and objective policy making (Thomas 2010).

Third, the policy agendas are often reactive to internal and external stimuli and largely driven by external agendas and requirements. This point comes across strongly in the emotive discussions of the contributors in describing the role of the European Union and the international community in driving the policy reform agenda. Two points are worth noting in this context: (a) The recent history of political instability across the region that sits on the borders of the European Union, occupying a historically significant space, and potentially important economic space in the modern economy (Sanfey 2010) explains the European interest and the considerable leverage exerted through the "EU pull"; and (b) The importance of external support in helping these economies to garner a sustained economic recovery (2000–2008) following the devastating political crises and conflicts and their continued importance in helping them to recover following the 2008 financial crisis.

1 Forecast: Cloudy with a Chance for Sunshine…

At the end of 2013, the European Bank for Reconstruction and Development issued its Transition Report for South East Europe (SEE) assessing the macroeconomic, structural, and institutional health of the region in light of the continuing impact of the financial crisis (EBRD 2013). The report's narrative – "stuck in transition" – and key highlights resonate particularly in the case of the Western Balkan countries. In summary, the report finds that economic growth remains below pre-crisis levels and the region's competitiveness is challenged, even as exports are recovering and deleveraging has moderated. The economic slowdown persists with high unemployment, reduced domestic consumption and investment. In addition, the report noted a significant downward shift in the pace of reform, particularly in the reform of economic institutions (including government effectiveness, regulatory quality, the rule of law, control of corruption, governance and enterprise restructuring, and competition policy) and structural policies (including economic liberalisation and privatization).

In many respects the EBRD report affirms the key policy areas that are covered by this book and places them in the context of the region's continued struggle to enhance competitiveness and increase investment in order to generate sustained economic growth and strengthen its position in the global economy and within the European neighborhood. What this book contributes is the examination of the political economy, design, process and implementation of policies that are necessary for sustained economic growth and competitiveness. Clearly there is still a lot of work to be done.

References

Cviic, C., & Sanfey, P. (2010). *In search of the Balkan recovery: The political and economic reemergence of South Eastern Europe*. London: Hurst.

EBRD. (2013). *Transition report*. London: EBRD.

Penev, S. (Ed.). (2009). *Improving the process of economic reform legislation in western Balkan countries*. Belgrade: GTZ.

Sanfey, P. (2010). *South-eastern Europe: Lessons from the global economic crisis* (Working Paper No. 113). London: EBRD.

Staranova, K. (2002). Cultural change into professional policy making: The case of Slovakia". Centre for policy studies. http://www.policy.hu/staronova

Thomas, M. (2010). *Public policy making in the transition economies of the Western Balkans*. Manchester: University of Manchester.

MIX
Papier aus verantwortungsvollen Quellen
Paper from responsible sources
FSC® C105338

If you have any concerns about our products,
you can contact us on
ProductSafety@springernature.com

In case Publisher is established outside the EU,
the EU authorized representative is:
Springer Nature Customer Service Center GmbH
Europaplatz 3, 69115 Heidelberg, Germany

Printed by Libri Plureos GmbH
in Hamburg, Germany